Phototype,　　　　　　　F. Gutekunst,　　　　　　　Philada.

REUBEN ROSS.

LIFE AND TIMES

OF

ELDER REUBEN ROSS.

BY HIS SON,

JAMES ROSS.

WITH AN INTRODUCTION AND NOTES

By J. M. Pendleton.

PHILADELPHIA:

PRINTED BY GRANT, FAIRES & RODGERS.

52 & 54 NORTH SIXTH STREET.

Printed By:

McQuiddy Printing Company
Nashville, Tennessee

TO

MRS. MARION R. DUDLEY, OF LOGAN CO., KENTUCKY:

THIS VOLUME, WRITTEN TO ACQUAINT HER WITH THE LIFE AND
TIMES OF HER VENERABLE GRANDFATHER, IS AFFECTION-
ATELY DEDICATED BY HER FATHER, THE AUTHOR,
WITH THE HOPE THAT SHE AND OTHERS OF HIS
DESCENDANTS, BOTH NOW AND HERE-
AFTER, MAY FEEL AN INTEREST
IN THE NARRATIVE.

CONTENTS.

5

CHAPTER VII.

BEGINS TO PREACH AND REMOVES TO THE WEST.

CHAPTER VIII.

REMINISCENCES OF EARLY DAYS.

CHAPTER IX.

THE JOURNEY COMMENCED.

CHAPTER X.

BEYOND THE MOUNTAINS.

CHAPTER XI.

AFTER THE JOURNEY.

CHAPTER XII.

RED RIVER CHURCH ; ASSOCIATIONS.

CHAPTER XIII.

RED RIVER ASSOCIATION.

CHAPTER XIV.
SKETCHES OF EARLY MINISTERS.

CHAPTER XV.
SKETCHES OF EARLY MINISTERS.

CHAPTER XVI.
REMOVAL; OLD SPRING CREEK CHURCH.

CHAPTER XVII.
SCENES AT THE OLD CHURCH.

CHAPTER XVIII.
LIFE IN STEWART COUNTY.

CHAPTER XIX.
CUSTOMS AND SCENES IN STEWART COUNTY.

CHAPTER XX.
WAR, INDIANS, COMETS, EARTHQUAKES.

CHAPTER XXI.

A NEW HOME IN MONTGOMERY COUNTY,

CHAPTER XXII.

OUR SCHOOL, BASCOM, MORRIS, CARTWRIGHT.

CHAPTER XXIII.

THE GREAT REVIVAL AND ITS PHENOMENA.

CHAPTER XXIV.

CUMBERLAND PRESBYTERIAN CHURCH.

CHAPTER XXV.

LORENZO DOW.

CHAPTER XXVI.

CLARKSVILLE AND ITS RECOLLECTIONS.

CHAPTER XXVII.

FAMILY AFFLICTION.

INTRODUCTION.

MEMORABLE among American years was the year 1776. It was the year in which our Revolutionary fathers adopted the "Declaration of Independence," and pledged for its support their "lives, their fortunes, and their sacred honor." They were noble men. How brightly did the flame of patriotism burn on the altar of their hearts! How pure was their love of liberty! How anxious their solicitude for the welfare of their posterity! There was something sublime in the fact that, though few in number, they fearlessly threw their banner to the breeze of heaven, resolved on victory or death. They contended against the mightiest nation on the globe, but their heart faltered not. Their military resources were scanty, but trusting in God, and sustained by the justice of their cause, they went forward under the command of the great Washington, till, after a struggle of seven years' continuance, during which their blood stained the soil from Massachusetts to South Carolina, they triumphantly achieved the object of their patriotic exertions. Let it never be forgotten that American independence was secured by as precious blood as was ever shed in the cause of human liberty. Degenerate sons of noble sires are those who do not appreciate the heritage which we enjoy—a heritage bought at such a price—a heritage covered with Revolutionary glory, and transmitted to us by the hands of our fathers.

In the remarkable year to which I have referred, that is to say, on the 9th of May, 1776, in Martin County, North Carolina, the infant, Reuben Ross, first saw the light, and wept at its entrance on the rough journey of life. Alas, the eyes that wept so soon, wept often, and continued to weep till more than fourscore years had fled.

The Ross family is of Scotch descent, and the grandfather of Reuben

11

settled in an early day at Roanoke, Virginia. The year of his emigration from Scotland cannot now be given. His son William, the father of Reuben, was a citizen of Martin County, North Carolina, and had. for his wife a woman of vigorous mind, superior in intellect to himself. They were both Baptists, and, so far as circumstances allowed, brought up their children " in the nurture and admonition of the Lord." Many, however, were the difficulties they had to encounter. The whole country was in a state of restless excitement for years before the commencement of the War, and from the battle at Lexington to the surrender of Cornwallis at Yorktown anxious fears filled the minds of the people. We may well imagine how such a state of things interfered with the regular training of children.

William Ross was the father of ten children, of whom Reuben was the youngest son. Three of his brothers were in the war of the Revolution, and two of them, Martin and James, became Baptist ministers.

Reuben went to school only nine months in all, at different times, in the course of seven years, and left school finally at fourteen years of age. He greatly desired an education, but could not obtain it. He considered it his duty to contribute, by physical labor, to the support of his father's family. To such labor he may have been indebted for that vigor of constitution which made him every inch a man, and lengthened out his days so far beyond the ordinary limit of human life. He knew in his youth and early manhood the inconveniences of poverty. And why? Because his father had sacrificed an independent estate to promote the objects of the War ; and his youngest son, when he had become old, was heard by the writer to say: " I was always proud that my father became poor by spending his estate to carry out the principles of the Declaration of Independence." Such language as this could not have been spoken if patriotism had not reached its climax and its perfection. Poverty is generally regarded as a calamity, but Reuben Ross rejoiced in his youth, in his manhood, and in his old age, that his father became poor by cheerfully surrendering his estate to help forward the Revolutionary contest. How safe would our country be if such a spirit of patriotism pervaded the hearts of all American citizens !

Young Ross was at school but nine months; and these months not consecutive, but interspersed through a period of seven years, so that he was at school only a few days at a time. "Dilworth's Spelling Book" and the "Psalter" were the books chiefly used in schools at that period. The educational facilities of the country were very meager. None but the rich were able to send their sons from home and give them th e advantages of Collegiate training. Hence there were but few scholars.

God had given to Reuben Ross superior intellect, and superior intel - lect will display itself amid the greatest disadvantag es. There is a buoyant elasticity in it which enables it to rise and throw off the in- cumbent mass with which untoward circumstances oppress it. Well is it that it is so. Owing to this peculiarity of a vigorous mind, the sub- ject of these Memoirs, in spite of the unfavorable surroundings of his youth, rose to distinction, and became a favorite preacher of the learned and the unlearned. For long y ears the educated and the unlettered listened with the deepest interest to the wondrous things he told them. But I am anticipating :

The mother of Reuben Ross was a woman of prayer, and maintained family worship in the absence of her husband from home. He was often absent during the War. She rose early and sat up late. Her domestic duties probably rendered this necessary, but she had another object in view. She wished to pray in secret without disturbance. Early in the morning and late at night she called on God, supposing that his ear alone heard her. It was not so. The ear of Reuben heard. Sometimes his slumbers were disturbed at night, and he heard his mother praying—sometimes he waked early in the morning and he heard the same imploring whisper. He afterward called them "whisper- prayers." He did not let his mother know that he heard them, yet they made an impression on him which went with him to his grave. In the days of his subsequent thoughtlessness he never forgot that his mother prayed, never forgot her "whisper-prayers." Who knows how much those prayers had to do with his conversion and usefulness in the ministry ? One of the greatest blessings known on earth is the blessing of a mother's prayers, and the most cruel manner in which children can be disinherited is not to be prayed for by their parents.

Though often impressed with the importance of salvation, Reuben Ross did not become a Christian till he reached his twenty-sixth year.

2

Then he was led to see and feel himself a sinner against God, and after experiencing much anguish of soul he was enabled, by divine grace, to trust in the Lord Jesus Christ. This brought peace and joy to his soul. He soon felt that it was his duty to make a public profession of Christianity, and was baptized by Elder Luke Ward. Not long after his baptism he became anxious to glorify God by doing good in the world; and, strange as it was to him, the thought of preaching would come into his mind. He tried to dismiss the subject from his consideration, ' for he regarded himself as utterly destitute of ministerial qualifications. He was tempted to believe that if the people knew he had thoughts of preaching, they would say he wanted to be like his two brothers. who were preachers. This annoyed him not a little. Preachers were not supported in those days, and he concluded to sell his land and engage in merchandise until he made money enough to sustain his family, thinking he might then with greater propriety devote himself to the ministry, if, indeed, his impressions continued. As soon as he began "to sell goods" his impressions in regard to preaching left him, nor did they return till he became embarrassed by the failure of his mercantile arrangements. Then they returned with great power, and he ever believed that his want of success was providential, because he was not employed as the Lord intended he should be. He now began to feel that he *must* preach the gospel, and was licensed by the church in the year 1806. When he made his first attempt at speaking in public he was ashamed to leave the house, after the services were over. He was unwilling for any one to see him, and wished to hide himself. Among many things that troubled him there was this fact: Many of the preachers of that section of country professed to preach by inspiration or its equivalent. They were accustomed to begin their sermons by saying that they had not studied their subjects, and had not seen their texts for a considerable time, and that, therefore, whatever they said must be received as coming immediately from God. The candor of Reuben Ross did not permit him to do and say this. He studied his subjects as well as he could, and told the people that he knew nothing but what he had learned. In after years he sometimes amused himself, in a circle of special friends, by referring to his statement of a truth too obvious to need statement; but at the time it was a serious matter with him.

The church of which he was a member encouraged him, and even called for his ordination the year after giving him license. This was done when he was about to emigrate to Tennessee. Under different circumstances he would have protested against ordination, for he attached much importance to the apostolic admonition, " Lay hands suddenly on no man." In 1807, having been solemnly ordained by Elders Joseph Biggs, Luke Ward, and James Ross, he left the State of his birth and turned his steps to Tennessee, at that time a place very attractive to North Carolinians.

It is a sad thing to leave one's native land. and the graves of kindred, and to go among strangers. On such occasions the most manly heart trembles with emotion, and tears come into eyes unused to weep, as the scenes of childhood are left forever.

> " Breathes there a man with soul so dead
> Who never to himself hath said:
> ' This is my own, my native land '? "

The " old North State" was dear to Reuben Ross, but he thought preachers were more needed in Tennessee, and supposed he could better provide for his rising family in a new State, where land was much cheaper and more fertile. He sighed and wept at the graves of his kindred and started on his pilgrimage westward. His prayer was that God would be with him, conduct him safely to the end of his journey, and then be his God and the God of his family forever. He reached the neighborhood of Port Royal, Tennessee, on the Fourth of July, 1807. Here he sojourned for a time, and his removal to other places is minutely described in the pages which await the reader's perusal. It may be said, however, that his permanent place of residence was about six miles from Clarksville, and that his ministerial labors were devoted chiefly to the Counties of Robertson, Montgomery, and Stewart, Tennessee ; and those of Logan, Todd, and Christian, Kentucky.

In all the early years of his ministry his hands ministered to his necessities and to those of his family. Having heard that he was accustomed to carry his Bible with him to his work, I once asked him if it was so. He replied that it was. In opening his farm, after cutting down a tree, he often sat on its stump to rest for a time ; and while resting he read his Bible that he might learn more about the word of

God, and prepare himself as well as he could to preach to his neighbors on the next Lord's Day. I have seen many likenesses of him taken in after years, but the likeness I should specially rejoice to see would be a representation of him with his coat off, sitting on the stump of a tree he had just felled, with the Bible open in his hands. I would intently gaze upon it, and I am sure I should weep. What a picture! Reuben Ross, with the sweat extorted by physical labor on his brow, the Bible in his hands, treasuring up the words of eternal life! I would hang up such a picture in every preacher's study, and in every theological seminary, that the present generation of ministers might be reminded of one of the ways by which one of the fathers became mighty, not in philosophy, not in science, but like Apollos, "mighty in the Scriptures."

It will, no doubt, be strange to many to learn that Reuben Ross, in the first years of his ministry, did not preach to impenitent sinners. Under the influence of the erroneous sentiments he had imbibed, he felt that he had no message to them. He considered the gospel as addressed to *elect* sinners, and as he could not tell who except Christians were elect, he confined his labors to the people of God, and dwelt chiefly on the consolatory topics of the Bible. He made the old English distinction, and classified sinners as "*sensible*" and "*insensible*"—a distinction which Andrew Fuller attacked with his mighty pen. A *sensible* sinner was a sinner who had feeling on the subject of salvation, while an *insensible* sinner had none. This sensibility, rather than the teachings of God's word, was allowed to decide to whom the gospel was to be addressed; for it was to be considered an intimation of God's purpose of mercy toward those who possessed it. Insensibility, it was argued, indicated, on the part of God, an absence of all merciful intentions. True, the *sensible* sinner, before the period of sensibility, was *insensible*, and this fact was very perplexing to the investigating, logical mind of Reuben Ross. He reasoned on it by day and by night. Amid the toils of his agricultural pursuits, his mind toiled and labored over this knotty point in his theology. He pondered the Apostolic Commission: "Go ye into all the world, and preach the gospel to every creature: He that believeth and is baptized shall be saved; but he that believeth not shall be damned." The common exposition of this passage was that the gospel was to be preached to every *elect* creature, and therefore ministers must wait till some evidence of election was given before they were authorized to preach the gospel to a person. This view could not long satisfy such a mind as that of Reuben Ross. He read, " He that believeth not shall be damned." He saw that the teachings of the pulpit at that day led to the conclusion that some of the elect creatures might refuse to believe, and bring upon themselves damnation—a conclusion at war with the dogmas of the ministry. After much thought, perplexity, and prayer, he began to look on the commission in its obvious sense. He saw its comprehensiveness—" Go ye into ALL THE WORLD." He could not deny its definiteness—" Preach the gospel to EVERY CREATURE." He, therefore, having in the meantime read Andrew Fuller's " Gospel worthy of all Acceptation," settled down in the belief, from which he never afterward swerved, that all men without exception are subjects to whom the gospel should be addressed. He renounced the doctrine which has received the designation Hyper-Calvinism. From that time, as long as his voice was heard from the pulpit, no one rejoiced more than he to proclaim, " Ho, every one that thirsteth, come ye to the waters."

The reader will learn from the pages that follow how effective were the labors of Elder Ross from the time of this change in his views to the end of his ministerial career. It will be seen that under the inspiration of these labors the Bethel Association was formed, composed of churches, some in Kentucky and some in Tennessee, and that the number of its churches at its formation has been more than quadrupled. He was often called the father of this Association, and was its Moderator for twenty-five years.

As a preacher Elder Ross cannot be easily described so as to give an adequate idea of either himself or his sermons. In his best days his person was not only impressive, but majestic. His appearance commanded respect and reverence. His presence awed wicked men into propriety of demeanor. His countenance, especially in the pulpit, was clothed with solemnity, so that his hearers at once felt that he had something of transcendent importance to tell them. After attending the old Triennial Convention in Philadelphia in 1844, I remember that, on returning to my home in Kentucky, I said to my friends that I had seen no man whose appearance impressed me like that of Elder Reuben

Ross. There was in the expression of his eyes and in the features of his face a union of intelligence, gentleness, solemnity, greatness, majesty.

In his sermons were combined exposition, argument, and exhortation. He was able in his interpretation of the Scriptures, and though he had no knowledge of the languages in which they were originally written, he was superior in exposition to most learned ministers. The reason, doubtless was, that the Spirit who indited the Holy Oracles dwelt in his heart and sanctified his large common sense, thus utilizing it in the explanation of the divine word.

When the nature of his sermons called specially for argument he displayed logical ability. He had no acquaintance with Logic technically; he knew nothing of its Moods and Figures, but he knew that if such and such things were so, then such and such results must follow, and *vice versa.* There was no artificial laying down of premises, and no scholastic deduction of conclusions, but the whole thing, for substance, was done. Positions were established and fortified by such reasoning as no sophistry could successfully assail. This argumentative power was of great value in doctrinal discussions, and the prevalence of truth in many places is traceable to its able advocacy by Elder Reuben Ross.

But it is not to be forgotten that his sound expositions and conclusive arguments were designed to furnish a basis of persuasion, so that he might prevail on his hearers to do what his expositions and arguments indicated ought to be done. Here, therefore, was the place for hortatory appeal, and who that has heard it has forgotten it? Sometimes the appeal would recognize "the terror of the Lord," and then the preacher seemed to be clothed with terror. He trembled while pronouncing the doom of the ungodly, and implored his impenitent hearers to escape that doom. Most usually, however, the love of God in the gift of his Son, the tragical death of the cross, the value of the soul, the advantages of piety in this life, and immortal glory in the life to come, supplied the hortatory element in his sermons, especially in their peroration. His appeals were generally fine specimens of impassioned eloquence, and at times their power was transcendent and irresistible. They carried everything before them. The intonations of the preacher's voice were melting, finding their way to every heart; his deep emotion was seen on the quivering lip and in the tearful eye, while the whole face was in a glow of ardent excitement. I have seen the wonders of Kentucky's great Cave, the thousand objects of interest in our Centennial Exposition, the magnificent scenery of mountains and vales, the wild, dashing, thundering waters of Niagara, and I have stood on the shore of the Atlantic, where wave after wave has rolled in majesty and power; but I do not remember anything that has impressed me more deeply than a sight of Elder Reuben Ross, with a countenance full of dignity, solemnity, anxiety, tenderness, and love, entreating sinners to accept Christ and salvation.

It remains for me to express my gratification that the public is to be favored with "Recollections of the Life and Times" of this good and great man. It is a beautiful thing that these Recollections are those of a son who intended them as a tribute of filial admiration, and also as a legacy to his daughter. The spare hours of about ten years were consecrated by the son to these reminiscences of the father, and the son has since passed away. There is no escape from the stroke of death. Parents and children are equally mortal.

In the "Recollections" which follow there is not only an account of the "Life and Times," but also of the death and burial of Elder Reuben Ross. He first saw the light in North Carolina—the greater part of his life was spent in Tennessee—and he died in Kentucky. His body was conveyed to his former home near Clarksville, Tennessee, and buried by the wife of his youth, under the spreading branches of a noble oak, and not far off a cluster of cedars, evergreens, fit emblems of immortality, on whose boughs birds of charming notes often perch. Sing on, sweet birds! You will not disturb the silent sleepers, and may the lightnings of heaven spare that oak.

J. M. PENDLETON.

Upland, Pa., February 1, 1882.

LIFE AND TIMES

OF

ELDER REUBEN ROSS.

CHAPTER I.

BIRTH AND PARENTAGE.

ON the right bank of the Roanoke River, in Martin County, North Carolina, stands Williamston. As I remember it when a child, it was a long straggling village, with one principal street running through its entire length, from south to north down to the landing on the river. On each side of this street, which was covered with sand, stood dwelling-houses, stores, shops, taverns, built with little or no regard to what might add to the beauty or attractiveness of the place. There stood on one side of the street the court-house, Williamston being then, as now, the county seat. This was even then, as I remember it, an ancient-looking structure of the rudest kind.

Near this town, but a little to the east, in a locality known as the "Islands," on the ninth of May, 1776, your grandfather was born. He was the ninth of ten children, six sons and four daughters. Among the dim recollections of my earliest childhood, there was a house with a large

2*   21

central, oblong room, with side rooms adjoining, all under
the same roof. In front of this grew a gigantic mulberry
tree, which, with its dense foliage, shaded most of the
front yard, and under which, in pleasant weather, the
family often took their meals. I remember being there
often with your grandmother, and feeling quite at home
there; and I doubt not that it was the place where your
grandfather was born. I have learned lately that there
is still in that vicinity what is known as the "Ross Place,"
long since deserted, where a number of neglected graves
may be seen.

Your grandfather's family was originally from Scotland.
The name is identified there with many places, and is also
borne by many persons. There was, as he used to say, a
tradition that in early times several persons of this name
left Scotland together, crossed the Atlantic, and settled in
Virginia; that their descendants—many of them—emigrated into Maryland and Pennsylvania; that their complexions were generally dark (Ross Dhu); and that almost
every family had a John, William, or James in it. The
name is not "unknown to fame," having been borne by
statesmen, philosophers, warriors, and navigators.

His grandfather, William Ross, a descendant of these
supposed traditional ancestors, emigrated from Virginia
to Martin County, North Carolina; date unknown. His
father, also named William, was born August 9th, 1731,
O. S. The maiden name of his mother was Mary Griffin.
They were married in 1756.*

* A further account of the family from an old family record was
brought from North Carolina in 1833.

"William Ross, Senior, of Martin County, was the son of William
Ross, formerly of the State of Virginia, who came to this State, namely

His parents were apparently estimable characters, both members of a Baptist church, and both adorning their profession by pious and godly lives. I have heard your grandfather describe them as a grave and thoughtful pair, having two prominent objects ever in view,—the faithful performance of all the duties of this life, and a diligent preparation ·for the life after this. All their religious duties were carefully observed, especially family worship. Every night before retiring, the children and servants took their seats, a chapter of the Bible was read, a hymn was sung, after which all knelt in prayer. When his father was from home, the mother took his place at the family altar, and prayed audibly with her children and servants. When in health, she was ever the last to retire to rest, and before doing so, she would kneel a second time at her bedside in silent prayer.

I infer from what your grandfather said, that professors

North Carolina, and settled in the above-named county. His son, the father of the children whose names are under-written, was born on the 9th of August, 1731, O. S., and departed this life the 25th of December, 1801.

"His funeral sermon was preached to a very large audience, by the Rev. Aaron Spivy, from Job 2 : 17. 'There the wicked cease from troubling and the weary be at rest.'

"The names and births of the children are as follows:

"John,	born September	3rd, 1757.
William,	" January	17th, 1760.
Martin,	" November	27th, 1762.
Winifred,	" March	9th, 1765.
Nannie,	" March	26th, 1767.
James,	" March	19th, 1769.
Mary,	" February	11th, 1771.
Nathan,	" November	2nd, 1773.
Reuben,	" May	9th, 1776.
Elizabeth,	" May	3rd, 1779."

of religion in those days were generally more grave and
serious than now. The members of the Baptist churches
at that time, almost without exception, believed that a
large proportion of the human race, including perhaps
many of those dearest to them on earth, had no chance for
salvation, but were doomed from the beginning to endless
wo. We can hardly conceive how they could feel joyous
and happy with a creed so terrible.

I have heard your grandfather say, that in prayer his
father was singularly impressive. That his earnestness,
together with the beauty and simplicity of his language,
could hardly fail to inspire feelings of veneration and devotion in those who heard him ; that, like Boyle, the
great Christian philosopher, the thought of coming into
the presence of the Deity, and pronouncing his awful
name, seemed to exalt all his faculties and feelings. I
have often heard him speak of a prayer he offered in my
behalf, that was long remembered in the family. When
the old patriarch heard of my birth, he hurried over to
see the young stranger, and to inquire after his mother.
After inspecting him, and deciding, as is usual in such
cases, that he was a " wonderfully fine boy," he proposed
that all should kneel down and invoke a blessing on him.
It was said that he seemed on this occasion almost like
one inspired, so many, so rich, and so appropriate were
the blessings he invoked, in language so elevated and beautiful. Those who heard it could but think of the patriarchal days. He entreated, in conclusion, "when his course
is finished, full of days and full of honors, may it be his
lot to ' die the death of the righteous,' and may he be
worthy to wear the bright unfading crown in reserve for
those who, by faithful continuance in well doing, seek for

glory, honor, and immortality." I was often reminded, when a child, of this prayer in my behalf, generally when out of favor on account of bad conduct, and I would be quite penitent for a time, and make many resolutions to do better; but, alas! then, as since, they were too soon forgotten.

His father was successful in accumulating property. The vast cane brakes on the rich alluvial lands along the Roanoke River afforded abundant food for cattle, summer and winter, and the mast that fell from the forest trees enabled him to raise hogs to good profit, but little corn being needed, and that only to keep them gentle. These products were sold chiefly to traders from New England, who ascended the Roanoke in their vessels. This enabled him and others, who were industrious and enterprising, to realize large profits for those times. All this prosperity, however, vanished at the commencement of the Revolutionary war. British cruisers filled the waters. Trade of all kinds was paralyzed, and at the close of that eventful period, he found himself a poor man, comparatively, with a large family to provide for. Yet he was never heard to complain on account of his changed circumstances, but rather to rejoice that, by the sacrifice of his property and by sending his three sons—William, John, and Martin—into the army, he had contributed his mite to obtain the priceless blessings of freedom. Your grandfather always spoke of this circumstance with evident *pride*.

At length the time appointed for him to leave this world arrived. On the 21st of December, 1801, "he finished his course." His faithful, affectionate wife soon followed him. They were separated a few months only. From what I have learned from your grandfather, and also from your grandmother, of these pious, amiable old people, I came to feel great reverence and respect for their memory, and to associate with it all that was venerable and good.

Of all these children, not one is now living. They all married and had families, except Mary, who died young. Your grandfather was greatly attached to this sister, and spoke of her in most affectionate terms. Two of his brothers, Martin and James, and two sisters, Mary and Elizabeth, died in Carolina. Two brothers, John and Nathan, and two sisters, Nannie and Winifred, died in Tennessee. His brother William, the first to leave his native State, soon after the war of Independence, settled in Missouri, and died near Cape Girardeau.

CHAPTER II.

THE Roanoke river is a fine large stream that rises in the mountains of Virginia, flows in a southeasterly direction, enters North Carolina at some distance above the town of Weldon, and finally discharges its waters into Albemarle Sound, which extends inland from the Atlantic some sixty miles or more.

It was famous in the early times for its valuable fisheries. In it were caught, at certain seasons of the year, fish of the finest quality in countless numbers. Families living near it during one of these seasons supplied themselves with enough of this article of food to last them till the next.

Of all the fish taken from this river the shad, as I think, was most highly esteemed. It was a broad flat fish weighing five or six pounds generally, but sometimes much more; and when properly prepared for the table, was unsurpassed in delicacy and richness of flavor by any of the finny tribes. It was what was called a pan fish, and while being cooked, a rich aroma, like that from fine ham, would pervade the whole premises. Great numbers of them were salted down and kept in this way; but were much less esteemed than when fresh. They moved in such immense shoals that many thousands were often taken in a single haul with a seine. Herrings also, a much smaller

27

fish, were taken in still greater numbers. These were
mostly salted down in barrels and shipped. Of these
every family kept full supplies. When kept for this purpose they were generally slightly salted, then hung upon
reeds passed through the head, and smoked. When hanging thus, in nice rows in the smoke-house, like tobacco to
be cured in a barn, they looked quite pretty. I remember
when a child, that on coming in from play between meals,
and begging for something to eat, your grandmother
would give me a piece of bread and one of these herrings
and send me off to broil it on the coals for lunch. I
thought them very good eaten in this way, but would
seldom taste them at the table. I remember what were
called rock or rock-fish were greatly prized. They were
of large size and delicious flavor.

But the sturgeon, generally four or five feet long,
though sometimes much longer, attracted my attention
most. They had a habit of leaping from the water perpendicularly into the air and then falling into it again
with a splash. When a little fellow I loved to stand on
the river bank and watch their performances. When
caught, as they often were, and laid on the bank, I considered them as monsters to behold. Many kinds of fish
that we are glad to get in this country were hardly ever
eaten there.

These various kinds of fish were mostly taken with
a seine, consisting of net-work made very strong and
wide, the lower edge being sunk down to the bottom of
the river by leaden sinkers, and the upper edge kept even
with the surface by buoys made of cork. The seine was
often of great length, and when used one end was made
fast to the bank and the rest of it put into a boat, carried

out into the stream, and dropped into the water as the
boat went towards the opposite shore. Then, making a
long sweep down the stream, the other end was brought
to the same bank. The fish in ascending the river in vast
shoals were thus caught and dragged ashore. Nothing
could be more beautiful than to see their bright silvery
sides shining in the water as they came in sight. I remember hearing the superintendent of one of the fisheries
say to one who inquired of him, that he thought he had
caught about sixty-thousand herrings at a *haul* they had
just made. This perhaps sounds to you like a genuine
fish-story, but if you will read the accounts from some of
the great fisheries lower down the Roanoke, and in some
of the rivers of Virginia, you will see that this story is not
incredible. In the bright days of early spring I often
stole away from home, and with other little boys, mingled
with the animated crowds along these fishing shores. On
this stream, as your grandfather has often told me, he
spent many of the most romantic and happy days of his
early life. He was selected, on account of his skill as a
fisherman, to keep his father's family supplied with fish.
Are we not here reminded of others in the olden times,
who after having followed the same pursuit, like him became "fishers of men?" It always seemed to afford him
pleasure to speak of this period of his early life. And
when doing so he would enter a good deal into particulars. When engaged, as he would say, in fishing on private account or to obtain family supplies, they generally
went out two together. One of them would sit in the
stern of the boat and manage the rudder and the other
hold the net deep in the water. When the fish in ascending the river would become entangled in its meshes, they
would be lifted out and dropped into the boat or canoe.

His fishing companion was a negro boy belonging to his father named Drewey, to whom he was greatly attached on account of his many good qualities. I do not remember to have heard him mention but one fault Drewey had. He would always consume on the first day all the provisions he had put up to last him for several. When expostulated with, and told how childish and silly it was to act in that way, he would say:

"Master Reuben, don't say anything more about it, please. I can fast as well as any nigger when there is no longer anything in my basket to eat, but till then I must be eating all the time, for I am all the time hungry. I aint like you no how."

Drewey died when young, but was never forgotten by his young master. He sadly missed his companionship and faithful services after his death.

I have heard him say, the highest success in fishing involved both toil and danger; that he was most successful when the nights were dark, the waters turbid and swollen, and the masses of drift passing swiftly by, often in dangerous proximity to his little craft. But when day had dawned upon him, and after a night of toil and danger he came safe ashore, his canoe laden with the trophies of his prowess and skill, his toils and dangers were soon forgotten in the pride of success.

His life among the fishermen brought him in contact with a great variety of characters of that class, and even late in life he used to repeat many amusing anecdotes, of which a few only are remembered.

People often came down from a distance to the river, with vehicles of various descriptions, in order to get fish for their families. Many of these were very superstitious, and could tell marvelous tales of witches, ghosts, and apparitions, to which, when a boy, he listened with great interest. Those who came down from the piny woods reported them in those early times as abounding in witches. These hags amused themselves, as was said, by taking men out of their beds at night and riding on them up and down the country, always selecting those they disliked, or who had offended them in any way. They were represented as merciless riders, going straight forward through thick and thin to their places of meeting, or those where they held their dances, without turning to the right or left. It was said that many a poor fellow had been found in his bed in the morning more dead than alive, covered with dust and mire, who had been ridden the previous night. These they would sometimes permit to rest a day or two, and then take them out again, and they continued to do so until the poor fellows would become weary of life, and, finally, sicken and die.

A hunter, as they reported, took his gun one morning and went out to hunt, but did not go far before he saw a fine doe standing near him. He raised his gun, took deliberate aim, and fired. The deer seemed rather amused than otherwise,—ran around him several times and stopped again. Again he loaded his gun and fired, more deliberately than before, with no better success. This was repeated, until, at length, he recollected that he had a small piece of silver in his pocket. With this he loaded his gun, and, taking aim at its side, fired. At this the deer fell, but soon sprung to its feet again, ran off through the woods and disappeared. On going to the spot where it fell, he saw blood. Following the bloody trail, it led him to the house where the most famous witch in all the country lived. On inquiring about the health of the family, a boy told him his great-grandmother had just died. On inquiring about her *ailment*, he was told she died of a *pain in her side*.

These witches could transform themselves into various animals. They seemed generally to prefer the form of cats. They did not always ride on *people* to their meetings. They were sometimes mounted on broom-sticks, pokers, hogs, goats, and dogs. At their assemblies the old Enemy always presided, in the shape of a large black goat.

After getting through with the witches, they would tell him about the famous Captain Kidd, the renowned pirate, whose black banner waved so long, the terror of the eastern seas; how he buried, somewhere on the Carolina coast, large chests of ill-gotten gold, and by his spells and enchantments had given these chests the power of moving under the ground, like fish in the water; how some men could, by a divining rod, tell exactly where these chests lay at any time; how large bodies of men had often gotten together to dig for them; and how they had sometimes been so close upon them as to be able to get a glimpse before they would pass out of sight. Many of them never seemed to doubt that, sooner or later, they would get possession of this golden treasure, and then adieu to all earthly troubles. Visions of wealth and magnificence would flit before their simple minds, and their eyes would sparkle with anticipated ease and splendor.

Such were some of the strange, wild stories he remembered to have heard these people relate when he was young, and what lent an additional charm to them was, as he said, their perfect faith in their truthfulness. His reminiscences

of these times, and of these singular people, always seemed
to afford him a melancholy pleasure, as they brought back
to his mind the happy years of his boyhood.

He took no little pains to give me, when young, some
general idea of the features of the country where he was
brought up, and of the character of the people at that time,
and according to my recollection it was pretty much as
follows:

All the country lying east and southeast of Williamston, on both sides of Albemarle Sound, was low, flat, and
inundated, to a great extent, when the waters of the Roanoke were high; it abounded in cane brakes and jungles,
almost impenetrable, and infested with bears, wolves, panthers, and other wild beasts destructive to stock.

There were also many " dismal swamps " of great extent, whose waters were nearly black, whence arose the
melancholy Cypress trees, whose roots, rising in many
places above the dark-colored water, and called by the
people " Cypress-knees," gave a weird and spectral character to the scene.

The country to the south and west was an extensive
sandy plain, covered with lofty pine trees, yielding lum-
ber, tar, rosin, and turpentine in great quantities, which
were shipped abroad, and formed the basis of a considerable trade. In this region of country, the land lying along
the rivers and smaller streams was productive, while in
the pine districts it yielded but little to reward the labors
of the husbandman. The lands lying north of Williamston and on the opposite side of the Roanoke were more
productive. The people inhabiting this region were, as
usual, divided into three classes,—the rich, the well to do,
and the poor. Those of the first-mentioned class were

very wealthy, one man owning, in many cases, hundreds of slaves, and land and other property in proportion. Being well educated (many of them abroad), they were refined and polished in their manners, and their style of living was almost princely. The females of this class, especially when young, were often of dazzling beauty, with clear olive complexions, fine large eyes, faultless in their forms and features, and distinguished for that air of elegant repose which lends so great a charm to feminine loveliness.

The men of these families were generally less prepossessing, being rather too delicate and effeminate to comport with manly beauty. This he thought was due to the malarial character of the country along the Atlantic seaboard, and to this he also attributed the swarthy complexion of the people, more especially of those much exposed to the weather.

This portion of Carolina was very unfavorable to the health of children, so that often out of a family of six or eight in number, not more than one or two would live to grow up and marry. And as the heir of one estate would often marry the heiress of another, should this continue any length of time, as it often did, the estates would finally become overgrown and unwieldy.

These families were very exclusive, and seemed to have a society very much of their own, visiting each other from a distance. I remember, when a little lad, hearing wonderful accounts of their splendid entertainments, brilliant assemblies of elegantly dressed ladies and gentlemen, and the profusion of gold and silver plate and costly wines. To these stories we children would listen with as much interest as to an Arabian tale.—The middle class, as he said, was industrious, intelligent, and enterprising, but, in general, poorly educated.—Those of the third class were light-hearted, improvident and thoughtless, and almost entirely uneducated. They lived mostly among the pine forests, collecting tar, turpentine, and rosin, as already stated, which they would carry down to the river in little primitive carts, without a particle of iron about them, drawn along the level sandy roads by a breed of horses, small, but capable of almost any amount of endurance. They generally returned with but little of the proceeds of their sales, most of it having been spent for oysters, beer, cakes, cider, and West India rum, and the remainder in a few flashy articles of finery for their wives, daughters, or sweethearts. These were the people who were wont to entertain him so much with their wild romantic stories.

Such, my dear Marion, as he used to describe it to me, was the country where your grandfather was born, the people, and some of the scenes and incidents of his early life. But on looking over these pages, as they have been written, I can but feel how much of that interest is wanting which he could impart by his manner of describing them.

CHAPTER III.

It has been said, with some degree of plausibility, that all which is absolutely necessary to influence and success in life, so far as education is concerned, is simply to know how to *read* and *write*. Since this, of itself, opens the door to all the treasures of learning and knowledge that have been accumulating since the beginning of time; that this, like the talismanic words of the story, when rightly used, will give admission into the cave in which are contained the treasures of silver and gold and sparkling gems. And the fact that so many beginners, starting with this, have made such vast accumulations of learning, knowledge, and wisdom, seems to confirm the sentiment, and discredit the notion of the poet who says:

> " A little learning is a dangerous thing."

It is not intended by any means, however, to convey the idea that a thorough course of general study is not in every way desirable.

Your grandfather affords a striking example of the great benefits that may accrue to one's self and others from a very limited education when rightly improved. His educational advantages were, indeed, small. All the time he spent at school was less than twelve months, and these

36

not consecutive : it would be a month or two at one time, and then a few months or weeks at another. After his fourteenth year he never went to school again. Why his attendance at school was so irregular and short, I do not remember ever to have heard him say; but I suppose it was in part owing to his own indifference, and in part to the want of schools in the country at that time. You will remember, too, that he was the youngest son, and the youngest child but one. There is reason to believe, likewise, that his parents, being then in their old age, indulged him a good deal, and permitted him to have his own way pretty much, and to go to school only when he chose to do so.

He learned, during this short and irregular attendance at school, to read well, to write a good hand, and enough of arithmetic to answer the ordinary purposes of life. I. is clear from this that his capacity for learning was above the average; for few boys have been known to do so much in the same time and in similar circumstances. Dilworth's spelling-book (of which you have probably never heard the name, though famous in its day), and the Psalter (a book in which the Psalms of David were arranged for the service of the Church of England), were the books with which education in those days began and often ended. As for grammar, he did not understand a single principle; though few who heard his public addresses or private conversations would have supposed this to be the case. A very critical ear only would have observed that he now and then failed to make the verb agree with its subject, and the relative with its antecedent, according to the rules of grammar. This purity of style I attributed to his natural good taste, improved by reading the

3

fine old writers in history, divinity, etc., whenever they fell into his hands in after years.

Few persons could master more perfectly the contents of any book they read, or more readily detect a flaw or sophism that might lurk in the reasoning. The exact words an author used he seldom took the pains to remember; but his thoughts and reasoning were seldom forgotten. In regard to the Sacred Writings it was different. Here, in his quotations, every syllable and word was in its proper place; and when repeated with faultless accuracy in his discourses, especially after becoming warmed with his subject, they gave to his style a solemn grandeúr and beauty bordering on the sublime, and left on the minds of those who heard him a deep and enduring impression.

No one ever more lamented the want of learning than he did, in later years. On two occasions especially did he lament this. The first was during the troubles that preceded his separation from his old hyper-Calvinistic brethren; the second, when a division among the Baptist churches was impending, on account of the views promulgated among them by Elder A. Campbell and his followers. He thought, had he been a ready writer, he could have rendered important service to the cause of religion and truth, on both these occasions. And we may well believe that many valuable thoughts, which would have been useful then and read now with both pleasúre and profit, have been lost. He would have been much gratified, too, as I know, to have been able to leave behind him his views on various religious subjects in which he felt a very deep interest. During the last visit but one I made him before his death, he took great pains to explain some of these to me, and, as I believe, to impress them on my memory with the hope that I would remember them after he was gone. I do not remember ever to have seen him more interesting, animated, or more eloquent than at this time; and I shall endeavor to reproduce them in the course of this narrative.

As regards your grandfather's *religious* education, or training, it was similar to that of the church to which his parents belonged, namely, the old Calvinistic Baptists. All or nearly all of these believed, at that time, in what are known as the *five points* of Calvin. These were, " Unconditional Election, Particular Redemption, Total Depravity, Grace Invincible, Final Perseverance of the Saints through Grace to Glory."

Those of this faith never thought that much could be done for their children, so far as salvation was concerned, by religious instruction. They believed that those of them who had been elected from the foundation of the world would be, at the appointed time, "effectually called" and brought into the fold; that until then the most that could be done for them was to teach them to show a decent respect for religion, to attend family worship and preaching, to be upright and moral in their conduct; and when the appointed time should come, the Holy Spirit would begin a mysterious work of grace in the soul, and carry it on with a power that nothing could withstand, till they were regenerated, pardoned, and saved; that it was best, while this was going on, for no one to interfere, but to leave the sinner entirely in the hands of the Holy Spirit, who knew far better than any mere mortal how to carry on and complete the work. The resistance on his part was, as they thought, often long, and the conflict fearful. It was all of no avail though, for when once the "arrows of conviction" had entered the soul, sooner or later it must submit; there was no escape. It was thought that there were always certain indications of what was going on,—a peculiar expression of the countenance, a disposition to silence and solitude, an indifference to the common concerns of life. At these indications, the good old brethren and sisters would look mysteriously at each other, shake their heads, and talk in whispers. They understood it all, having "travelled the same dark road themselves," as they were wont to say.

The individual thus exercised inspired a kind of awe. He was looked upon as one for whom the powers of the invisible world were contending,—Spirit with spirit. And how they all rejoiced when they heard the conflict was ended, the victory won, and another of the *elect* saved from the power and dominion of Satan! The "stronger the convictions and the more powerful the conversions," the greater the rejoicing on these occasions. None, I presume, who have had opportunities of seeing and hearing these old Christians talk, will think the above account too highly colored. But alas, for those of their children who were not of the elect! They were doomed from the beginning; for, not being included in the plan of salvation, they could only live on during their allotted time, die, and be lost forever, "to the praise of his glorious justice," as they would express it.

Your grandfather, even when a boy, seems to have learned a good deal in regard to the views and sentiments of his predestinarian parents, as one would infer from such anecdotes as the following, which I have heard him repeat more than once.

On one occasion, while playing among the apple trees in his father's orchard, he so managed as to get on the back of one of the horses, rather vicious in disposition, without either saddle or bridle. He had no sooner done so than the horse started off at full speed. At this he was well pleased until, on looking before him, he saw with terror the horse was going directly under a large limb, extending horizontally from the tree, so low that it seemed impossible to pass under it without being killed, *unless it had been decreed* otherwise. So far as he could see, his time had come, and escape was impossible, when suddenly the thought flashed across his mind that, by entwining his left hand in the horse's mane, keeping his left leg only over his back, and lying close to the horse's side with the rest of his body, he might possibly pass under it. He carried out the plan, and escaped unhurt.*

After recovering somewhat from his terror and thinking it all over, he concluded that he was indebted for his life to one of those *decrees* he had heard so much about, and thought that any boy ought to consider himself fortunate, who had one of these in his favor in time of trouble, espe-

---

* It would be well, not only for boys, but for persons of mature years, to remember that God's purposes or decrees furnish his rule of action, and that their execution does not interfere with the freedom of human agency. So far from it, they are often, to say the least, carried into effect through the free agency of men. Thus, while it was decreed that Christ should die, the decree became effective through the voluntary agency of the Jews who procured his crucifixion.—Acts xi. 23. They acted freely, and their sin was fearfully great. Whatever the views of the boy Reuben Ross may have been concerning the divine decrees, when the time of danger came he immediately resorted to the best means for saving his life. He cut in a moment what has been called the "Gordian knot of theology." We may well rejoice that God is sovereign and that man is free.　　　　　　　　　　J. M. P.

cially if it was an "*eternal decree*," which he thought much more powerful and efficacious than any other kind. And if it had been made "before the foundation of the world," it must be much better than one of later date.

He was, when a little fellow, very fond of his bow and arrow, and by practising a good deal, at length became so expert, as now and then to kill a bird, or other small game.

On one occasion, being about to shoot at a dove, he felt a good deal of compunction, the bird appearing so innocent and unconscious of its danger. He finally concluded that all these things had been settled long ago, even down to the death of a sparrow, and that he had nothing to do with them whatever. All he had to do was to shoot, and if the bird's time had come, he should kill it; if not, he should miss it, just as it had been *decreed*, and he not to blame one way or the other. Had he but known it, he was now on the confines of one of the darkest and most perplexing subjects that ever "confounded the wisdom of the wise," namely, the foreknowledge of the Deity, and man's accountability. I am not certain how it fared with the bird, but rather think it escaped unhurt.

These anecdotes are curious as showing on what subjects his thoughts sometimes ran, even when quite a small boy.

Nothing would afford me more pleasure than to be able to present your grandfather, in his boyhood and youth, as a model to others, but, as a faithful chronicler, I fear I cannot do this; I fear I cannot class him even among what are commonly called *good* boys.

There is reason to believe that at this time he had a very decided will of his own, which, as a rule, he was pretty much bent on following, regardless, too often, of where it might lead him. His parents thought dancing very sinful (at least such as they then had), and did all they could to keep him from engaging in it. But he was so fond of this amusement, that he would often leave home at night, when they were asleep, and go to disreputable frolics of this kind, without duly considering the distress it would cause them should they ever come to know it.

Once, when behaving very badly, his mother called him to her and said to him, with tears in her eyes, " Reuben, you are my youngest son and my youngest child but one, and my heart's desire is to love you dearly; but you are so bad, I cannot do it; it seems impossible."* These words, and her manner while saying them, made a deep impression on his mind, and long after she was sleeping in her silent grave they would seem, at times, to be sounding in his ears.

Thus will thoughtless children, by their perverse and wayward conduct, often entail upon themselves sorrows and regrets for the coming years, as perhaps many of us know but too well.

---

* If Reuben Ross was a " bad boy," let not parents who have way-ward sons despair of their conversion to God. Almighty grace can do great things, and under its influence the hardest heart is subdued.

J. M. P.

CHAPTER IV.

ANECDOTES OF EARLY YEARS.

Your grandfather remembered quite a number of amusing anecdotes which he had heard when young, and would sometimes relate some of them when speaking of his early life. He told them well. One could see that he greatly enjoyed the wit and comic humor they contained. I propose relating two or three of these before proceeding further with our narrative.

One of these related to an old Englishman, who had somehow found his way to the region of country where your grandfather lived. He was of dissipated habits, but light-hearted and frolicsome as a boy. His only business was to travel around the country and teach school for a livelihood. His rule was to teach a few months at one place, collect the little sums when due, and then, with a set of lively fellows frolic around till all was spent; then to take up another school and go to work again. Nothing could induce him to teach longer than a few months at one place. His scholars considered him a prodigy of learning. He could tell how many barley-corns, placed one at the end of another, it would take to reach round the world, and how many seconds of time were contained in any given number of years. But what astonished them most of all was the marvellous beauty of his penmanship. This, to them, seemed little less than supernatural. Be-

sides these accomplishments, he knew a great deal about
ghosts, witches, apparitions, and haunted places. The
boys took great delight in gathering around and hearing
him tell of these wonderful things. On one occasion, a
youth, a boy of the larger class, who wished to see his
future wife, told the old man he had heard that people
sometimes had been permitted to see the images of their
future wives, and that nothing in the world would delight
him so much as to be able to see his. To this the schoolmaster replied that nothing in *his* country was more common than this; that he knew exactly how it was done,
and if he really desired to see his future wife, and would
meet him at a certain time at the schoolhouse, exactly at
midnight, he should be gratified by seeing her face to face.
The young man thanked him again and again for his kindness, and promised to be there punctually to the time, if
his life was spared. Here all the other boys began to beg
that they might be permitted to attend also. This was
readily granted, and everything settled to the satisfaction
of all parties. At the appointed time, punctual to the
hour, not only the school-boys, but every vagabond and
reprobate in the country was there, with torches and candles sufficient to illuminate the old house brilliantly. A
rude curtain having been drawn across the room, the old
man took his seat before it. Just at the bleak hour of
midnight he rose from his seat, uttered some strange, bad-
sounding words in an unknown tongue, took his seat again
and waited motionless a few minutes. Then he rose again,
and said in sepulchral voice, " She has come; she stands
behind that curtain!" The crowd now began to show unmistakable signs of uneasiness, to look over their shoulders towards the door, and many to wish themselves safe

3*

at home. Soon the curtain began slowly to rise, and the lower part of a long white female dress to appear. Here terror could be seen depicted on every countenance. But when the curtain rose still higher, and the face of a pale, death-like female * form stood before them, one wild shriek arose, followed by a rush to the door, through which the terror-stricken multitude swept, one over another, in mortal terror. Neither the dark night, the dismal swamp, briars nor thorns were heeded until, breathless and half-naked, they reached their homes and buried their heads in their bedclothes.

When the rest made a rush for the door, the poor fellow who wanted to see his sweetheart so badly, sprang to the schoolmaster, caught him around the neck, and said: "Lay her, master, lay her! for God's sake, lay her! Oh, I wouldn't see her again for a thousand worlds!"

This frolic broke up the old man's school; though for this he cared but little, and would have given up a dozen schools, at any time, for another like it. The beauty of his penmanship alone, whenever he wanted one, would give him a school. The old schoolhouse had a bad name after this, and people seldom went near it afterwards, especially when alone.

THE PIONEER SETTLER.

At the period of what is called Braddock's war, an old pioneer settler lived among the mountains of Virginia. It was a time of trouble and danger. The French and Indians held in strong force Fort Du Quesne, situated where Pittsburg now stands. From this place the savages were

---

* A boy had been dressed up for this purpose.

supplied with the arms and ammunition which they used in carrying on hostilities against the frontier settlers of Pennsylvania and Virginia.

As but little human aid was to be expected at that time, the old man, as is usual in such cases, became very devout, and prayed earnestly, night and morning, for the protection of Heaven for himself and family, in a prayer he had prepared to suit the times, and which it required the best part of an hour to repeat. It so happened that, just about the middle of this prayer, he invariably implored the Almighty to crown the efforts of Braddock and the colonies with victory, and to overwhelm the French and Indians with defeat and ruin. His two sons, Bill and Tom, finding it too much for human nature to keep awake during this long prayer, repeated almost word for word, night and morning, and observing also that Braddock always came in just at the middle of it, conceived the idea of turning this circumstance to advantage by *dividing* the *time* equally, and settled it between them that Bill should always go to sleep at the beginning of the prayer, and Bob keep awake until the old man " prayed up to Braddock," then to give Bill a nudge and awaken him, and go to sleep himself. Bill would then be awake, ready to stir up Bob in time, so that all could rise together. This arrangement gave each a good half-hour of much-needed sleep, and no one the *worse* for it. On trial, the thing worked beautifully, and went on like clock-work for some time ; but alas ! one unlucky morning Bob, instead of keeping watch as he ought to have done, went fast to sleep too. The old man, having finished his prayer, rose to his feet, and on looking round saw the two poor fellows on their knees asleep, Bill having been awakened just enough by the rising of the others to

ask Bob, in a drowsy whisper, if the old man hadn't got
to Braddock yet. Eyeing them a moment, he reached up,
took down his cane, and gave each a rap on the shoulder.
Supposing they were attacked by the Indians, they "raised
a murder shout" and sprang to their feet. Waiting till
they became a little composed, he opened his mind freely
to them, saying that he considered them little better than
two uncircumcised Philistines; that he had been praying
for them the best part of an hour, and they fast asleep all
the time, dreaming of Braddock. They were very much
afraid of Indians, he perceived; but there was something
worse than Indians, he would have them to know; and if
they went on as they were then doing, they would find it
out in the end, to their cost.

I always suspected, from your grandfather's manner of
telling this story, that he knew by experience, to some
extent, how Bob and Bill felt when they were thus caught
napping.

JACK HUNTER AND THE CATS.

The hero of the next story was a young fellow, as I
think, named Jack Hunter, and, as reported, was young,
gay, handsome, very rich, and well educated. It was even
said he knew Latin; for when invited to join in a frolic,
he used to say, "Semper paratus," which he told the boys
meant *always ready*. He properly belonged to the very
highest class of society, but somehow took a downward
course, and landed in the lowest. It was said he had
prettier sweethearts and more of them than any other
young fellow in all the country.

Court day, in Williamston, was a kind of jubilee for all

the idle fellows around. The piny-woods boys especially were then out in great force, drinking rum, beer, and cider and eating oysters, gingerbread, etc.,—mostly at the expense of Jack, who was as liberal as a prince. This would continue till late in the day, when the whole crowd would become so happy as to forget entirely that there was any such thing as care or trouble in the world.

It so happened that Jack once, on the night previous to a court day at Williamston, staid at Washington, the county town of Beaufort, situated about twenty-five miles distant. On his way home the next day to join his party, being a great way, he studied up a plan to have some fun when he joined them; and pretty late in the evening, when they were enjoying themselves to their hearts' content, and only unhappy on account of his absence, he was seen coming down the long street, on his fine horse, at a full gallop. He was soon in their midst, and pulled up his horse. All gathered round, shook hands with him, and after chiding him gently for having been absent so long, asked for the news. He told them that the news he brought was highly important, and at the same time very wonderful: that just before he left Washington, a ship had sailed into the harbor and cast anchor. That the news she brought was that a strange and fatal disease of some kind had broken out among the cats in England, and that the last one of them in the United Kingdom was dead, and the Norway rats were about to ruin the country, and added that the King of England had sent this ship over to Carolina, to buy up every cat she could spare, regardless of price; and he advised them to hurry home as fast as possible, catch all the cats they could lay their hands on, and carry them to the ship.

This news had the effect to sober every one of them instantly. All hurried home without delay, never expecting to have such another opportunity to fill their pockets with gold. The dear old court-house in a few moments was deserted, and looked as lonely as a country meeting-house on a week day.

The next morning, bright and early, vehicles of every kind were seen pouring into Washington loaded with cats. The citizens in amazement inquired of the owners what they were bringing *cats* to town for. They replied : " For the ship." " For what ship ?" " For the ship the king of England has sent over for cats." " Who told you there was any ship here, or that the king of England wanted cats ?" " *Jack Hunter.*" All was now explained. Nothing more was necessary. The golden vision vanished. The poor fellows turned round and started for home, disappointed and angry. Jack thought it prudent to keep out of the way for several days. But all was soon forgiven and forgotten. They loved him dearly, and could not think of breaking with him.

Such were some of the stories your grandfather used to hear when young, and would sometimes repeat, long afterwards, when something brought them to his remembrance.

CHAPTER V.

HIS MARRIAGE—THE YARRELL FAMILY.

UNTIL the twenty-second year of his age, your grand-father seems to have passed his time in assisting his father on the farm, fishing, hunting, and amusing himself with his young associates, unfortunately without any books to read suitable to his age and taste, everything of the kind being scarce and dear in those early times.

Had this been otherwise, he might, during these invaluable years, have stored his mind with an amount of general information that would have been of priceless value to him in time to come. For such was the character of his mind, that there is no doubt whatever, had valuable books been in his reach, he would have read them with great pleasure and profit.

It so happened that about this time he became acquainted with your grandmother, then about sixteen years of age. I have heard that he first met her unexpectedly, as she and some other girls were out enjoying a walk, and that she was at the time dressed in white, with a wreath or chaplet of wild flowers on her head, and that he surrendered on the spot, or, as the young folks say, "fell in love at first sight." He seems to have pressed his suit earnestly and with gratifying success, for they were married on the 30th of September, 1798, a few months only

51

after becoming acquainted. It is said he was then a very
handsome and prepossessing young man.

I have heard, also, that she was very pretty at that
time, and you who remember her late in life can well
believe it. Your grandfather always thought her a great
beauty, and was as proud of her good looks as we children
were. He, as you may remember, thought himself quite
a judge of female beauty. Her form, features, and fine
presence, as I remember them in my childhood, are so
impressed on my memory, that were I a painter or sculp-
tor I could reproduce them with great accuracy. But the
beauty of her life and character remain still more deeply
impressed on my memory, and I think I may say with the
great Scottish poet:

> "Time but the impression deeper makes,
> As streams their channels deeper wear."

Her maiden name was Yarrell,—Milly or Mildred Yarrell. She was the daughter of Matthew Yarrell. He was
born and brought up in Halifax County, North Carolina,
but finally settled in Martin County, where he was living
at the time of her marriage. He was an orphan child,
brought up by an old uncle named Day, who, during his
nephew's minority, took good care of his property, which
was considered a fine estate for the times when he came
into possession of it. But, taking to politics, high living,
and speculation, Mr. Yarrell had but little of it left when
his daughter was married. I have often heard it said that,
when he was in his prime, he was uncommonly handsome,
and, as I remember him in old age, his features were very
fine.

The maiden name of his wife was Mary Wheatly. She

was related to the Wheatlys of Montgomery County, Tenn. Dr. James Wheatly, one of the first citizens of the county, and his brother Albert, you may perhaps remember. Grandfather Yarrell removed to Tennessee several years after she did, in order to be near his daughter, to whom he was greatly attached, and he lived with us most of the time until his death, in 1829, in the seventy-sixth year of his age. He had been a widower several years when your grandmother was married.

He had a proud and independent spirit, and disdained the thought of living on others after having lost his own property. In order to avoid this, being naturally handy with tools, he took up, in his old age, the business of trunk-making. These he covered with deer skins, which he bought of the hunters, some nearly red, some bluish, and some spotted, being the skins of fawns. These, when finished off by him, were quite pretty, and highly prized by his customers, the girls and young ladies of his acquaintance, to keep their nice things in, and such articles of apparel as they did not choose to hang up about their rooms. For bureaus, presses, and wardrobes were not often seen in those days. This business afforded him the means of supplying all his wants, and enabled him to keep a good horse to ride, which was always a great pet with him.

He had been brought up in the Episcopal Church, and for this he had great respect, but very little for any other. In fact, he considered all others very much as heretics. He placed a very low estimate on the preachers of other denominations, and used to say your grandpa could preach very well, it was true, but that he had no more *right* to do so than he had, as he had never been ordained by those authorized to confer ordinations. He kept his prayer-book by him, and generally read the lessons for the day himself, or got some of his grandchildren to read them for him.

He read his Bible a good deal on Sundays, giving the Psalms of David the preference. I am sorry to say those passages in which the Psalmist uttered heavy imprecations on his enemies seemed to have a particular attraction for him. I fear he often included his own enemies with David's, and rather wished them to have the same portion. His enemies were those who had betrayed his confidence and swindled him out of his property. He seems to have been one of those who, when young, consider all men fair and honest, and only find out to the contrary when too late.

There were some new-fangled notions, as he called them, which he especially abhorred. He believed the sun, literally, rose and set every day. That the earth was placed exactly in the centre of the universe, and that it was the business of the sun, moon, and stars to revolve around it every twenty-four hours to give it light and heat and beauty.

The changing of the Christmas and the style from the old to new he thought was a special enormity, showing the degeneracy of later times and the little reverence men felt for the past and the traditions of the fathers. I mention these things to give you some idea of the thoughts and feelings of many old men as late even as the beginning of the present century.

In all his dealings with men he was scrupulously just and honorable. In his last illness, he sent for me and told me he had a number of small outstanding debts which he

wished me to settle for him, as he did not think he had
long to live, and wanted no one to have any reason to
complain of him after he was gone. He told me at the
same time where I would find a canvass bag containing a
sum of silver money, which he wanted me to use for that
purpose. Taking the money, with a list of the names of
his creditors, most of whom were living in Clarksville,
I paid them all off and brought in his receipts. He seemed
to think I had done him a great favor, and thanked me
again and again. His mind now being easy, he fell into a
state of unconsciousness, and soon after breathed his last.

He sleeps at Cedar Hill, your grandfather's residence,
in Montgomery County, Tenn., near the grave of the
daughter he loved so well, and who ministered to him to
the last. For a number of years he and I were much
together, and I have for his memory an affectionate veneration.

One circumstance during his last illness deserves notice.
Until then he never manifested any particular attachment
for your grandfather, but now it was quite different. He
often spoke of him as his "dear friend," and seemed pleased
to have him sit near him at the bedside.

Your grandmother had two brothers, Thomas and Garrard, and likewise two sisters, Rosa and Mary, more frequently called Polly.

Her brother Thomas married and raised a large family,
and continued to reside in the old State till 1834, when
he went out to Alabama, intending to purchase a farm
and remain there. But while attending to this business,
he fell sick and died. Several of his children had previously settled in Alabama. Her brother Garrard followed
the sea till late in life. When a little boy he was appren-

ticed to the captain of a merchant ship, and he remained
till he became thoroughly acquainted with his business as
a sailor, rose steadily in his profession, and finally became
sole owner of a fine merchant ship, which he named "The
Live Oak."

When war was declared between the United States and
Great Britain, in June, 1812, he and his ship were in the
Gulf of Riga, in the north of Europe. When the news
reached him, he attempted to return home, but was cap-
tured by an English man of war and was carried into
Leith, near Edinburgh, Scotland. Here he was detained
a prisoner until the close of the war, when he and his vessel were released; after which, he returned to the United
States with his wife whom he had married in Scotland.

While on another voyage, some time later, he was cap-
tured by French cruisers, acting under Bonaparte's infa-
mous "Berlin and Milan Decrees"; his ship and cargo
were confiscated and he thrown into prison. He was now
ruined, having only his papers left. These would have
entitled him to an indemnity sufficient for the support of
himself and family; but on his way home with these papers, just as he came in sight of land, the vessel caught
fire and everything on board was burnt up, the crew and
passengers only escaping with their lives. After this, he
remained in Carolina until about the year 1834, and then
removed with his family to Tennessee, and lived here until
his death in 1838. He was a very able seaman, as I have
learned, and an upright and excellent man. The early
part of his life was unusually bright and promising; the
latter darkened by the cloud of adversity.

Her sister Rosa married and came to Tennessee when
we did, raised a large family, and died a few years ago.

Her sister Polly was twice married, and was living near Fort Donelson during the civil war, was ruined thereby, and died in its vicinity. Thus this melancholy record closes. Knowing the desire most people feel to know something of the history and fortunes of their families, I give you this brief sketch at the risk of appearing tedious.

We may now return to your grandfather. That he might be near his aged parents in their declining years, he built a house on the tract of land upon which they lived, and which was to be his at their death. This house was built of pine and cypress timber, and I have often heard your grandmother, when speaking of her early housekeeping, tell how sweet and pleasant the rooms were when new, being perfumed by the fragrant wood of which they were built. I infer from what I have heard her and your grandfather say, that the few years they lived in this house were among the happiest of their lives. They were both young, both hopeful, and both in happy ignorance of the long and weary journey that lay before them. Here the little twins, Nancy and Polly, the first-born and pride of the family, first saw the light, and here, too, I was born September 3, 1801.

While living here, your grandmother made a profession of religion and joined the Baptist Church. The name of the church of which she became a member was Skewarkey. It belonged to what was then, and still is, called the Ke-hú-kee Baptist Association. These were Indian names, and both accented, as I think, on the second syllable. Many places in that region of country still retain the names given them by the Indians.

This old church I remember well, though I was very

young. It stood in a grove of lofty pines, among whose tops, when a gentle breeze was passing, a low and melancholy sound was heard. The Carolina negroes used to say it was the moaning of unhappy spirits, and it always produced in me a superstitious awe on that account.

At this church I rather distinguished myself on one occasion. I was standing by my mother during the preaching, and observing that many of the old brethren were frequently saying "Amen," I concluded I would do so too, and to the great astonishment of everybody present, cried out "Amen" nearly at the top of my voice. This, coming from a chap so tiny as I was at two years of age, sounded very strange, and attracted a good deal of attention. Your grandmother gave me a shake, and told me, in a whisper, not to say another word. I was so pleased, however, with the sensation first produced, that I could not resist the temptation to try it again, and, after a while, repeated the "Amen" still louder than before. This was too bad, quite a commotion was caused, many so far forgot themselves as to laugh out, and the preacher made a slight pause in his discourse. At this your grandmother became quite confused, rose from her seat, led me out under the pines, and told me I had behaved very badly, that little boys did not know when to say "Amen," and ought not to think of doing such a thing, adding that she was ashamed of what I had done and did not love me a bit. She did not venture to take me back into the church again, but kept me out under the trees till preaching was over. It was long ere I heard the last of this performance.

Now you must know, my dear Marion, that it is one of the greatest pleasures of an old man to think and speak of himself when young. One can hardly understand why this is so, for many of his stories are generally poor enough. I suppose, though, it is because they bring back to his memory his young and happy days, when all before him looked bright and hopeful, and behind were no dark shadows of sorrow and regret.

A very kind friend, in a letter dated Williamston, N. C., March 8th, 1872, in answer to one addressed to him previous to that date, says:

"The Skewarkey Meeting House, that your mother used to take you to, was about a mile and a quarter from Williamston, on the road leading to Washington, in a southeasterly direction. The present house is about one-fourth of a mile nearer town. It was built a few years before the war, and is in a piny grove beautiful to look upon, with seven acres of land and a burying ground attached. Number of members belonging to the church about eighty.

"Your recollection of Williamston is correct. It is the same little town yet, with one long main street leading down to the Roanoke River. The fishing on the opposite side of the river became unprofitable, and has not been used for many years. There are valuable fisheries, however, lower down on the river, in the neighbourhood of Jamesville (which used to be called Jameston) and Plymouth. We have a great deal of steamboating on the river now, extending to Norfolk and Baltimore."

I hardly need say I was much gratified to learn from this letter that my early recollections were so correct, as described in the beginning of this book.

The same friend in another letter says:

"I profess to be a Baptist minister, and belong to the Skewarkey Church, near this place, which church is a member of the Kehukee Association, of which Association I have acted as Moderator for a number of years. * * * I knew your father well and loved him dearly. Your uncle James I was also well acquainted with, and had a high regard for him. With your uncle Martin I had no acquaintance. He was, no doubt, a very able minister, and was the first one, perhaps, to introduce a resolution favorable to missions in the Kehukee Association.

He and his brothers were all members of the Kehukee Association, I presume, before the Chowan Association was formed out of it. The Chowan is by far the largest Association in N. C., I expect."

These extracts are interesting to us,—first, as showing the estimation in which your grandfather's memory is still held by his old Carolina brethren; and secondly, as showing that the old Kehukee Association, to which he first belonged, has passed through precisely the same ordeal the Red River Association did in this country; viz., that on account of difference in doctrinal views, a separation took place among them, and that the Chowan Association was formed out of the Kehukee as the Bethel was formed out of the Red River Association.

The Carolina Baptists of that region seem ever to have felt a lively interest in their Tennessee brethren. And as far back as 1810, when the Red River Association held one of its sessions at our old Spring Creek Church, the Kehukee Association sent a letter of correspondence and kindly greetings to them from distant Carolina, as may be seen from the published minutes of that session now in my possession.

All denominations, indeed, feel a strong attachment for their organizations. The very name of Baptist, Methodist, and others strikes a chord in the hearts of the brotherhood that seems to vibrate whenever touched. And no other words fall more pleasantly on the ear than these. It awakens in the mind the memory of the great and good who have lived and died in their communion, with all their eventful history. This feeling of love and veneration for the religion and the church of their fathers is often very strong even with those who make little or no pretension to religion themselves.

CHAPTER VI.

HIS CONVERSION.

WE now approach the most important event in the life
of your grandfather,—his conversion; but before giving
you an account of it, as I have heard him relate it, I propose making a few general remarks on the subject.

Nothing seems to be more clearly taught in the sacred
writings, than the fact that man, in his natural state, is
not in harmony with his Creator; that he is not disposed
to love and serve him as he ought. And of this, I suppose, no candid individual, who has ever reflected, has any
doubt. He has the "witness within himself" that all is
not right in that direction; and as regards others, his own
observation and the melancholy history of the race in all
ages of the world afford ample proof that this is true.
This indisposition to love and serve his Creator as he
ought must therefore be removed before he can enjoy the
divine favor and blessing; just as the perverse and rebellious disposition of a child must be, removed or changed
before he can be received into the favor of an earthly
parent. And this change of heart in man from a sinful,
wicked, and rebellious disposition or state to one of love,
reverence, and obedience to his Heavenly Father is what,
in the figurative language of the Bible, is meant by being
converted, regenerated, or born again, and is beyond all
comparison the most important event in human life, since

4   61

on it depends heaven and eternal happiness beyond the grave.*

For when through the new creating power of the Holy Spirit, the love of that which is holy and good is implanted in the soul; when this indisposition to love, serve, and reverence the Creator is removed; when that golden link which was broken and lost in the Garden of Eden is found and restored, man emerges from the ruins of the *Fall*, and is again in harmony with his Creator, the Fountain of all that is holy, pure, and good. And since this change in man is an absolute necessity before reconciliation and pardon can be obtained, it is not strange that it was said to Nicodemus, "Marvel not that I said unto thee, ye must be born again." There is indeed nothing marvellous in this, since in the very nature of things, the spirit, which after death returns to the God that gave it, cannot be happy in his presence, unless it has come to love and reverence him; for as all know, nothing is more intolerable than to be confined to the society of those for whom one entertains feelings of dislike and aversion.

This disposition to love and serve the Creator, to walk in "all his commandments and ordinances blameless," constitutes the very soul and essence of religion,—a *word* of beautiful and interesting signification, meaning *that which re-unites* or binds again what has been broken or severed. With this disposition to love and serve God,

---

* The critical theologian may object that the biographer identifies conversion and regeneration. In popular style this is often done, and no evil results; though the two terms are not identical in import. This, however, is not the place to point out the difference, only so far as to say that regeneration gives the *disposition* to turn to God, while conversion is the *actual* turning.　　　　J. M. P.

and to trust in Christ as his only Saviour, and to become his humble follower, one is a Christian. Without it all else avails nothing, so far as salvation is concerned. Riches, power, glory, and honor are as dust and ashes. With it the beggar becomes a king and priest of the Most High.

Although all men, before conversion, are indisposed to love and serve the Creator, this indisposition seems to be much more fixed and obstinate in some than in others. In some, the remembrance of the goodness of God and the gentler influences of the Holy Spirit lead them to repentance. Like some beautiful plants, their religious life seems, as it were, to grow up almost spontaneously, bud, bloom, and bear its golden fruits. Happy these beyond the common lot! But the conversions effected thus, with less emotion, are no less necessary on that account.

Others are more manifestly and stubbornly indisposed, as already stated, to love and fear God and keep his commandments. They wander far away into the paths of sin and folly. The still small voice of conscience is seldom heard or heeded. Their eyes do not perceive the perils by which they are surrounded, until they are awakened by some sudden or unexpected event of an alarming character, and see themselves standing, as it were, on the brink of a fearful abyss, from which they recoil with alarm and terror.

Something like this seems to have been the case of your grandfather. He never doubted, as he would say, the divine origin of the Bible, or the great truths of the Christian religion, or undervalued their importance. But he had come to look upon it as something solemn and gloomy, and better suited to persons in the declining years of life, intended chiefly to solace those who were no longer able to enjoy the gayeties and pleasures of this world.

After your grandmother made a profession of religion and became a member of the church, he came to look upon religion with a kind of aversion, as something in his way, interfering with his enjoyments, as already stated. Under the influence of these feelings he would dismiss it almost wholly from his thoughts.

Thus matters stood when he and a number of his gay companions got together on a certain occasion and, to use his own expression, "spent a Sabbath evening very wickedly." I do not remember ever to have heard him say in what this wickedness consisted. When he came to reflect upon it, however, his mind was ill at ease. While in this unpleasant state of feeling, he heard that one of the gayest of their party had been taken ill and died suddenly. This seems to have moved him to a degree hardly to have been expected in one of his age and exceptional firmness of character. It had the effect to change, almost at once, the whole course and current of his life. The thunderbolt said to have struck down the young Alexius at his father's side does not seem to have produced a more deep and lasting effect upon the great Reformer, than did this sudden death of his young friend on your grandfather. The uncertainty of life, the certainty of death, and after death the judgment, and the danger of procrastination were most painfully realized by him. He trembled, when he thought of his young friend cut down in the flower of his days, all unprepared as he was for the solemn change. Oppressed with these thoughts, on his knees he implored God, in his mercy, to spare his life for repentance and reformation, and to save his soul from death and ruin.

To add to his unhappiness, the effects of his early teaching were now painfully felt by him. He feared at one

time he was one of the non-elect.* Then he feared that
he had committed the unpardonable sin, whatever that
might be. Then again he was afraid that his day of grace
was passed and gone forever. The remembrance of his
thoughtless and sinful life lay heavy on his conscience;
and so little did he know of the Bible, that in this hour
of trouble he could derive no consolation from the blessed
promises it contains for those in trouble on account of
their sins. Had he known these, how they might have
cheered him in this dark hour! This unhappy state of
mind was of long continuance, during which he in prayer
earnestly sought the forgiveness of his sins and the salvation of his soul.

At length, having retired to a lonely place for self-exami-
nation and prayer, he became conscious of a great change
that had taken place in him, in many respects. He could
now hardly recognize himself as being the same individual as before. The ways of sin no longer seemed pleasing and attractive. To be a Christian was now his greatest
desire. For all whom he regarded as followers of Christ
he felt esteem and love. His soul overflowed with love
and gratitude to God, at the remembrance of his goodness
and mercy in not having long since cut him down in his
sins as a cumberer of the ground; and finally his heart
felt submissive and penitent, rather than hard and rebellious. It now began to dawn upon him that he had experienced that change which in the Bible is denominated

* There is nothing more useless than a sinner's anxiety on the subject
of *election*. It is a matter with which he has nothing to do. His business is to repent of his sins and believe on the Lord Jesus Christ. Then
he will know of his election, and can appropriate all the comfort arising
from the doctrine.

being born again. This produced a degree of happiness and joy that was new and strange to him. And in conclusion he would say, the time when and the place where this occurred, he thought would be among the last things that would fade from his remembrance at the close of life.

I have thus given, almost in his own words, your grandfather's account of his conversion; for I had many opportunities, when young, of hearing him speak of it.

It was not unusual in those days, when several of the older brethren and sisters would spend an evening together, for them to devote a part of the time in giving an account of their conversion, or relating their experiences, as they commonly expressed it; and on these occasions he would speak of his, also, if requested to do so. On these occasions I was always present, if possible, listened with profound attention to all that was said, and heartily rejoiced as one after another was relieved of his burden. This was generally a happy time with these Christians; their brotherly love would seem to increase, and their faith and hope grow bright and strong when thus communing with each other. Their joys and sorrows, hopes and fears, on account of their striking resemblance, seemed to unite them in closer bonds of love and sympathy.

Many of these recitals, as I remember them, were very interesting, and were often expressed in simple, unaffected language. They would generally begin by referring to some circumstance or incident that first turned their thoughts to the subject of religion; such as the death of a beloved friend or relative, a dangerous illness that had brought them near the gates of death, an impressive discourse from the pulpit, or perhaps some nameless sorrow that had turned their thoughts away to another and a better world. Sometimes they would refer to a state of feeling that seemed like a solemn warning to prepare for death, for which no especial cause could be assigned.

The change in your grandfather, consequent upon his conversion, was very remarkable, and seems to have been, to some extent, both mental and physical. The gay and lively expression of countenance for which he seems to have been noted in his youth and early manhood, now disappeared, and was replaced by that grave and solemn expression which followed him through life, and which is still remembered by all who ever knew him. The solemn views he came now to entertain of life and death, time and eternity, endless joy and endless woe, seemed to have left their shadows on his mind and features. And what I regard as very singular is that, though his grave and solemn presence was felt by all, it was repulsive to none. Even little children liked to be near him. His pastoral visits among his brethren and their families were highly prized by all, children and servants included, and were long remembered by them. An elderly lady, while speaking of him to me, said that nothing she remembered during her childhood ever delighted her so much as his visits to her father; and that when he would call her to him, let her stand by him, lay his hand upon her head, and talk to her, her happiness was greater than her words can express.

But the power of his presence was never so much seen or felt as when he rose in the pulpit to address an audience. Instantly it would pervade the whole assembly, and the hum of voices be no longer heard. The greetings of neighbors and friends and the conversation so agreeable and pleasant to them on meeting would be at once arrested,

and all become still and silent listeners.   No one seemed
disposed to break the spell that was felt by all.   I doubt
if any one ever heard him administer reproof from the
pulpit.   If any slight disturbance arose, a short pause or
a look was sufficient to restore order.   This power was
felt likewise in later years, when acting as chairman or
moderator over large deliberative bodies in associations or
conventions,—a service which, as we shall see, fell often to
his lot.

CHAPTER VII.

AFTER his conversion, your grandfather thinking it his duty to make a public profession of religion, and to become a member of the church, repaired to the old meeting-house and related his experience. When the brethren heard this they pronounced it in their judgment a genuine work of grace, congratulated him on having "found the pearl of great price," and bade him God-speed, on his heavenly journey.

Soon after this, in the twenty-sixth year of his age, he was baptized by Elder Luke Ward, then pastor of the old Skewarkey Church. Of this church your grandmother was already a member. This was a day of special rejoicing with her. Soon after his baptism he began to feel a great desire to persuade others to come to Christ also; that they might enjoy the promises of the gospel, and escape the fearful consequences of dying in their sins. At times this desire became very great, so much so, that he often felt as though he would have been willing to rise from his bed at night and go among his friends, in order to persuade them to forsake their sins, and warn them to flee from the wrath that was to come upon all those who obey not the gospel. I have heard him say, that this desire for the salvation of others was not, at first, accompanied by a sense of duty, but was simply a restless anxiety for their welfare and happiness after death. At length, however, a sense of duty was superadded; and with it an abiding impression, that he would not be held guiltless if he did not endeavor to perform this duty. This weighed heavily on his mind, especially when taken in connection with the absence of all the qualifications, as he thought, for speaking acceptably in public. Could it be the duty, he would say to himself, of one under these circumstances to appear as an ambassador for Christ, to pray men as in Christ's stead to become reconciled to God! There must be some mistake; this could not be. Such were his reflections.

After he had been perplexed and oppressed some time, with these thoughts and impressions, he took occasion to make known the state of his mind to some of the brethren. These encouraged him to make the attempt, and he soon after obtained from his church a *license* to speak to the people on the subject of religion whenever he might feel disposed to do so. I doubt not the church granted this license the more readily, because he had two brothers who were already distinguished Baptist preachers, and they were the more hopeful of him, perhaps thinking there might be some natural aptitude in the family for public speaking, which is often the case. The names of these brothers were Martin and James Ross. The former, born in 1762, and living in Perquimons County, North Carolina, on the north side of Albemarle Sound, near the town of Edenton; the latter born in 1769, and living in Bertie County, higher up the Roanoke River.

I have heard your grandfather say, that his brother Martin was a preacher of ability and influence among the Carolina Baptists; clear, argumentative, and impressive

as a speaker, and more dignified and polished in his manners than was common in those days; and possessed of
more learning and general information than any other
member of his family. His brother James was considered
less able in the pulpit than his brother Martin, but, nevertheless, he was popular and influential as a preacher. He
was of a cheerful and lively disposition, greatly beloved
by all who knew him, and especially so by the young and
happy, many of whom were brought into the church under his ministry. I have often heard your grandmother
speak of him as one she loved and esteemed very highly,
on account of his pleasant manner and affectionate disposition.

It would afford me much pleasure to give you some
particulars or incidents connected with your grandfather's
early ministry, but I know little to relate on this subject.
He used to say, that his first efforts seemed to him so imperfect, that he generally felt relieved when at a distance
from those whom he had first addressed. There is reason
to believe, however, that the people, from the first, listened
with much interest to what he said. I remember, almost
as far back as my recollection reaches, his asking me one
day if I did not want to ride with him to meeting. Of
course, I was very ready for the ride. I was then so
small that he had to keep one hand behind him a good
deal of the time to prevent my falling from the horse.
On reaching the place, which was, I think, a private residence, there was quite a number of people present. On
going into the house, I saw on one side of a large room
a table, and a chair placed near it. When the people
came in and filled the room, to my astonishment, he took
the place by the table, sung a hymn, prayed, and com-

menced preaching. I was greatly astonished, for I had never heard him preach before, or even knew that he was a preacher at all. All seemed to pay the greatest attention, and there was at one time much feeling manifested by the audience. This must have been very soon after he commenced preaching, and from the number of people present he must have been able even then to fix the atten· tion of his hearers on what he was saying.

No incident of my childhood is more distinctly remembered than this. What surprised me beyond measure was the number of bad words, as I considered then, your grandfather used on that occasion. In order to make us children avoid everything resembling irreverence or profanity, my two sisters and I were taught to substitute other words for many in common use. Instead of saying God, we were taught to say "the Good Man;" instead of devil, "the bad man;" instead of heaven, "the good place;" instead of hell, "the bad place," or "the fiery place." I felt very much scandalized at hearing him use these bad words so freely, but got on after a fashion, though sorely puzzled, until I heard him use the awful word "damnation!" Then I thought he had ruined himself and gave it up completely. I could think of no excuse to make for him after that.

Many of the preachers of those times, and long afterwards, often spoke and acted as if they believed that what they should say would be given them at the proper time; after entering the pulpit they would often say they had no idea, even then, what their text would be, but did not doubt that a subject would be presented to them in due time, thus intimating that their thoughts were directly under the guidance of the Holy Spirit, as well as those of the inspired apostles of old. No such delusion as this, however, ever entered your grandfather's mind. However hopeful that what he might say would prove a blessing to those who heard it, like seed sown in good ground, he thought it necessary to use the greatest diligence beforehand in preparing something if possible that would interest and benefit his hearers.

There is little doubt that most of his preparation, then and afterwards, was made while on horseback, especially after he became more fully engaged in the work of the ministry. When this country was thinly settled, his rides from one appointment to another were often long and solitary. This was favorable to deep thought and reflection on what he intended to say when he met his audience. A friend once told me that he had heard him say that so distinct and clear would his discourse, when thus prepared, appear to his mind's eye, that it resembled an edifice, sharply defined in a clear atmosphere, exact in all its parts and proportions.

It was not until he entered upon the ministry that he became aware of the importance of learning and general information, and of the priceless value of the time he had wasted when young. The great events, recorded in history, the rise and fall of kingdoms and empires, the vicissitudes and sorrows of the human race, were things of which he had hardly heard. The great achievements of the human mind in science, art, and literature were almost wholly unknown to him. Had he been questioned of Egypt and the Red Sea, Horeb, Sinai, and Palestine, the land of miracles and wonders, or of the distant Jordan, he could hardly have told whether they lay beneath the rising or the setting sun. All these things, besides the great truths revealed in the Bible, must now be learned, if learned at all, amid the cares of a busy life. But his resolution was fixed and unalterable to do what he could to promote the salvation of his fellow-men.

At the death of his parents he came into possession of the farm on which he had been brought up. He now found it hard to decide what was best to be done. There were two duties, as he thought, pressing on him at the same time—the one, to provide for his family; the other, to preach the gospel; and these seemed to conflict one with the other.

There are few sadder pictures to contemplate than that of a lonely wife, neglected children, and a cheerless home; and he knew it had fallen to the lot of few to look upon that picture oftener than those who, with small means of their own, and unaided by their brethren, had thought it their duty to preach the gospel. The Calvinistic Baptists of those days, and even later, doubted the propriety of paying their ministers for preaching, fearing it would induce some to follow that as a calling who had never been called and sent for that purpose; and many of their honest and conscientious ministers had grave doubts themselves on the subject. The consequence was that many of them were very poor and their children sadly neglected, giving rise to the belief with many that the worst boys of the neighborhood were the sons of the preacher.

Hoping to avoid this, after much reflection, he concluded to sell his farm and stock, and invest the proceeds in merchandise, and commence selling goods in Williamston, thinking that the profits from this business would enable him to support his family, and give him more time to devote to preaching, which he had so much

at heart. Accordingly, a sale was effected, a lot purchased, a dwelling, store-house, and other necessary buildings erected, a partner found, and business commenced.

He soon discovered, however, that he had made a sad
mistake! His partner failed to supply his part of the
capital, owing to some unexpected disappointment. This,
together with the unforeseen cost of preparing for business, left him but a small capital to carry it on with, and
it soon became apparent that he must fail. He now determined to sell out and pay off all his debts before it was
too late. He found he had not done this a day too soon;
for when they were all paid off a few hundred dollars only
were left him to begin the world anew.

His situation had now become not only perplexing, but
alarming even; and for a time he almost lost sight of the
other great object of his life so dear to him. I doubt if
he ever told any one except your grandmother, how much
he suffered mentally at that time. It was a rule with
him never to burden others with his troubles and per-
plexities, but to keep them very much to himself; and
this course added dignity to his character, as it always
will. Nor were his fears and anxieties groundless, as is
often the case; for before we bring the narrative to a
close, it will be found that many trying scenes awaited
him in the coming years, to test him both as a man and
as a Christian.

About this time glowing accounts were in circulation,
of a beautiful and fertile region, lying far away towards
the setting sun, beyond the blue mountains of his native
state. Cumberland was the name given to this goodly
land by the early explorers. It included what is now
known as Middle Tennessee, and that portion of Kentucky lying north of the Green River of that state.

This region, when first seen by the white man, seems to have justified all that has been said or written in its praise. When Boone, Finley, Clark, Robertson, Sevier, Donelson and others first beheld it from the western slopes of the Cumberland Mountains, they were enchanted with its beauty. Its wooded hills, crystal streams, vast forests and flower-enameled plains seem to have possessed more than Arcadian attraction and beauty ere the deadly strife for its possession between the white man and the savage began. It was the most magnificent park the world had ever seen, abounding in game, where a few hunters have killed more than a hundred fat bears, seventy-five or eighty buffalos, and as many deer in a few days only.* It was truly the hunters' paradise. It was considered by the Indians exclusively as a common hunting and battle-ground, and from the banks of the Tennessee to the Ohio, not an Indian village, or wigwam, was to be seen in it.

At first these accounts were considered somewhat doubtful, and the people hesitated; but when in process of time they were confirmed, an exodus from Virginia and the Carolinas commenced. Your grandfather now being broken up, with but little inducement to remain longer where he then was, and hoping to find a home for himself and family in this new country, decided promptly to remove to it, and see what fortune might have in store for him in what was then considered the "Far West."

When the brethren of the old Skewarkey Church heard this they said, "He must, at once, be set apart and or-dained to preach the gospel, that he may be qualified to build up churches and administer the ordinances in the

* See Putnam's History of Middle Tennessee.

land whither he is about to journey." Accordingly, early in the year 1807, he was ordained as a minister of the gospel, by Elders Joseph Biggs, Luke Ward, and his brother James Ross. Elder Ward, it will be remembered, had baptized both him and your grandmother.

The 6th of May, 1807, was set for the commencement of the journey, on which day all were to meet at a deserted Episcopal Church, in a pine forest a few miles west of Williamston, and there pitch their tents for the first time. Several other families had concluded to emigrate with us. Among these was that of our uncle, Charles Cherry, the husband of your grandmother's sister Rosa.

Before setting out, however, on our distant journey, I will relate some of the scenes and incidents that I still remember during our sojourn in the little town where we had lived before our removal.

CHAPTER VIII.

REMINISCENCES OF EARLY DAYS.

WHILE the emigrants are preparing for the journey, I will relate some of my childish recollections during the time we were living in Williamston. Among the earliest of these was the interest everybody seemed to take in the little twins,—your aunts Polly and Nannie. Ladies making their purchases at the store, before leaving, would often call on your grandmother, and ask to see them. They were two bright little specimens, faultless in form and features, and almost exactly alike in every respect. When on exhibition, they generally stood side by side with their little hands before them, one in the other, in an easy attitude, free from all embarrassment, on account of their familiarity with the situation. After being inspected, questioned, praised, and dismissed, they would again run out to their play.

After this, these ladies would sometimes call for the baby, and I would then be brought in. They would often, when this was done, make me stand by them, and taking off a glove put their pretty white fingers in my hair, which was very thick and curly, and turn it about in a way that was very pleasant. One of them once said: "When he is grown up, his hair will be as beautiful as Absalom's." I did not know then that Absalom was the naughty fellow who wanted to kill his father David and be king himself.

These ladies, I think, must have used choice perfumery of some kind in those days. For, when standing near them, I was charmed with the delicate aroma which, as I thought, exhaled from them like the fragrance from flowers. And from this association of ideas, as I suppose, it seemed to me quite as proper to speak of a sweet lady as of a sweet flower.

I used to stay in the store a good deal and watch the customers coming and going, and hear them and your grandfather talk about the goods and their prices. I would likewise often take my seat in the door to watch for witches as they passed along the streets. We village urchins could tell a witch as far as we could see one, as we thought. When they came to town, they always appeared in the form of little old women, with bright scarlet cloaks and hoods drawn over the head so as nearly to conceal the face. If they were very much bent with age, and shaking a little with palsy, so much the better. They generally supported themselves each with a long staff, which they held in the hand, a little above the middle. Their skin, where it could be seen, was like old parchment; their eyes black and restless. They came to town, as they *said*, to buy a little tea, chocolate, tobacco, or snuff; but this was all a pretext, as we thought. They were always, really, bent on mischief of some kind. On seeing one of these approaching us, we children would dart like so many partridges and watch them from around the corners. He who pointed his finger at one of them, or in any way offended her, was a doomed boy! Perhaps in less than a week he would be attacked by some strange disease that no doctor in the world could cure. These were the terrible witches, according to our belief, that took men out of their

beds at night and rode them to the places where they held
their dances, around a tree that had been struck by lightning in some wild, desolate place. Alas! that these poor
old women should have had so bad a name.

Old women, in former times, used to have their thumbs
tied together and be then thrown into deep water. If
they sank and were drowned, they were considered innocent. If they did not sink, they were considered guilty
of being witches,—taken out and burned. It is to be
hoped people will never again make themselves such idiots
as they then were about witches.

Another cause of dread and fear we foolish children had
was the *Guinea Negroes*. The slave trade was lawful at
that time, and great numbers of negroes were brought from
Africa and sold to the Carolina planters. As I remember
them, they were generally very large of stature and perfectly black. When first brought over, they could not
speak a word that any one could understand except themselves. Rich men in and near Williamston owned great
numbers of them.

The other negroes, who had been longer in the country
and considered themselves *highly civilized*, looked on these
new-comers not only with scorn and contempt, but with
intense hatred and fear, which they largely instilled into
the little white children also. They believed them closely
leagued with the *Evil One;* and that, when they chose to
do so, they could prepare a mixture of noxious herbs, roots,
and poisonous reptiles, and lay it under the door-sill of
another negro against whom they might have a grudge,
which would, sooner or later, produce death unless coun-
teracted by some more powerful conjurer.

Many poor negroes in good health, imagining they had

been thus foully dealt by or tricked, would pine away and die notwithstanding all that could be done for them. Sometimes they would make up a poison of a different kind and conceal it in the path the negro they hated passed along to his work, and if he happened to stop *over* it he would soon, as they thought, begin to feel its effects in every part of his body, and gradually grow worse and worse as the poisonous articles decayed more and more, and just as decomposition of the poison took place, death would ensue. This belief brought out another set of im-postors, who professed to be able to relieve those thus affected, by counteracting remedies, which often produced death likewise. Those who are acquainted with the ac-counts travellers give of the sad condition of the poor negro in his native land, on account of these and other dark superstitions, can but feel pity for their unhappy lot.

Very often, early in the morning, one of these large black Guinea negroes would be seen going along the street carrying a small negro child on his back, with its little black woolly head sticking out from the blanket. We white children were told by the other negroes that these Africans were carrying the little fellows out where they were at work to eat them for breakfast, as there was nothing in the world they liked to eat so well as a fat baby. I can remember when we believed this implicitly, and supposing they would not object to a white chap if they could conveniently pick one up, we generally gave them a wide berth, as you may well suppose. Your grand-father, on learning how we were exercised on this subject, relieved us greatly by telling us it was all false from be-ginning to end; that the Guinea negroes were really very fond of their little children; and that their masters, when the weather was fine, would often permit them to carry them out to the fields where they were at work and set them down on their blankets under a shade tree, so as to be near them.

Most of my recollections of those times are pleasant. They are not all so, however. On one occasion your grandfather gave me a piece of money to buy a knife with. I went, accordingly, into a store and made the purchase. Soon afterwards, having lost the knife, I went back to the store-keeper and told him as I had lost it, I thought he ought to give me my money back. I cannot imagine what put a notion so absurd into my head. I soon perceived I had made myself ridiculous. Everybody present was laughing at my expense. Among these was a boy I very much disliked. I now became very angry and struck him. We then had a long, hard fight, a crowd of boys forming a ring around us as is usual in such cases. At length I became completely exhausted and could fight no longer. The boys told me I was whipped and parted us. I left the crowd, went off a little distance, and sat down very disconsolate. This had been an unlucky day for me,—"*dies notandus carbone.*"* All in one day to lose my knife, my money, get a whipping, and make myself ridiculous, was too bad.

One of the larger boys, however, for whom we all had great respect, seeing my forlorn condition, came to me and said I must cheer up,—adding that I had done exactly right; every *man* ought to fight when insulted; being whipped was nothing; he had been whipped twenty times and was not a bit the worse for it; I had fought bravely; all the boys said so, and he thought a great deal more of

---

* A day to be noted with a black mark, or charcoal.

me than he did before. This talk comforted me wonderfully and all my trouble soon vanished. It is true my
ribs felt sore for several days, but I cared little for that.

I remember the story of a boy who lived in Williamston
at this time, which i will tell you. His father, who was
a store-keeper, invited some of his friends one day into his
room to take a glass of toddy with him. West India or
Jamaica rum was the favorite and almost universal bever-
age in those days. These gentlemen took their glasses,—
mixed, stirred, and tasted; then dropped in another lump
or two of sugar, poured in a little more water, and then a
little more of something else; then taking up something
like a dear little baby's shoe, as the old woman said, grated
some fragrant nutmeg over the compound; then seated
themselves, and sipped and talked and talked and sipped
in a way that was very pleasant to see. After all was
disposed of, they kept their seats and chatted a short time,
then rose, took up their hats, bade each other adieu in
the most friendly manner, and went their several ways.

Somehow it happened that the boy of whom I am speaking went into the room while this was going on. Did you
ever observe how apt this is to be the case with children ?
When all were gone this naughty boy, seeing everything
ready to his hand, concluded he would have a toddy too,
and prepared one stiff enough probably for a grown man.
After drinking this off, he sat down in his chair and rested
awhile. Then he got up and went into his mother's room.
She not knowing what he had been about, told him to go
out and pick up some chips to put on her fire, the weather
being a little cool at the time. He told his mother he
should do no such thing, that he was done picking up
chips,—never expected to pick up any more, that she knew

where the wood-pile was, and if she wanted chips she could go and get them herself or send some one else, he didn't care which.

His mother, who had never heard him use such language to her before, rose from her seat in amazement. Then, seeing what was the matter, in the greatest alarm, threw her arms around him, exclaiming: "My poor child, my poor child!" And this, as I have heard, was about the last this boy remembered. The people of the town, who knew from *experience* what was best to be done in such cases, were called in, and I have heard it said that for a long time no one could tell certainly whether this boy was dead or alive, so near did he come to death's door. It is to be hoped he never behaved in this way afterwards, and that others who read this story will take warning.

The war feeling born of the Revolution still lingered in Carolina at this time, to some extent. Every man of the military age was enrolled, and companies organized in all the counties were required to muster so many days in every year, armed and equipped as the law directed. The company musters were called petty musters. The others were styled regimental and general musters. A general muster was a great affair with us boys. Then all the different companies of the county met in some old field near town, and formed, as we thought, a mighty army. Early in the day the boys, white and black, would repair to the place of rendezvous to witness the arrival of the different companies. It was a beautiful sight to see them coming in from the different points of the compass, with their guns gleaming brightly in the sun, the officers richly dressed in their uniforms, with cocked hats, nodding plumes, drums beating, fifes playing, colors waving in the breeze, and all falling into line as they came up. In my childish opinion there would be men enough there to conquer the world.

After performing a great many evolutions, in one long column they would march down into the town. It was a glorious sight to gaze upon this proud array. The ladies, in their fine dresses, would crowd the doors and windows, clap their hands, and wave their handkerchiefs. Every fellow now would straighten up and step proudly forward, imagining every eye was fixed on him alone. I would have given all the gold of Ophir had I possessed it to have been large enough to march in this proud column. You must remember that I describe things as they seemed to me then, in my childish fancy. So impatient was I to attain the proper age and height to muster, that I requested an officer one day to make me a mark with his pencil on the door; and he promised that when I should reach it he would let me muster under him. For a time, I often went and stood under this mark to see how I was getting on, and sometimes, to help me on, I tried to do a little extra eating, but I went up so slowly, that I finally became discouraged and gave it up.

To the left of the principal street in Williamston, if I remember rightly, stood the old Court-house, the object of affectionate remembrance long years afterwards. Here I used to see sights that just suited the taste of the idle village boy, whose chief delight was to ramble about from place to place to see whatever could be seen. It had a venerable look, even then,—this old Court-house. It stood on wooden posts or pillars, high enough from the ground for vehicles of every description to pass under it. There was a kind of rude stairway rising from the ground outside

5

the building, leading to a door in the end of it next the street. This was the only entrance to the room above where the courts were held. I do not remember ever going up *into* this room, though I would sometimes go up the steps high enough to look into it and observe what was going on there. I noticed there would be a man seated on one side of this room, before whom first one man and then another would rise up and speak in what I thought rather a threatening manner at times. While this was going on above, a lively scene would generally be enacting in the *lower* regions. In those times Court days were a kind of Saturnalia. Everybody would seem to be there either buying or selling rum, beer, cider, oysters, or gingerbread. Early in the morning the *elite* of the piny-woods would be seen hurrying in on their little horses, so low that the toes of their long-legged riders would almost reach the ground, and generally at about half speed. I believe all uncivilized people are hard riders. The Indian squaws even, as I have been told, ride like Lapland witches.

Towards the close of the day, the *boys* would become "unco happy," and be seen walking about, shaking hands, hugging each other in the most affectionate manner, and making vows of eternal friendship. While all were in this delightful frame of mind, suddenly, perhaps, the startling sound, "a fight! a fight!" would be heard. Then a simultaneous rush would be made to the scene of conflict, a ring be formed around the belligerents, and so intense would be the desire of the outsiders to see the fight, that they would often climb up on each other's shoulders to look down into the arena below. Soon a friend of one of the combatants would break through the ring to help his

comrade, and the cry of " foul play " be heard.   Then a
friend of the other party would throw off hat, coat, and
shirt, and spring upon the interloper.   Then another and
another would go in, until the battle would wax fierce and
general.   After a little, one fellow would cry out "enough!"
and be dragged out.   Then another would make a similar
announcement, and be pulled out also by his friends, and
this would continue until the fight ended, and perhaps,
after all, no one could tell what it was all about.

For all this, no such thing as pistol, dirk, or bowie-
knife would be seen or thought of.   When all was over, it
would be found that no serious mischief had been done.
Perhaps next day, on *coming to*, one might find that he
had gained a black eye, or lost a small piece of his ear.
In those days there was no meddlesome police to interfere
on such occasions and mar the happiness of the people in
their sports.   I would not be understood as saying that
scenes similar to the one described *always* occurred on
court days.

Under this old Court-house I ate many a fine mess of
oysters.   On court days they would be brought here in
carts, nicely prepared for use.   Each dealer would have a
table for his customers to eat from.   When one called for
oysters, they would be set before him with a piece of white
wheaten bread, vinegar, salt, and pepper.   These oysters
were nearly fresh, and beyond comparison superior to any
I have ever seen since.   At least this is the impression
left on my mind.   Your grandfather was very fond of
them, and frequently went down among the carts to feast
on them.   When he did so, if I could be found, he generally took me with him.   On these occasions, I stood or
sat by him and had a good time of it.

Few things that I can remember afforded me more pleasure than to go on a fishing excursion with him. He would take me in a canoe and paddle either up or down the river, until he came to a place shaded by the trees that leaned over the water. Here he would soon catch a basket of the finest fish. It seemed strange that they would bite for him so much more freely than for me. I would drop my hook just as near to his as I could get it, and not have a nibble even, while he brought them out, fluttering one after another in rapid succession. At length, becoming disgusted, I would throw down my pole, and go to playing in the water. Why the fish manifested so great a preference for his bait was then and still is a mystery to me. I could see no reason for it whatever. My bad success though did not prevent my enjoyment. The beautiful river, the beautiful trees that bordered it, and the sandy shores all combined to fill the mind with a succession of pleasing emotions.

The woods around Williamston, at certain seasons of the year, abounded in wild grapes, chincapins, huckleberries, &c. To ramble among these woods, gather and eat grapes and huckleberries, collect chincapins for winter, and, when tired, to roll up great heaps of fragrant pine straw to wallow in, were among our most agreeable pastimes.

On the outskirts of the village grew a gigantic willow tree, which made a beautiful playground, and all the children of the place used to meet there to play under it. There was nothing left behind that we children regretted more than this beautiful tree. Among others that often met us there I remember a little girl attended by her old nurse. For her we boys had the profoundest admiration. Her hair was dark and very glossy, her eyes large and of a deep hazel color, her complexion fair as the lily, and her expression inexpressibly sweet and pleasant. At least so I thought. She usually sat a little apart from the rest, watching our pranks, and occasionally clapping her tiny hands. When something very amusing would occur, she would lay her head down on the grass and laugh to her little heart's content. The power of grace and artless beauty, as shown even in this child, must be great, for there was not a young scape-grace among us that was not gentle as a lamb in her presence.

But I know you must be weary by this time, and so I will stop, after saying once more,—Good-bye, my dear old native State, stretching far away beyond the blue mountains to the deep Atlantic. Good-bye, fair Roanoke, my native stream, dear to my childhood's memory, as the winding Ayr, or bonny Doon, to the great Scottish bard. Good-bye, dear old Court-house, with all your pleasant memories. Good-bye, grand old willow, with your long pendent branches waving in the breeze. And Good-bye, too, little beauty of our play-ground. I trust your bark has glided smoothly down the stream of time. But if, as is most likely, long ere this, you have found your last resting-place, may the birds sing and the flowers bloom sweetly around it. Good-bye one and all.

CHAPTER IX.

THE JOURNEY COMMENCED.

THE time for beginning the journey at length arrived; and I propose to give you some of the scenes and incidents connected with it, as they arise in my memory. You will, no doubt, be surprised to find that it retains so many of these, as I was then only six years old. But what things I shall relate, and many besides, were themes of conversation in the family circle long years afterwards, and thus became fixed in my memory.

Several other families had concluded to emigrate with us, with their large families of children and servants. It was agreed that all should leave their homes the same day, in the morning, and meet at a deserted Episcopal church that stood in a forest of pines some distance from the town, and there encamp the first night.

There were many of these deserted churches in Virginia and the Carolinas at that time. When the law was passed depriving the clergy of that church of the sixteen thousand pounds of tobacco to which they had been entitled annually, the Established Church was broken up, and these lonely and decaying buildings might be seen in many places in the country. As many of these churches had grave-yards attached, which were likewise neglected, the superstitious imagined they often saw forms that did not seem properly to belong to this world—not only by night, but sometimes in broad day—standing still or moving about; people generally went a little out of their way to pass around them. This was especially the case with the boys and negroes, who had many tales to relate of what they and others had seen at these places.

On the 6th of May, 1807, according to appointment, all bade adieu to their friends and relatives, the scenes of their early life, the graves of their fathers, and many objects besides around which memory loves to linger, and turned their faces towards the setting sun. It was customary then, and I believe is so still, when a family was about to remove from a place where they had long resided, and seek a home in a distant country, for the near neighbors and intimate friends to call and bid them farewell. This is usually a time when there is much tenderness of feeling; many, in taking leave, would not venture to speak; a tender embrace, a silent tear, and a pressure of the hand in many cases would be all. But few of the aged men and women now living do not remember such parting scenes. In those early times the emigrants that left Carolina or Virginia to settle in Kentucky or Tennessee hardly expected ever again to see those from whom they parted, especially if somewhat advanced in years. The great distance, the intervening mountains and rivers, the difficult roads, and the cruel savages that roamed in and around these States forbade the indulgence of this hope. They parted much as do those who part at the grave.

We children and the negroes that were along kept up our spirits pretty well by thinking and talking about Cumberland,—the name of the beautiful new world we were to find at the end of our journey. We loved to hear the word pronounced, and when journeying on towards it, if a stranger asked us to "what parts" we were going, we answered proudly, "To Cumberland." We always lost heart though a little when told there were no shad or herring, chincapins, huckleberries, or pine-knots to kindle fires with in all this beautiful country. The negroes made a serious matter of the pine-knot question, and thought the lack of these a great drawback on any country, however blest in other respects,—even on Cumberland itself.

On the day appointed, the whole party met at the old church; and as the night came on, the tents were pitched. Two or three stakes, forked at the upper ends, were cut, and firmly planted in the ground. On these a ridge-pole was laid, and against it other poles were leaned like the rafters of a house. Over all these a large tent-cloth or piece of canvas was spread, to keep off the rain and dews; then another piece of the same material was hung up opposite the front, which was always turned from the wind, to keep the smoke from being blown in. Then, if the leaves on the ground were dry, some of them would be brought in and spread down inside the tent. A bed was then brought in from the wagon and laid on quilts and made comfortable to sleep on, a blazing fire kindled at the mouth of the tent, and supper cooked and served. This would be followed, perhaps, by a stroll around the camp-fires, and then to bed.

The first night we children camped out we were ill at ease. We thought ghosts could not find a more desirable place for their walks than the lonely church. The scarred trunks of the pines, white with the indurated rosin, the moaning of the wind in their lofty tops, and the red glare of the camp-fires among their branches worked on our

imaginations, and caused the whole scene to appear weird
and spectral. But at length "tired nature's sweet re-
storer" came to our relief, and in the deep slumber of
happy childhood all was forgotten. Next morning betimes
all were up. The teams were fed, breakfast prepared and
served, the tents struck, and the long journey began in
earnest.

Other emigrant families soon joined us, and their wagons
and teams, in addition to ours, formed a long line that
moved slowly over the white sandy roads, bordered by the
stately pines. Among these families was that of a man
named Long, with his wife and three or four children
They seemed to be in better circumstances than any others
of the party,—better dressed, better equipped for traveling, more cheerful and lively, and in these respects in
strong contrast with their fellow-travelers. We soon
learned they were Methodists, a kind of people we young
Predestinarians knew but little about.

The first night we encamped together the Long children
joined us in our plays; and after things began to grow a
little dull the oldest daughter, a lively girl ten or twelve
years old, proposed that we should have a camp-meeting,
and all get happy. Then she began to sing a lively song, in
which her little sisters joined her, clapping their hands,
shouting "glory! glory!" and swaying their little bodies
backward and forward in a way that astonished the rest
of us greatly. Their parents did not seem to think this at
all improper; but ours looked grave and shook their
heads, thinking it a kind of mockery.

One evening the little Long girl and another got up a
discussion about religion, in which the former remarked
that her papa said everybody had a spark of grace in

5*

his soul, which, if he would blow and fan it, would kindle into a bright flame, and make him a good Christian. To this it was replied, " If one was not of the elect he might blow and fan a long time, before he would see any bright flame make its appearance." This subject was discussed more or less frequently for several days, among the larger children, and indicated the hard-shell and soft-shell elements very clearly.

After journeying with us for several days, the Longs took another road and left us, very much to our regret. We missed the camp-meetings and songs, especially at night, after they were gone. I do not remember where they were to settle, if I ever heard.

The first town through which we passed, after leaving Williamston, was Tarboro, in Edgecombe County, — the county where the General Assembly of North Carolina met in 1787. Here we crossed the Tar River, on a long narrow bridge. The water under the bridge looked nearly black, and I imagined was very deep. I thought it a dangerous-looking place, and was glad when we were safely over it. The next place that I remember was Hillsboro, in Orange County ; and the next Guilford Court-House, now Greensboro, where the famous battle was fought between General Green and Lord Cornwallis, in 1781. Here we all stopped, and remained several hours on the battle-field, trying to find some vestige of the conflict. We only made out, however, two or three trees cut off a considerable distance above the ground by the cannon balls. This was not much, it was true, but all seemed thankful that they had seen that much. I remember there was a good deal of jesting about the time it took some of the North Carolina militia to reach Martin County, after the fight. One fellow, of marvellous speed and bottom, got in some time before any one else, and reported that he was the only one left alive of General Green's whole army,—that all the rest were lying stark and cold on the bloody field of battle, and he alone was left to tell their sad story.

Some days after leaving this place, we children had loitered behind; on coming up with the wagons, we found them all stopped on an elevated part of the road. On inquiring the cause, we were shown what seemed to be a light blue cloud lying far away to the west, on the verge of the horizon. It was indeed to our young eyes a vision of beauty. In its vast outline not a rent or fissure could be seen; and we gazed upon it with mingled feelings of won-der and admiration. And this, then, was the famous Blue Ridge, about which we had heard so much, and be-yond which lay our distant homes. As for crossing over it, how was that possible? Could wagons and teams ascend perpendicular walls? or pass over the clouds?— so thought and spoke the children.

Some time after this, if I remember rightly, we passed near the base of the Pilot Mountain, a conical peak of great elevation, and, as I think, in Surrey County, around the lofty summit of which some wonder-loving chap told us shapes like men with wings had often been seen flying in the clear blue sky. This was something to study about; and for years afterwards, your two aunts and I talked about it, so much did it haunt our imaginations. I have thought since that perhaps eagles might have sometimes built their nests on this mountain, and that this gave rise to the story, if there was any foundation for it at all.

North Carolina is divided by geographers into three sections,—the eastern, or alluvial; the middle, or hilly; and the western, or mountainous. We were now in the section last mentioned. As we approached the Blue Ridge, it seemed every day to rise higher and higher towards the zenith. At length our tents were pitched at its base. In vain they tried to make us believe that this was the same calm and beautiful mountain which we had seen many days before when it first came into view. The vast masses of rock, piled one above another in wildness and confusion; the lofty summits beaten and scarred by wintry storms; and the deep ravines worn in its sides by descending torrents,—forbade our believing it to be the same beautiful mountain first seen. "Distance" had indeed lent "enchantment to the view." ·

We did not cross the Blue Ridge by the road which the State of North Carolina, in 1776, ordered to be opened from Morganton on the east to Jonesboro on the west of the mountains, but farther north. Nor do I remember the name of the Gap or Pass at which we crossed. A good deal, though, was said at the time about a pass called Ward's Gap.

After the pass had been reconnoitered the ascent began. A wagon was lightened by having a part of its load taken out. Then as much team, from other wagons, added to it as could be conveniently managed. After which, one man would be placed at each wheel to assist in turning it, and two behind it, each with a large stone in his hand. It was the business of the scotchers, as they were called, to save every inch of ground in the ascent, by placing their stones, or scotchers, behind the wheels, to prevent the wagon from rolling back and dragging the team after it.

All things being ready, the driver would throw himself

into the saddle, crack his whip, yell at the horses, in which he would be joined by others, and if your grandfather were not too near, perhaps some bad words would be heard. After a hard pull, the driver would ascend probably eight or ten yards, and then make his team stop just as he perceived they were about to do so themselves. The scotchers quickly placed their stones behind the wheels, to save all the ground gained. Then resting a minute, the word would be given again and a similar feat performed. In this way all the wagons finally reached the summit of the mountain, and a shout of triumph was heard by those below.

While this was going on the boys had a sort of side-show, which made them nearly frantic with delight. They persuaded a stout lad to play wagon for them. He got down on all-fours, with a string around his neck, which was held by another boy, whip in hand, and scotchers were behind with stones to prevent his rolling back ; in this way they carried him up the mountain too. They enjoyed every part of the show in a high degree; but when the boy would balk, as he sometimes did, and kick up his hind legs like a horse, the mountain fairly echoed with their yells of delight.

I do not remember the number of emigrant wagons then with us. Perhaps there were half a dozen, perhaps more. Some had taken other roads and parted from us before we reached the mountain. All finally gained the heights in safety, prepared, after a night's repose, to resume the journey on the morrow.

The east of the Blue Ridge is the boundary between North Carolina and Tennessee. On these lofty heights the emigrant might take his stand, and turning his face to the east, gaze for the last time on his native State and bid it a final adieu. First and last, how many sorrowful hearts, young and old, have performed this sad rite!

The journey thus far had been one of no little anxiety to your grandfather. Soon after it began, your grandmother took a deep cold from which she did not fully recover before it ended. At one time she was so much indisposed, that a physician was called in to prescribe for her, and fears were entertained that she would not be able to finish the journey. I well remember her pale and sorrowful face, as she lay on her bed, and was moved along over the rough uneven roads.

CHAPTER X.

BEYOND THE MOUNTAINS.

We must have made a considerable *detour* after crossing the mountains, for Abingdon, in Washington County, Virginia, was the next town I remember. Its locality in the old times, I think, was known as the " Wolf Hills." Here lived the Crabtrees, who killed an Indian while the treaty of Watago was being negotiated, which brought so much trouble upon the early settlers. This town was on the great highway traveled by the early emigrants from Virginia, who, turning to the right and passing through the famous Cumberland Gap, entered Kentucky, while those from Carolina, turning to the left down the valley of the Holston, entered Tennessee.

Along this route Boone and his large party of emigrants met with a bloody defeat, by the Indians, in 1772, in which one of his sons was killed. On this route, also, the father of the famous Peter Cartwright and his family traveled in these perilous times, when on their way to Kentucky, of which he has given an account so deeply interesting in the first chapter of his autobiography, and which culminated in the murder of "the seven families" near Crab Orchard, in Kentucky, by the Indians. On this route the famous pioneers of Kentucky, Boone, Calloway, Henderson, Clark, Rogers, and others traveled to explore this wild and perilous region when in its primeval state; as also Robertson, Donelson, Sevier, etc., so famous in the annals of the early settlements in Tennessee.

Abingdon was even then a pretty town. Here we children had a feast of gingerbread given us by our parents, and most of us received some small presents besides. Mine was a bright, tin cup, which I carried many days suspended from my neck, and used in drinking water from the pretty streams which we so often crossed. It was long ere we juveniles forgot Abingdon, and its name even now sounds pleasant to my ears.

Journeying on, we at length reached Bean's Station, a place about which the emigrants had a great deal to say, long before we reached it, as being the place where the first settlement was made west of the mountains, in what, as I think, is now Grainger County. But its being the place where the first white child was born in Tennessee, seemed to have given it more dignity and importance than anything else. They could never cease talking about that child, and I came at length to envy its good fortune to some extent, and to wonder why *I* could not have been born there instead. To me, except for the child, the place seemed to have no interest whatever, ignorant as I then was of the bloody Indian wars and thrilling incidents that had occurred long before, on the banks of the historic Watauga and Nolichucky rivers, and also of the famous old beech tree that bore until lately, if it does not still, the inscription carved in its bark by Daniel Boone, in 1760—about forty-seven years before we passed through that country.

After leaving Bean's Station, while among the moun- tains of Tennessee, we saw much that was picturesque and beautiful, hills and mountains, covered with vast primeval forests, and robed in the light green of early summer, with valleys of surpassing beauty and fertility, through which flowed streams of bright and sparkling water. No wonder the poor Indian struggled long and hard to retain possession of this beautiful and romantic region.

It was among these mountains that I got into trouble. Passing near a beautiful stream, where some men were engaged in catching a quantity of fine fish, I could not resist the temptation to stop and look at them. I waited too long. The wagons got far before me. Starting off in a hurry to overtake them, I took a wrong road. After proceeding some distance I turned back to get in the right one again, having found my mistake. 'In the meantime I had been missed; the wagons were all stopped in the road, the horses unharnessed and mounted, and the neighborhood scoured in search of me. They feared I had been drowned in the river. All were in distress, and some in tears, for I had many friends. At length I was seen toiling up the road, weary with my long walk and anxiety. A shout was raised; all gathered around me and manifested, for a while, the most lively satisfaction for my safety. But some who had been in tears, when they thought me dead, after they came to think of the trouble and detention I had caused, suddenly turned against me and rather, hinted that some punishment would do me no harm : I was quite surprised at the sudden turn things had taken. I escaped punishment, however, but was in disgrace for several days.

Long before we reached it we heard of a portion of country we had to pass through called the wilderness; and what made it more appalling to us children was that sometimes the word "howling" was added. The phrase

"howling wilderness," sounded ominous in our ears. Visions
of wolves, bears, lions, tigers, panthers, and Indians rose
before us. This wilderness lay on the Cumberland Mountain, between the Clinch River, a northern tributary of
the Tennessee and the Caney Fork, a southern tributary
of the Cumberland.

In consequence of some misunderstanding about what
was called the treaty of Holston, it was uncertain at the
time to which race it belonged, the white or the Indian,
and consequently neither held it in possession. It commenced, I believe, about forty miles west of Knoxville,
and terminated about sixty miles east of Nashville. And
as the distance between Knoxville and Nashville is two
hundred miles, it must have been about one hundred miles
across. A beautiful description of this wilderness you
may find in Parton's Life of Jackson, Volume I, chapter
16. It was written by Francis Bailey, the celebrated
English astronomer, who crossed it in 1797, about ten
years before we did.

It was necessary for all who passed through this wilderness to provide food for themselves and their teams,
before attempting to do so; especially for themselves.
There were many places where the teams could find an
abundance of grass and wild pea-vines. These pea-vines
were preferred by horses and cattle to any other food
whatever. And it was said to recruit them when in low
condition faster than any other known. These were abundant among the hills and mountains of Tennessee in early
times, and afforded the richest pasturage.

Soon after entering the wilderness, we descended a very
long and steep hill, not far from Crab Orchard, in Morgan
County, Tennessee, I think, and encamped near a pretty

stream of water. It was a beautiful and romantic spot. The little stream was called Daddy's Creek. This name greatly delighted us children. We would have given anything to know how it came by that name. The hill we had just descended was the famous Spencer's Hill, so called from a pioneer of that name who had been killed upon it by the Indians. There was a great deal said that night around the camp-fires about poor Spencer, how he and another man named Holiday crossed the mountains together and traveled on until they reached the neighborhood where the City of Nashville now stands; how each built a rude cabin and cleared a little field; how Spencer would cut down a large tree, take a rail-cut on his shoulder, and carry it to the place where he was making his fence, split it into rails, and lay them upon it, all of which he was enabled to do on account of his prodigious strength; how a hunter, not knowing he was in the country, and seeing his enormous foot-prints in the snow, became frightened, fled from it, and reported it full of giants; how Holiday lost his knife, and Spencer broke his own in two and gave him half of it when they parted; and how, after he had finished his cabin, and fenced his little field, when on his way home to bring his wife and children to the beautiful country he had found for them, he was killed by the cruel savages on the hill which bore his name.

The children shed tears for the noble hunter, when we thought of his manly form lying stark and cold far away in the lonely mountain, never again to be seen by his sorrowing wife and fatherless children; and gave vent to our feelings of abhorrence by heaping every opprobrious epithet we knew upon his murderers. I may observe here that most, if not all of what we heard that night relating to Spencer is, I think, historically true.

We were alarmed on several occasions while in the wilderness, two of which I remember. One evening, after our tents were pitched for the night, a solitary Indian came to us with some venison for sale. He told us he was "good Injun." Our people, however, thought differently, and set him down as an Indian of the very worst kind, sent as a spy by his tribe, perhaps not far off, to ascertain our strength and means of defense; and if he found us weak, to return and bring a party down upon us during the night, to tomahawk and scalp the last one of us before day. The more we thought about it, the greater the danger seemed. A council was held, and the "conscript-fathers" decided to buy the Indian's venison, and to invite him to stay with us all night. Should he consent to this, well and good; if not, to place him under arrest, and keep him prisoner till morning. When the proposition was made he readily consented, and at bedtime rolled up for himself a bed of dry leaves, got into it and went to sleep. Not so your grandmother, .Aunt Rosa, and others. All night they watched that pile of leaves, expecting every moment to see the Indian crawl stealthily from among them, and start off to bring his gang upon us. But this did not happen. When morning came he was still there, remained with us till after breakfast, then shouldered his rifle, bade us adieu, disappeared in the forest, and this was the last of our "good Injun," as he really turned out to be.

The next trouble we had in the wilderness occurred when at the close of a day's journey, we reached a stream of water too late to cross over it. Other emigrants, though, who reached it earlier in the evening had crossed, and encamped on the opposite side.

I must inform you, if you do not already know it, that large reeds, or canes, when thrown on a hot fire, will swell and burst with a report very much resembling the crack of a rifle. The children on the other side of the stream, after all had become quiet, and before going to sleep, got into a frolic, and commenced throwing armfuls of large canes on the fire, and shouting when they burst.

We on our side took this to be the report of rifles, accompanied by the yells of Indians, and thought all on the other side were being massacred by them, and that it would soon be our turn. Wild shrieks now arose among the women, children, dogs, and negroes, and dire was the din that followed. The people on the other side, hearing the uproar among us, and never dreaming that the bursting of the reeds and the shouting of the children of their party was the cause of it, concluded the Indians were among us, and would soon be on them, and raising a regular murder shout, joined in the concert. It would be useless to attempt a description of the scene that followed. Some new words would be needed for the purpose. At length, however, quiet was restored. On reflection, we were heartily ashamed of what we had done, and those who had us in charge thought theirs was a hard lot indeed.

After leaving the wilderness behind us and crossing the Caney Fork River, while going towards Nashville we met a gentleman in the road, who getting into conversation with your grandfather, advised him to purchase land, and settle in what, I think, was then called the Dutch River country, describing it as being a beautiful and fertile region, telling him at the same time that he owned land there, on which he had built a good cabin, which he might occupy until he could find land to suit him, and gave him at the same time an order to his agent to let him have possession of the house. I have heard that this gentleman told others he was very much pleased with your grandfather's appearance, and wanted him to settle in the part of the country where his lands lay, believing he would attract others to settle near him. I judge he was one of those great land speculators, who were then engaged in securing a portion of the rich lands lying south of Nashville.

We accordingly went to the place, found his cabin, and took possession. It was situated in a vast cane-brake, a description of which would be incredible to one who had never seen anything of the kind. The canes reached half way up the tall trees, and were so thick that a bear, or Indian, could not have been seen at the distance of a few yards. Where a road or path was cut through it a wall, almost solid, seemed to stand on the right hand and on the left. The wild and lonely appearance of the country, and the constant dread of Indians, however, had a depressing effect on most of the party, and they begged to be carried away from the dismal place, so the idea of settling here was finally abandoned. But your grandfather always regretted that he did not remain, as he thus saw the lands were wonderfully fertile, and to procure such had been his chief inducement in leaving his native state and moving to the West.

Leaving this place, we journeyed on in the direction of Nashville, which a few days afterwards we reached. Here I was sadly disappointed; a few log houses and two or three brick kilns constituted the Nashville of that day, according to my recollection. But I suppose we must have passed through the suburbs only. For I see from Putnam's History of Middle Tennessee, that two years before we passed by it or through it, Nashville could have boasted of about twenty houses, scattered around here and there, in various directions. What a change had come over it when next seen by me some thirty-five years later! It had grown to be a beautiful city, the seat of wealth and refinement. A bridge spanned the Cumberland; steamboats lay along its wharves, and its spires and domes glittered in the sun.

From Nashville, after crossing the Cumberland, we traveled in a north-westerly direction to Port Royal, a village situated in Montgomery County on the left bank of the Red River, a tributary of the Cumberland. This was virtually the end of our long journey, which we reached on the 4th of July, 1807, having been on the road two long and eventful months.

CHAPTER XI.

AFTER THE JOURNEY.

On the opposite side of Red River, about two miles from Port Royal, there was living at this time an elderly gentleman named McGowan, who gave your grandfather permission to occupy, for the present, a small cabin standing in his yard. He was a grey-headed man, gentle in his manner, with a pleasing expression of countenance, a widower at the time, and a member of the Baptist Church. His residence was a short distance to the left of where the road leading from Port Royal to Graysville, Kentucky, and the one leading from Clarksville to Keysburg cross each other, and in what is now a field, opposite the brick house, formerly built by James Reasons, Esq., a man of some note in his day, and occupied at present, I think, by a gentleman named Powers.

A short distance from this house and in the direction of Port Royal is what was formerly known as the Woolfolk place, where there is a spring breaking out in a sink-hole, the water from which is conducted off in a wooden trough. This place is noted for the mysterious murder, in former times, of a young man near it, which threw all the country around into the greatest excitement. No one was ever brought to trial or punishment for the bloody deed, as no satisfactory explanation of it, I think, was ever obtained. Woolfolk was the name of the victim, a young man highly

108

esteemed by all who knew him. It was generally believed he was killed by mistake for another who was at the time riding with him.

When we drove up to the little cabin, your grandfather told us children that we were now at the end of our journey, as he had decided to settle somewhere in this part of the country. Could this be so? Was this place the Eldorado of all our young dreams, the beautiful Cumberland on which our thoughts had delighted so long to dwell? It could not be. There must be some mistake. Our little feet, sore with the sharp stones, had not crossed so many hills and mountains to find a home like this. Our hearts were nearly broken. We laid down on the ground and shed bitter tears. Our parents sympathized deeply with us in our disappointment, but there was no help for it. All was soon taken from the wagon and carried in. And here, in the language of antiquity, " our household gods were set up " for the present. As it was now too late in the season to think of renting land and planting a crop, your grandfather, after looking round a little, decided to teach a school for a few months.

He was then about thirty-one years of age, straight, well proportioned, just under six feet in height, and weighing one hundred and forty-five pounds, which was his weight for many years. All his features were good. His eyes were grey, his hair dark brown. His voice was pleasant to the ear, and finely adapted to sacred music. In the prime of life, when he became animated in his discourse it had considerable strength and power, growing feeble though as he advanced in years. His complexion was dark. The expression of his countenance was thoughtful, and this deepened perceptibly as he grew older.

6

In a large and mixed company he was rather taciturn, but a close observer of all that was said and done around him. In the company of a few friends his conversation was free and animated. His self-possession and sense of what was becoming and proper in himself and others were remarkable traits in his character. I doubt whether any person living or dead ever saw him thrown off his guard. It mattered not how sudden and unexpected a turn things might take, he always seemed to have foreseen what was coming and to be prepared for it. This was often seen in after life while presiding over deliberative bodies as chairman or moderator. I think he had a genius for the management of affairs of great moment in church or state, had he been called to do so.

Soon after stopping here his voice as a preacher was first heard west of the mountains. The place was near what is now known as the Port Royal Mills, where he was then living. His stand was under the branches of a spreading oak, his audience sitting around him on rude seats or on the ground during the services. I supposed when I commenced this writing that I could find some grey-headed man still living who was present on that occasion; but I have failed to do so. They, like him, have passed away. There are some left though who have heard others speak of being present at that time. Would it not be interesting to know how many sermons he preached after that until he delivered his last short address, long years afterwards, in the old Bethel Church, Christian County, Kentucky? At two hundred for each year they would have numbered more than ten thousand.

In the month of November of this year (1807) the first great sorrow fell upon our family. While your grandfather was lying on a sick bed, we children were playing in an outhouse near by. Our little sister Mildred, so called after her mother, about three and a half years old, was with us. We were amusing ourselves gathering dry leaves and throwing them on the fire to see them blaze up and burn. She ran out and brought in her little apron full of leaves, like the rest of us, threw them on the fire, and turned her back to it. They caught, blazed up, and soon she was enveloped in the flames. The alarm was given. Your grandfather sprang from his bed, hastened to her, and tore off her clothing. It was too late. The burns were incurable; and after a few days of intense suffering she died. We larger children mourned the loss of our little favorite, and thought to ourselves she had traveled a long, long journey to find her tiny grave. Her parents were almost broken-hearted. These were dark days in our family history, but many such were in store for us in the coming years.

There was a burying-ground near by, and neglected graves may still be seen in a cluster of trees to the left just before reaching the cross-roads already mentioned. There she was buried, and in this lonely place her ashes still remain, far from those of her kindred in other places. There is a touching reminiscence connected with her grave. When she was buried, two rough stones were set up to mark the spot where she lay. Several years later your grandfather stopped to visit the grave, as he always did when passing that way, and found to his surprise that some unknown friend had removed the former ones and replaced them by others of gray limestone, with the name and dates accurately carved on them. It was indeed a delicate act of friendship. They have long since disappeared, and the exact spot cannot now be identified. It is likely they were removed by some person destitute of respect for the memory of the dead, to be used for some other purpose.

While living here your grandfather was visited by his brother William Ross, who had heard of his arrival in this country. This brother, soon after leaving the army at the close of the Revolutionary War, had come west and settled in what is now Missouri, but was at that time known as Louisiana, a part of the then vast domains of Spain.* The place he selected for a home while still unmarried was near the Mississippi River below the old French town called by the early French adventurers Cape Girardeau, and in a "bottom" famous for its deep and fertile soil. They had not met before since your grandfather was a little boy.

I was present at their meeting. It was very affectionate. They held each other in a long embrace and shed tears freely. He had wandered so far from home—nearly a thousand miles—and been so long absent and lost sight of by his family, that he had come to be regarded very much as one dead. I have heard that he encountered almost incredible hardships and dangers during his long journey on foot, from the shores of the Atlantic to the Mississippi, while passing with his rifle on his shoulder

* This is a historical mistake. The Louisiana territory originally belonged to France, but in 1762 was ceded to Spain. In 1800 it was ceded back to France, and in 1803, during Mr. Jefferson's administration, it was purchased by the United States for fifteen millions of dollars. If this were the place, it would be interesting to show why the great Napoleon was willing to sell so valuable a possession at that time.

J. M. P.

through.the deep forests and savage Indian tribes. He was very gentle and affectionate, and in consequence we all became much attached to him, considering the short time he remained with us.

He greatly desired your grandfather to remove from where he was and settle near him, describing the country in which he lived as surpassed by none in point of fertility of soil, and in the fall of the next year your grandfather went to see him and to look at the country. But from what he saw of it he concluded it must be unhealthy, and was afraid to take his family there.

In the autumn of 1836, long afterwards, I had occasion to visit that country myself. I learned that he, his wife, and some of his children had been dead many years, and the rest had left there and gone farther west, no one could tell me where. I went to the house where he had lived, but it was occupied by strangers, who knew nothing of the family. It was a pretty place, situated on a little stream called Cape-la-Cruce, near the western bank of the great river.

Although not a great deal could be said in praise of the little village of Port Royal itself, near which we were now living, it would perhaps be safe to say no finer citizenship could have been found anywhere at this time than in the country around it, extending into Robertson and Montgomery Counties. In evidence of this one need only mention such names as Fort, Norfleet, Northington, Dortch, Baker, Cheatham, Washington, Bryant, Turner, Blount, Bailey, Johnson, and others, too numerous to mention. They were generally men of large stature, dignified and patriarchal in their bearing, many of them wealthy, very hospitable, and always ready to assist those who

needed it, especially the stranger who came to settle
among them.

Of these some were professors of religion, and those
who were not generally manifested great respect for it
and for all whom they considered pious Christians. Most
of them were Carolinians who had been attracted to this
section of country by its noble forests, fine springs, and
beautiful streams of water, which caused them to prefer
it to other portions where the land was richer, but which
were less favored in other respects.

A mutual friendship and esteem soon sprang up between these people and your grandfather's family, which
lasted while they lasted, and descended to their posterity.
In after years he built up a flourishing church among
these people, called Harmony, where he preached to large
audiences; and there, it is said, he delivered some of his
ablest discourses. It is not to be inferred, however, from
what has been said of this population, that there were no
exceptions to be found among them. There were many
wild, rough characters, as in all new countries, who would
drink, gamble, and fight, often for no other reason whatever than to show their pluck and muscle. These would
sometimes collect in considerable numbers on court-days,
and at elections and horse-races.

Before closing this chapter I will say a few words about
the country that constituted the principal field of your
grandfather's labors as a minister of the gospel after his
settlement in it. It was included within the limits of six
counties—Robertson, Montgomery, and Stewart, in Tennessee; and Logan, Todd, and Christian, in Kentucky.
In 1788, nineteen or twenty years before we came here,
the territorial government of Tennessee authorized a new

county to be organized, taken from the northern portion of Davidson, and to be called Tennessee County, extending along the Kentucky line westwardly and across Cumberland River, embracing quite a large extent of territory. (See Putnam.) Clarksville was made the county seat. Afterwards, however, this county was divided into three, Robertson, Montgomery, and Stewart. Springfield then became the county seat of Robertson, Dover of Stewart, and Clarksville of Montgomery.

The northern portion of these counties bordering on the State line is level or gently undulating, and the soil very productive, yielding rich crops of corn, wheat, and tobacco, producing also the fruits and vegetables peculiar to the climate in great perfection and abundance. Farther south, bordering on the Cumberland and Tennessee Rivers, the country becomes broken and hilly; and in early times, before the forests were cut down, and the hills left bare and unproductive, it was quite romantic, in some places assuming an Alpine character. Among these hills are various minerals; iron ore especially, in inexhaustible supply, and said to be the finest article of that metal to be found in the world.

It would not be easy to give an adequate description of the beautiful streams descending from the hills and hurrying along their rich narrow bottoms to unite with those still larger, and thence to the rivers, bordered by a growth of poplar, beech, walnut, wild-cherry, sugar-maple, buckeye, hackberry, as seen in the early times.

In these narrow alluvial bottoms the first settlers built their cabins, fished in the streams, and hunted among the hills; often cultivating a few acres to raise a crop of corn, pumpkins, etc. Among many of these hills and valleys your grandfather was the first to carry the glad tidings which he loved so well to publish.

Tennessee being settled mostly by emigrants from North Carolina, was considered the daughter of that state.

These three counties in Kentucky, viz., Logan, Todd, and Christian, lying on the state line parallel to Stewart, Montgomery, and Robertson, in Tennessee, resemble them in this respect: the portion of each nearest the state line is rich and level, and that farthest from it broken, hilly, and less productive. The southern portion of these Kentucky counties may be considered one of the garden spots of the state; and had not its advancement in prosperity and wealth been checked by our civil war, it is probable that in no distant future it would have borne the palm.

The face of the country is beautiful, spreading out into wide plains, and producing the same crops as the northern portion of the three Tennessee counties across the line opposite. Its value as an agricultural region was long not even suspected. Being destitute of water and timber to a great extent, and in many places nothing but grass and a few stunted trees to be seen, they were called the "Barrens" of Kentucky. Their appearance too was dreary and forbidding during the winter months as the bleak winds swept over the dry and withered grass, from which, as in the great prairies of the North and West, there was no shelter to be found. But even while this idea of sterility prevailed, during the spring and summer months when far and wide the ground was covered with deep green prairie grass and myriads of bright wild flowers, the scene was one of enchanting beauty.

When its wonderful fertility came to be known, it filled up apace with immigrants mostly from Virginia, many of whom stood high for intelligence, wealth, and refinement. Your grandfather soon became greatly attached to this people, and began to feel deeply interested in their spiritual welfare, and they in turn to love and reverence him almost as a father.

He and his brother ministers preached among them with great success. Flourishing churches were organized, and Baptist influence fully established over all this beautiful country, which might be called the natural home of the Old Bethel Association. But I fear I have detained you too long in endeavoring to give you some idea of the field in which your grandfather labored both in his early manhood and in his declining years.

6*

CHAPTER XII.

In the immediate neighborhood of Port Royal, in the year 1791, about fifteen years before your grandfather came to the country, a church had been organized, known as the "Red River Baptist Church." When this church was first constituted there was no meeting-house, but the meetings were held first at the residence of one and then of another of the members. At length a rude meeting-house was built, such as was common in those days, on the left bank of the Red River, and from this stream received its name. The word church among the Baptists was generally applied to the members rather than to the house in which they worshipped. In those times the custom of naming the church or meeting-house for the creek or river near which it stood was almost universal. Hence we have the "West Fork," the "Spring Creek," and the "Little River" Churches.

The members of the Red River Church—the oldest in the Bethel Association—as their congregations increased in size and their circumstances improved, from time to time built houses of worship more commodious, and they have lately built in the old neighborhood a large and handsome edifice at what is called Adams' Station, on the railroad leading from Nashville to Henderson, on the Ohio River, about eighty years after the first was built

118

in which their fathers worshipped. Verily this old church does not seem wanting in vitality.

The original members of this church—many of whom I remember to have seen when young—a highly respectable body both as citizens and Christians, exercised a happy influence in their community. Most of them were Carolinians and members of Baptist churches before leaving the old state. They soon manifested the kindest feeling for your grandfather, and had heard of his brothers, Martin and James Ross, who stood high among the Carolina Baptists as preachers.

This church had at first belonged to the Cumberland Baptist Association, which, on becoming too large for convenience, was divided into two. The one formed from it took the name, Red River Association, either from this church, or because most of the churches that composed it were in the country watered by the Red River. The association from which it was taken still retained its former name. .Of this famous old Red River Association we shall have much to say hereafter.

What is called an Association among the Baptists is a voluntary union of a number of churches of the same faith and order, prompted thereto by feelings of brotherly love and friendship, and a desire to promote the great interests of religion. Each church belonging to one of these Associations is expected to send one or more messengers to it at its annual meetings, with a letter containing a statement of its progress, present condition, and wants. These letters are read publicly before the body, and give it a general view of the present state of all the churches within its bounds. The messengers elect their Moderator, or Chairman, with other necessary officers.

Each of these bodies has its rules of order, by which its deliberations are to be governed; and when its session closes a brief synopsis of its proceedings is printed and distributed among the churches. During the session some individual will be appointed to write what they call a *Circular Letter*, to be printed with the synopsis of the next year, and sent out with it. A subject is sometimes given, on which he is required to write, but the subject is at other times left to the choice of the writer. Finally, a place is appointed for the next year's meeting, and the body is adjourned. Petitions are often sent up by several churches that the next Association meet with them, and there is sometimes a spirited contest for that honor.

These Associations are often very attractive to the communities in which they are held. All the preachers belonging to them are expected to be present, and while the business is being transacted at one place some of the best preachers address the people at another. The old brethren in the early times were delighted to show their hospitality to brethren and friends from a distance. And families in the vicinity who belonged to other denominations would often open their doors to visitors. Most of the beauty and fashion of the country was present also, which lent an additional charm and interest to these meetings. Many ladies, members of the churches, would travel quite a distance on horseback with their babies in their laps to be present, and might be seen days beforehand converging to the appointed place. On their return it was to them a most delightful task to tell neighbors and friends who had gathered in, of all they had seen and heard. Especially would they tell how their great preachers plunged into the deep, dark mysteries of re-

ligion, and made subjects that had before caused them
to feel giddy even to think of appear so clear that a child
might understand them. And they would often return with
all their doubts and fears dispelled, and a deep religious
determination to press forward along " the narrow way."

How much soever Baptists may be divided in their
views, in other respects there are two points on which
they are a unit wherever found. They all believe that immersion is the only proper act of baptism, and that believers are the only proper subjects. They think the
teaching of the Bible is clear on these points, and, therefore, can never be induced to abandon them. In the
next place, they consider every church a separate and
independent body, and that it is answerable to no other
saintly tribunal or power whatever. If it choose to con-
nect itself with an Association, and is accepted, well and
good; if not, it can stand unconnected, and attend to its
own business in its own way. But although opposed to
being governed, there is a strong tendency to union and
co-operation among them. When young I used to hear
them talk a great deal about their union quarterly and
yearly meetings. At these no business was transacted.
A number of churches would agree through their messengers to meet periodically, interchange letters of kindly
greeting, and worship together for several days in succession. These reunions were held first at one church, and
then another in regular order. The attendance was large,
and their best preachers addressed the people.

As a body the Baptists constitute one of the leading
Christian denominations. I see from the statement of Dr.
Bailey of Chicago that at this time they have 17,445
churches, and have increased in the ratio of one church

per day for the last forty years.* They are numerous in
England, Ireland, Scotland, and Wales. In Sweden and
Germany their increase is now rapid. In the United
States the independence and simplicity of their government and worship, together with their religious views
commend them to the people, and it is estimated that one-
fifth of the people, at least, are under Baptist influence.

In regard to doctrine the Baptist denomination, like
many others, has been divided in sentiment, and to some
extent is still so, some adopting the views of John Calvin ; others, those of Andrew Fuller ; and others still the
sentiments of James Arminius. Hence, we sometimes
hear of Calvinists, Fullerites, and Arminians, among those
whose general designation is Baptists. It is supposed
that a decided majority of the Baptists of the United
States are in accord with the views of Andrew Fuller,
that there is in the atonement of Christ an "objective fulness" sufficient for the salvation of the world, and that
this "objective fulness" is the ground on which the
gospel is consistently preached to every creature.

Baptists, it should be remembered, do not like to be
called by the names of men. They profess to derive their
views from the word of God, to which they appeal as the
supreme standard. While, therefore, they do not undervalue the writings of good men, a subordinate place is assigned to such writings. No persons more cordially
adopt the sentiment that the holy Scriptures are the "only
and sufficient rule of faith and practice."

* According to the "Baptist Year Book" for 1882, issued by the Am.
Bap. Pub. Society, the churches have increased to 26,373, and the members to 2,336,022, This large increase brings with it great responsibility.
                                           J. M. P.

CHAPTER XIII.

RED RIVER ASSOCIATION.

I DO not know the number of churches that composed the Red River Association when it was organized. But in 1810, they amounted to twenty-seven scattered over a wide extent of country.

The number of members was 1020. Of this session Anthony New was Moderator, Wm. Aingell, Clerk, and Elder Reuben Ross, Assistant Clerk.

During my boyhood and youth my opportunities of forming a correct estimate of these old Baptists were much better than those of most boys of my age, had I possessed the requisite discrimination. Your grandfather always insisted on my attending the meetings, if possible, hoping, I suppose, that at some time my attention might be arrested, and my thoughts take a religious turn. I not only attended preaching with him near home, but often at some distance, both in rude and newly settled districts, and also where society was more refined and polished. At Hopkinsville, Elkton, Russellville, etc., were many fine Baptist families fifty years ago; and the impression left on my mind is that they were worthy of all esteem. Their Christian spirit and reverence for religion were every where noticeable, and, notwithstanding their creed, their hearts seemed to glow with love and gratitude to the Creator for the great and merciful scheme

123

of redemption through the sufferings and death of His Son.

As far back as I can remember, what I considered a fine sermon delighted me very much, and I am even now surprised at the impression that remains on my mind, not only of the spirit of some I heard on those occasions, but in many cases of the words and sentences. Next to the fine sermons I was most interested in the experiences that used to be related among the Baptists. And though I rather considered myself a very good judge of a sermon I prided myself on my opinion of an experience, and thought I could tell whether it would pay or not before the vote was taken.

There were, besides your grandfather, four preachers of notoriety in the Association whom I remember well, and whom I have heard preach many times. Of their personal appearance and the character of their preaching, I have a distinct recollection. These were elder Lewis Moore, Jesse Brooks, Isaac Todevine, and Sugg Fort. I will attempt to describe them, that you may have some idea of the men with whom your grandfather was for many years associated in the ministry.

They were staunch Predestinarians, and gloried in the doctrine they preached. All were of excellent character, and some of them of fine talents. In point of ability it was generally admitted that Elder Lewis Moore stood foremost. He was not above medium height, heavily built, with a short neck, large head, full face, and was rather careless in his dress. Out of the pulpit he had little to say, but in it he was certainly no common man. Before coming to this country in 1728, he was pastor of the Reedy Creek Baptist Church in Warren County, N. C.

(See Burkitt and Reed's Church History, page 260).
When I first knew him he was pastor of the Muddy
River Church and of several others in this country. This
church was, I think, situated somewhere north of Russellville, Logan County, Kentucky. In his style of speaking he was nervous, vehement, and sometimes startling.
He seemed to carry in his memory every text in the Bible from Genesis to Revelation that bore on election, predestination, and kindred subjects; and could apply them
with great force and effect. His tact in explaining away,
and weakening the force of those texts that seemed to
militate against his views, I thought little less than marvellous. His irony, too, was exceedingly sharp and cutting.

It was customary in those times for the preachers while
arguing their points to call on a brother, or sister even, to
say if what they affirmed was not true. They would do
so many times during a sermon after becoming heated by
the argument, and the brother appealed to would sanc-
tion with great energy. After piling text upon text, and
argument upon argument, and making his position seemingly impregnable, he would say:

"Tell me now, Brother Todevine, is not this doctrine
true?"

"Yes, Brother Moore, it is true, and the gates of hell
shall not prevail against it."

"Sister Owens, is this doctrine true?"

"Yes, brother, and bless the Lord for it."

"And yet," he would continue, "there are men in the
world, and not a few of them either, who deny the truth
of this glorious doctrine of election that has made glad
the hearts of God's people for thousands of years. They
say, forsooth, it is partial and unjust, and does not give

every one an equal chance to be saved. Now just reflect.
We are all miserable sinners, conceived in sin and
brought forth in iniquity ; and if we had our just deserts
would every one be sent to hell, and that speedily ; but God
in his infinite goodness and mercy has condescended to
elect and save a few of us. And instead of adoring his
holy name because all are not lost, they are raising a
great clamor because all are not saved. A. has money
and chooses to give B. a part of it. The money is his own,
and he can use it as he pleases. But it is no sooner known
that he has bestowed a portion of it on B. than every vagabond in the country denounces him as partial and unjust, because he does not give him some, too. Who is
injured by this ? I would like to know. Some are bene-
fited, but does that defraud any one else ? One man makes
a feast, and invites his friends to come and partake with
him. Those who have not been invited raise a howl as if
victuals had been taken out of their own mouths. Alas !
for the folly and presumption of human beings ! It is
really past finding out."

"But let me tell you, my friends, what is really the
matter. I am sorry to say it, but the truth is the Almighty don't properly understand his business. That is
clear from the mistakes he is constantly making. Would
it not be a blessed thing if he could have some of our
wise men to assist him ? Some that have studied Latin,
Greek, and Hebrew in the colleges and high schools, to help
him govern the world ? Or might it not be better still as
the poet has said to

> "Snatch from his hand the balance and the rod ;
> Rejudge his justice ; be the god of God."

Then would follow one of his perorations, or conclusions, which I used to think very fine.

"But, my dearly beloved brethren and sisters, let not
your hearts be troubled at these things. Your bread shall
be given you, and your water shall be sure. Your house
is built upon the rock. Let the heathen rage and the
people imagine a vain thing. Greater is he that is for
you than they that are against you. Let us contend earnestly for the faith once delivered to the saints. The conflict will soon be over, and we shall be where the wicked
·cease from troubling, and where the weary are at rest.
In those bright mansions not made with hands, eternal in
the heavens, crowns and diadems and palms of victory
await you, which shall be placed on your brows by the
Great King himself."

It was delightful to see how happy the brotherhood
seemed to feel on occasions like this. Every countenance
was radiant with these inspiring hopes, but no hands
would clap or shouts be heard. These preachers would
stop instantly in the midst of one of their loftiest flights
should any one give way to his emotions,—and wait for
him to get composed.

Elder Moore believed that long before the morning stars
sang together, and the sons of God shouted for joy at the
glories of the new creation, the Almighty looked down
upon the ages yet unborn, as it were, in review before
him, and selected one here and another there to enjoy
eternal life and left the rest to the blackness of darkness
forever ; and so he preached. I do not think he lived to
be an old man. When a youth I used to pass by his
dwelling on my way to Drake's Pond Church. His residence was in the extreme southern part of Todd County,

Kentucky. The situation was low and flat, and had an air of loneliness and solitude about it even during his lifetime. I regret that I cannot tell you his age or when he died.

Elder Jesse Brooks, though of the same school of theology as Elder Moore, differed from him in several respects. He was more social, cheerful, and pleasant out of the pulpit. His coat was always brushed, his linen clean and white, and his boots or shoes nicely blacked. He wore a broad-brimmed hat, made of the genuine fur of the beaver, which had perhaps been caught by some trapper among the Rocky Mountains. It used to be said that one of these hats, with what the ladies called a "little doing up, now and then," would last twenty years! He, like other traveling preachers in those times, used to carry on his left arm his saddle-bags, containing his Bible, hymn-book, and a change or two of linen, if he expected to be from home some time. The umbrella was carried in the right hand, and used as a walking-cane when not needed to keep off the sun or rain.

He was above the medium height, and his frame large, without any unnecessary weight. His complexion was fresh for an old man, and his expression mild and prepossessing. Your grandfather used to admire his manners at home, which were those of a pious Christian who made all around him cheerful and happy.

I think he was a silversmith by trade, but had long since quit the business, except as an amusement. He once put a very pretty silver band around the ivory head of a cane belonging to your grandfather, which had been fractured. I would infer from what I used to hear, that he had saved enough from this business while young to make himself and family comfortable in old age.

Elder Brooks, like other Calvinistic preachers of the day, had but little to say to sinners, as those were called who had never made any profession of religion or connected themselves with any church. Indeed, they seemed at a loss to know what to do with sinners any way. They were tough subjects, and they seemed very much disposed to let them alone. If they were not of the elect, all the preaching in the world would do them no good, so far as salvation was concerned, since they believed Christ died for the elect only. Why then preach to them at all? On the other hand, if they were of the elect, nothing could prevent their being saved. They would be sure, sooner or later, to come into the fold. Many of the Old Order of Baptists still doubt the propriety of making sinners the subjects of gospel addresses, and the late Dr. Watson, who stood high as a man of great learning, benevolence, and zeal in religion, (in a work published after his death called the " Old Baptist Test,") complains of his brethren for *not* doing so.

I have heard the subject of hereditary depravity discussed many times. The argument was about this:— That we are all parts of our father Adam; and when Adam, who was the whole, sinned, we the parts sinned also in him; and as he deserved punishment, so do we, as being Adam drawn out at length, as they expressed it. I used, when a boy, to try hard to comprehend this mystery, but never succeeded. We know that one can receive a taint morally and physically by hereditary transmission, as in pulmonary consumption, and bad tempers and dispositions both in men and brutes. But how one can be really guilty for this inherited defect is not so easy to conceive. Sinners were advised to shun outbreaking sins if possible, such as horse-racing, card-playing, cock-fighting, profanity, drunkenness, and fiddling and dancing especially.

Election, predestination, the nature and extent of the atonement, the final perseverance of the saints, effectual calling, and the glorious and happy state of the elect after death were the themes on which Elder Brooks and others loved to dwell. In lofty style, like Elder Moore, he would exhort his brethren and sisters not to be discouraged or faint by the way, telling them the day of their redemption was drawing nigh, and that they would soon behold the city of the Great King in all its apocalyptic beauty and splendor; their spotless robes, their golden harps, were there awaiting them, which would continue to shine and sparkle in unfading brightness when the sun, moon, and stars shall grow dim with age and pass away.

Elder Brooks also lived in what is now Todd County, Kentucky. He was long pastor of the "West Fork of Red River Church" the old site of which is hardly known. He was, I think, a native of Virginia. I do not know the date of his birth or death, though I have taken some pains to learn. He and your grandfather often traveled and preached together, and together assisted in organizing churches and ordaining ministers in the early times.

I have taken unusual pains to recall my early impressions of these two old pioneer preachers, who may be considered representative ministers among the Baptists of those days.

Their preaching was chiefly directed to the defense of their doctrines and the feeding of their sheep; that is, to comfort and encourage the members of their churches; and this was done so much to their satisfaction and delight, that the aged men and women of that generation who are left still look back to those as the palmy days of their church, about which they love to think and speak, though now comparatively few in number.

Of the soundness of their doctrines and the purity of their faith they had the most exalted ideas, and no doubt many of them considered themselves as much superior, in these respects, to the surrounding Christian denomina- tions, as did the ancient Jews in comparing themselves with the heathen nations around them.

But there was one dread thought that often brough these old Christians low even unto the dust. "Am I, after all, one of the elect? May I not, after all, be mis- taken? And if so, then all hope is gone!" The storm- tossed mariner, when his boat goes down, may find a plank or broken spar, and on it may reach the friendly shore; but for him who is not of the elect there is no plank or spar or friendly shore; he must sink in the deep, dark waters. There is ground for believing that by this dread apprehension the reason of many has been de- throned. Cowper, one of England's sweetest poets, was unable to bear up under it, and Cromwell himself, if I remember rightly, whose iron nerves never quailed before mortal foe, trembled at the bare thought of this.

I have heard many, whose minds were filled with doubts and fears on this subject, converse with your grandfather in regard to it. While troubled with these gloomy apprehensions, they might often be heard singing the plaintive old hymn :

> " 'Tis a point I long to know,
>   Oft it causes anxious thought;
> Do I love the Lord or no?
> Am I his or am I not?"

Their fear was that Satan, who can transform himself into an angel of light, and deceive the very elect themselves, were it possible, had tempted them to conclude they were the children of God when they really were not, and that they would ultimately be lost after all their fond hopes to the contrary.

Before passing on to our next chapter we will add, that there was one theme of which these old Christians never grew weary, and which filled their hearts with unspeaka-able love and gratitude. That the Almighty should have loved them with an everlasting love, chosen them to be lively stones in his holy temple, made them the special objects of his regard, vessels of honor, while others, as good by nature as they, perhaps better by practice, were vessels of wrath fitted for destruction, seemed at times to fill their hearts with love and gratitude beyond expression. Had he shown his loving-kindness in this way to all alike, it would not have been so wonderful, since all were in the same lost and ruined condition. But this act of peculiar and *special* favor, when there was no merit whatever in them, that they should be made kings and priests of the Most High rather than others, was unlike anything known before among mankind, and it seemed to them that their hearts ought to overflow with love and thanksgiving on account of it every moment of their lives. Indeed, there was a simplicity or artlessness in the way they talked on this subject that was really interesting. Is it not possible that many of them, almost without knowing it, thought they were after all just a little better than others, and were chosen or elected on that account?

CHAPTER XIV.

Elder Isaac Todevine emigrated from Virginia about the year 1785. He was an ordained minister belonging to the church of London Bridge, Princess Anne County. He lived six or eight miles north of Clarksville when I first knew him.

According to my recollection of him he was short of stature, rather thick set, with a full round face, large black eyes, and olive complexion. He was, no doubt, of Italian extraction. He wore what was called a round-breasted coat and waistcoat, short knee-breeches, and stockings. His shoes, instead of strings, were fastened with large buckles nearly covering the front. This costume was quite common among elderly gentlemen in the early part of the present century. On the whole, his appearance was rather respectable, though his motions were too brisk and quick to be graceful and dignified.

He was never at a loss for subjects of conversation. I used when a boy to think his talk very amusing. His utterance was distinct though rapid, and his sentences short and abrupt. He would often, when no one was expecting it, commence singing one of the fine old hymns of Newton, Watts, or Cowper. It was useless for any one to join in with him, for no other person could sing a hymn of the same length in the same time. He would

7   133

finish it by the time another would get fairly started.
Many times late at night, while in bed, he would break
out and sing one of these hymns.

He lived in a solitary cabin on the bank of a pretty
stream called Spring Creek, on account of the number of
fine springs whose waters unite to form it. Some of these
in classic times would have been thought favorite abodes
of the nymphs, "*domus nympharum,*" on account of their
romantic beauty. The maple, poplar, beech trees, and
wild flowers that once grew around them have mostly
disappeared, but their sparkling waters still flow on as
when first seen by the pioneer hunter. When at home,
the only companions the old solitary had were his horse
Snip and his dog Pup. The farmers of the neighborhood
gratuitously supplied food for himself and his two companions. Your mother's father, a very kind-hearted gentleman, often filled Snip's little crib with corn during the
old man's absence. On returning home he would be very
much pleased, and if asked who had been so kind would
say, "Either Charles Barker or the Lord, he didn't know
which."

He prepared his simple meals himself. His lady friends,
kind-hearted and good as they ever will be, supplied him
with clothes. Mrs. Rebecca Dudley, who lived near this
old hermit, told me not long since that she and the Misses
White, sisters of Willie White, Esq., all of whom you have
seen when a little girl, often made up clothing for him.
I do not remember to have heard any one say in what
way he spent his solitary hours. I think, though, he was
fond of reading; have heard him speak of Flavel, Top-
lady, Bunyan, Booth, and Gill, as if he were familiar with
those fine old writers. He read his Bible much, lingering

no doubt with special delight on the passages which to his mind established his favorite doctrinal views.

When tired of home he would saddle up Snip, lock the door of his cabin, and, together with Pup, set out on a circuit among the churches of the Association to which he belonged, and they were all kindly received wherever they went. Pup was permitted by the kind sisters to take his place at meal time near his master, who would from time to time give him a part of whatever he had on his plate. The young darkies waiting round the table thought Pup got a greater number of good things than a dog was entitled to, were quite unfriendly to him, and often gave him a kick when they could do so on the sly. He was a good-natured, lazy, worthless fellow, but none the less beloved by his master on that account. Pup used to have a gay time at the big meetings playing and romping with the other dogs while his master was preaching. The old man was quite uneasy at times for fear he would leave him. It was said on one occasion, while preaching, he looked out from the window and seeing Pup, as he thought, going off with a stranger, stopped short in his discourse and requested one of the brethren to please go and bring Pup back, as he feared he might lose him, and then went on with his discourse again. This reminds one of the anecdote told of the venerable Elder Craig of Kentucky, who, while preaching, happening to see from a window the limb of a tree that had a crook exactly suitable for the frame of a pack-saddle, stopped immediately, told his audience the discovery he had made, informed them that he claimed the crooked limb by the right of discovery, and then went on with his sermon. Such crooked limbs were hard to find and highly prized in those days when packsaddles were in great demand.   These two old preachers, from what I have heard, seem to have resembled each other very much in their eccentricities.

Every morning after breakfast, with a biscuit or two in his pocket for Snip, the old man would go out to the stable or lot.   Snip, so soon as he saw his master, would go up to him.   He would then ask him how he was getting on, and whether they gave him enough to eat and drink.   At this the horse would lay back his ears, indulge in a low whine, and paw the ground slightly.   I used to think this was carrying things a little too far, that it looked like a sort of witchcraft, and could not help feeling somewhat afraid of them.   Snip seemed to expect something to eat, and would smell about his master's pockets for it, which amused the old man greatly.

In prayer Elder Todevine was quite fluent, and on that account would be requested to conduct family worship when visiting the brethren.   He would commence by invoking the choicest blessings on the family under whose roof he then was, then on the surrounding community, then on the nation and its rulers, then on all men everywhere; and finally on the church, that she might awake and put on her beautiful garments, and that her glory might fill the whole earth.

He and the darkies were far from being on good terms. When preaching on the duties of master and servant, he would take great pains to convince the latter they ought to be very thankful they had some one to whip them when they needed it, adding at the same time, very shrewdly, that it would be a good thing if some white people had some one to do the same for them.   He would tell them that a good whipping, when they needed it, was worth more to them than a suit of new clothes. They were highly offended at this kind of preaching, and called him all sorts of ugly names. Neither was he very popular among the boys, as he would sometimes cut them up pretty sharply.

His belief in election and predestination was unwavering. According to his theology the condition of one not elected from the foundation of the world was as changeless and as hopeless as if he were already in the bottomless pit. On the other hand, if he were one of the elect, neither his own wrong doings nor all the powers of darkness could prevent his salvation. Strange that so many great and good men should have believed a doctrine so terrible! And when Elder Moore or others would preach one of their powerful discourses advocating it, the old man's countenance would beam with delight and he would say, "Glorious day for *my* soul."

Elder Todevine when preaching always divided his discourses into a number of heads, or topics, often into half a dozen or more. These he would take up and discuss in order. Sometimes, however, in his more advanced age, he would forget some of them. Might not his method prove useful if adopted by some preachers of the present day, many of whom have but little method in their sermons?

Many years before his death he told his friends he had had a dream in which it was shown to him at what age or at what date he would die. This dream had been so strongly impressed on his mind that he often made it the subject of conversation. According to it he was to die in the year 1821. Early in the month of March of that year he left home for Blooming Grove Church in the western part of the county. On his way he stayed all night with his friend and neighbour Mr. Bryan Whitfield, who told him he was too old and infirm to ride so far by himself, and tried to persuade him not to go. He replied there were two souls there he was to be instrumental in awakening before his departure which was near at hand, and Mr. Whitfield, supposing it to be one of his fancies, said nothing more. He went on to the church, preached to the people, and returned home. Some days after he rode over to Mr. Whitfield's, called him to the gate, told him his time to die had come, and as he would rather not die at home by himself, he would be very thankful if he would permit him to die at his house. Mr. Whitfield, after joking him a little, invited him to get down and go in. He did so, took his bed, and, as one account says, died the next day; another, a few days afterwards, on the 23d of March, 1821. One hardly knows what to think of such cases of presentiment as this; but, as there are so many on record that seem to be well authenticated, it is, perhaps, best simply to state the facts and leave each one to form his own conclusions regarding them.

It is said when his remains were carried to the grave, his dog followed them, and after it was filled up laid down beside it, and remained there several days, until Mr. William Watwood, an old friend of his master, tied a handkerchief round his neck and led him away. Thus ended the life of this singular but interesting old preacher. His name has nearly passed into oblivion, but brings back to my mind " the memory of the days of other years." He was buried on the hill to the right of the road leading from Clarksville to Trenton, Kentucky, just before crossing the creek on which his cabin once stood; and far away from the home of his childhood.

Elder Sugg Fort, fourth in order of the preachers mentioned above, was highly esteemed and popular in his day. He was below the medium height, a good deal disabled by rheumatism, of a pleasant and engaging countenance, and always neat in his dress and person. He was much beloved by all who knew him, the young especially, on account of his affectionate, cheerful, and affable manner; and of all the preachers who visited your grandfather your two aunts and I loved him best.

Children and young people generally used to stand in much greater awe of preachers than at present, and kept out of their way, if possible, fearing they might be questioned and lectured by them. When they did take us in hand, though, we were pitiable-looking objects, and almost as happy when released as birds out of a cage or criminals when reprieved. This was not the case when Uncle Sugg, as we familiarly called him, talked to us about being religious. On the contrary, his manner was such that we liked to listen to him, and generally felt like trying to improve in consequence of what he would say. This was because he divested himself of that stiff and solemn manner which others were apt to assume on such occasions. He would tell me sometimes, that he intended to make a preacher of me, that I might take my father's place when he was gone; but I must first become a good Christian.

He and your grandfather loved each other as men not related seldom do. They were both born the same year —1776—both from the old North State, and from adjoining counties, Martin and Edgecombe. When a free salvation to all who would accept it began to be preached by your grandfather, which, as will be related hereafter, resulted in his separation from his high Calvinistic brethren,

Elder Fort was the first, or among the first, to enlist in the same cause. And side by side, they passed through all the troubles that agitated the Baptist churches previous to the organization of the Bethel Association. They travelled and preached together, not only in their respective counties,—Montgomery and Robertson,—but also in distant localities where the people were destitute of Christian religious instruction. On these tours they were always received with the greatest kindness and respect, and the attention paid to their preaching showed that the religious feeling among those early settlers was much greater than is generally supposed.

I still retain a very pleasant recollection of a trip I made with them among the hills and valleys of Stewart County east of the Cumberland. The people among whom we went were thinly settled along the pretty streams bordered by the rich narrow bottoms already mentioned. The ridges dividing these streams were often high and steep, and covered with heavy timber in many places affording wild and romantic scenery. Uncle Sugg and I had a great deal of pleasant chat riding along together over these hills and across the streams, while your grandfather would often ride on before studying, as we would say, upon his sermons.

They usually left home early in the morning for some place where an appointment for them to preach had been made some time before. This was generally the residence of some well-to-do settler or some rude meeting-house made of round logs covered with boards kept in place by poles laid upon them near a spring or on the margin of some pretty stream. Here two sermons would be preached, one immediately after the other by day, and another somewhere in the vicinity at night, and this would be the order until they returned home again.

In the neighborhood where these meetings were held all business was suspended, and the most marked attention was given by the audiences, many coming from a distance guided to the place by trees, from which the bark had been chipped off. On these occasions the hospitality of these people knew no limits. You were welcome to all they had, and to see that you enjoyed it and were satisfied with it seemed to afford them the liveliest pleasure. You were sure to have plenty to eat, a big fire to sit by, your horse well cared for, and the best accommodations for sleeping they had.

The flattering attentions I received on your grandfather's account showed plainly how much children are indebted to the good name and respectability of their parents. Yet how few ever think of this! The child of honored and respected parents has, on the day of its birth, what the child of the poor outcast can hardly obtain after a long life of good and virtuous conduct

I imagined the preachers were abler in their discourses among these people than when nearer home. Perhaps I was not mistaken, and the idea of carrying the gospel where it was seldom heard, and to people who listened with so much interest kindled unusual zeal.

Your grandfather on this tour preached a sermon, by which the audience was greatly moved, and which seemed to sound in our ears for many days afterwards. It was from these words: " Thus it is written, and thus it behoved Christ to suffer and to rise from the dead on the third day."

Although Elder Fort was an interesting preacher at all

7*

times, he was particularly so, as I thought, when he
adopted the style called *spiritualizing*, which he sometimes did. At the house of my uncle, Nathan Ross, who
then lived on Saline Creek, in Stewart County, he preached
a sermon of this kind which all very much admired, and
I think I can give you some idea of it even now.

But I will first remark that it is believed by many that
much of the sacred writings has a twofold meaning, one
plain or obvious, the other more recondite or hidden, and
that he who sees the former only has but little or no conception of all their marvellous beauty. Those who had
fine imaginations and could perceive and elaborate to advantage these hidden beauties and relations, were considered as little less than inspired. How strange that a
text they had read again and again and never supposed
meant anything more than just what it said, should have
concealed in it, as the rough ordinary looking stone sometimes has, a gem so rich and beautiful. People would go
far to hear one of these gifted preachers and consider
themselves well repaid for their trouble. When characterized by good sense and taste this preaching was very
pleasing, as, beside the religious element, it had all the
charm that invention and novelty throw around a subject.

At the time alluded to Elder Fort took for his text
Exodus 15 : 27. "And they came to Elim, where were
twelve wells of water, and threescore and ten palm trees;
and they encamped there by the waters."

"The ordinary reader of the Bible," he said, "will only see in this
text the simple statement of the fact that the Jews, after leaving the
land of Egypt, while journeying on encamped at a place called Elim,
where were twelve wells of water and threescore and ten palm-trees;
and could find nothing more. But in the first place observe, my friends,
this journey of the Jews through the wilderness to the land of Canaan,

lying far away beyond the distant Jordan, is beautifully typical of the Christian's journey through the wilderness of this world before he reaches the Jordan of death, after crossing which it will be his unspeakable happiness to enter the heavenly Canaan, where will be found pleasures forevermore.

" You will observe, also, that the Jews, just before reaching Elim,'had been encamped at a place called Marah, whose waters were bitter, unfit for use, tending to produce disease and death. Need I tell you that Marah and its bitter waters are typical of a sinful and wicked state or course of life, which, if we do not abandon it, will result not only in temporal, but also in spiritual or eternal death. Let me therefore entreat you, as you would enjoy eternal happiness beyond the grave, to leave these bitter waters of Marah and journey with us to Elim, and with us refresh your spirits at these delicious fountains.

" The twelve wells of water at Elim are typical of the twelve holy apostles, whose writings contain the waters of eternal life of which he that drinks shall never die. The doctrines and blessed promises to be found in them are more refreshing to the Christian while on his journey, than all the fountains that ever gushed from Carmel or Lebanon to travellers from the desert. They contain treasures hidden from the careless eye. Search them diligently. They will make you wise unto salvation, and enable you to obtain an inheritance among them that are sanctified.

" And should we not bless and magnify the name of our Heavenly Father who has given us these living oracles, these writings of the twelve holy apostles, these wells of water at Elim to refresh us on our journey, as they did the Jews when journeying to the beautiful land promised their fathers long years before ?

" But did they find aught beside the twelve fountains when they arrived at Elim? Yea verily ! Threescore and ten palm-trees rising above the sands of the desert in matchless beauty, casting a delicious shade from their long dark green leaves, where the Jewish host might rest their toil-worn limbs. What beautiful emblems these of the seventy sent out by Christ, as recorded by Luke, to publish the glad tidings of salvation to those sitting in darkness and in the shadow of death."

Thus in a style of preaching both pleasing and instructive would Elder Fort often delight his audiences.

On another occasion he preached an interesting discourse

of the same kind from Proverbs 30 : 26. "The conies are but a feeble folk, yet make they their houses in the rock."

The coney, he told us, was a small animal of the rabbit kind, very weak and unable to defend itself from its enemies, and for this reason was always found near large masses of rock, in which it made its house, and to which it would flee in times of danger. Here, protected by its stronghold, it was safe from all its enemies, how powerful soever they might be. These weak but sagacious little animals he considered typical of the Christians, who have chosen a tower of strength—the Rock of Ages—to which they can flee in the hour of danger, and where they can rest in safety while storms and tempests are raging without.

It was delightful to sit and listen to him while running the parallel between this little animal and his antitype, the Christian, and bringing to view so many interesting points of resemblance between them.

Elder Sugg Fort was pastor of the Red River Baptist Church until his death in 1829. It was organized by his father Elias Fort and other pioneer Baptist brethren in 1791, and is the oldest church in the Bethel Association. It worships in a handsome new house near Adams' Station, on the Nashville & Henderson railroad.

Elder Fort and your grandfather lived in adjoining counties. Their fields of labor were consequently nearly the same. I well remember how much they seemed to enjoy each other's society, and how heavily the news of his fellow-laborer's death fell on your grandfather. They were separated more than thirty years. May we not suppose there was joy unspeakable when they met again on the shining shore.

CHAPTER XV.

SKETCHES OF EARLY MINISTERS.

BESIDES Elders Moore, Brooks, Todevine, and Fort, there were two others who occasionally visited us, viz., Elders Daniel Parker, and Garner McConnico, the former a messenger sometimes sent from the Wabash Association, Indiana. The latter was from the Cumberland Association, Tennessee, already mentioned. They were very different from each other in many respects, but both were men of note.

Elder Parker, I think, I only saw and heard preach once, which was during an Association held at Spring Creek Church about the year 1820. He was a small, dry-looking man, of the gipsy type, with black eyes and hair and dark complexion.

On rising in the pulpit to speak, he soon gave us to understand that he meant business,—pulled off his coat and vest, laid them deliberately on the pulpit near him, and unbuttoned his shirt collar. After this preparation it is almost incredible with what ease and fluency he spoke. He seemed full of his subject, and went through it in a way that was truly wonderful. He was an able man in his way, but afterwards gave his Calvinistic brethren a great deal of trouble, from which they have not yet fully recovered. The famous "two seed" doctrine originated with him, which heresy shook the churches of the Old Order to their foundations long after the Bethel Association had been formed.

It seems that when Elder Parker in reading his Bible found such expressions as, "Your father, the devil," or, "Child of the devil," it set him to thinking, as did the falling of that famous apple Sir Isaac Newton,—which was, in his case, too, attended with important results.

He decided in his own mind that these texts were to be understood literally and not figuratively, as they had been heretofore, and that without any figure of speech Satan had a host of lineal descendants in the world. And when we look around us and see how enormously wicked people sometimes become, this fancy of Elder Parker does not seem so absurd after all.

But in order to make out that Satan had children in the world directly descended from him, he had to adopt the violent presumption that the souls of one part of mother Eve's children were of celestial origin, as, for instance, that of Abel, and those of another part, as that of Cain, were supplied in some way by Satan. And thus came the *two seeds*, which are now so mingled together that no being in the universe but the Omniscient can tell one from the other—the wheat from the tares, the sheep from the goats—with any degree of certainty. At the last day, however, a complete and final separation will take place. Satan's seed will then be sent to dwell with him forever in outer darkness, while the *good seed* will be permitted to enter into the joy of their Lord. According to Elder Parker, the devil's children were the non-elect, and their being such was a sufficient reason for their being left out of the plan of salvation.

This doctrine was received with great favor by numbers

of the Old Order of Baptists, and it required all the learning and talent of those opposed to it to prevent its general adoption. Any one who is anxious to look further into this subject may consult the great argument of the late Dr. Watson against this heresy in his work the "Old Baptist Test," before referred to. He was a professor in the Medical Department of the University of Nashville, and one of the luminaries of the hyper-Calvinistic Baptists.

I am not able to tell you when or where Elder Parker died, but think, when he used to come among us, he lived in Indiana, and belonged to the Wabash Baptist Association in that State.

Elder Garner McConnico, who belonged to the Cumberland Association, used to come down now and then and preach among us. He was a large, handsome man. His voice was singularly rich and powerful, and his talents of the first order.

On one occasion he had an appointment to preach under some shade trees on the banks of Big Harpeth River; but there fell a heavy rain the night before, and when he reached the river it was past fording, consequently, he could not join his congregation. He spoke to them, however, from the opposite bank, and told them if they would seat themselves and be quiet they should hear what he had to say. This being done, he raised his voice a little above its usual pitch, and preached a fine sermon, every word of which was distinctly heard on the other side, notwithstanding the distance, and the dashing of the swollen stream against its banks. Elder Todevine used to say when speaking of him, "Brother McConnico has a voice like a trumpet."

The following sketch of him is condensed from an old record now before me.

Elder McConnico was born in 1771, in Lunenburg County, Virginia, and was the youngest of three brothers His mother was a woman of great piety, from whom he received when young many kind admonitions. An old Baptist preacher who had belonged to the British army, and remained in the United States after the Revolutionary war was over, was instrumental in awakening him to a sense of his lost condition.

This old soldier had an appointment to preach in his mother's neighborhood, and she requested Garner to go with her to hear him. To this he objected. The request was slightly modified so as to take the form of a *command*. With this he thought it prudent to comply. He hated the very name of Englishman, having when a youth been often compelled by the British and Tories to leave his home, and lie out in the woods when they were in that part of the country. And he determined, if he did go, not to listen to a word the preacher had to say—his mother could not make him do that any way.

On reaching the place, however, he concluded to go just near enough to look at the preacher. He proved such a diminutive, unsightly dwarf of a man, that young McConnico felt some curiosity to hear him talk a little. He did so, and never heard mortal man speak with such power. To use his own expression, "He seemed to bring the very heavens and earth together," and when he came to himself he was standing near the old man in tears. From this time he never rested until he embraced religion, and united with the Baptist Church at Tusekiah.

Soon after this he was married to Miss Mary Walker,

and commenced trying to preach.   He was, however, so disgusted with his efforts, and annoyed by the ridicule of his brother that he and his young wife left Virginia, crossed the mountains, and in 1795 settled in Davidson County, Tennesee, hoping to get rid of the impression that it was his duty to preach.   Fully resolving never to do so any more, he enjoined on his wife, when they should seek their new home, not to let it be known he had ever presumed to be a minister of the gospel.   Here he resided two years after his removal, in a state of great darkness, to use his words.

After this he was in search of his horse that had strayed off in the spring of the year.   As he was walking along a narrow path cut through the tall cane, in deep thought on the subject of preaching, he saw a small venerable-looking man advancing towards him.   The thought at once came into his mind that this was just such a looking person as the apostle Paul, and when they met after the usual salutations, the following dialogue ensued.

"What sort of a country is this we are in?" said Mc Connico.

"A very rich woody country," responded the old man.

"Any religion in it?"

"A few scattered about here and there."

"Any Baptist preaching in it?"

"There will be Baptist preaching in it next Lord's Day."

"And you are the preacher?"

"I try to preach here sometimes for want of a better."

Here they parted.   This old man afterwards proved to be Elder Dillahunty, a pioneer Baptist preacher, well known in that part of the country in the early times.

Young McConnico could hardly wait for the day of preaching to come round, so great was his desire to hear the venerable old man preacher. Punctual to the time he was there; and when Elder Dillahunty at the close of his sermon made an appointment to preach on a certain Lord's Day at Richland Meeting House, young McConnico in his excitement rose up and said :

"And I will be with you there."

"And who are you?" says Father Dillahunty.

"The man you met in the cane brake."

"A Baptist?"

"Yes."

"And a preacher?"

"Why, yes, *I have* tried to exercise a little in that way."

And now the great secret he and his wife were going to keep so close, was out, and he was in great trouble on account of what he had done.

At the time and place appointed, he attended, but tried hard to beg off from preaching; Father Dillahunty, however, held him to his promise. He had not gotten more than half through his sermon before the good old man rose from his seat, took him in his arms, wept aloud, and thanked God for having found a young brother on the frontier both able and willing to assist him in spreading the glad tidings in the wilderness.

This Elder Dillahunty was a Baptist preacher belonging to the Neuse River Association, North Carolina; before he came to the west. (See Burkitt and Reed, page 309). Richland Meeting House where this took place was the name of the first Baptist Church ever planted on the south side of Cumberland River, in Davidson County.

In the fall of 1797, Elder McConnico removed to the neighborhood of Franklin, Williamson County. Here he built up the Big Harpeth Church, which was organized in 1800. It was the third Baptist church planted south of Nashville. He was ordained to the ministry by this church in 1800, and took the pastoral charge of it the day he was ordained. He continued pastor until his death in August 1833, in the sixty-second year of his age. All his life after he joined the church, about forty-five years, was spent in preaching the gospel. He loved this church to the last, and in the dying hour when all else seemed forgotten often repeated its name.

One thing in this connection strikes us as a very singular coincidence. It so happened that he preached his first and his last sermon from the same text. " Examine yourselves whether ye be in the faith." Probably such a thing never occurred before. It seems to have been purely accidental.

At the organization of the Cumberland Baptist Association he was chosen its Moderator, and remained in that honorable office till his death. This showed the high estimation in which he was held by his brethren, and his ability to preside over their deliberations.

An extract from a notice of his life says : " Elder Mc Connico was peculiarly commanding. He was of a stout, robust person—his face intellectual—his eye penetrating —his whole demeanor marked with perfect dignity, and his voice singularly powerful, manly, and pleasing."

Such I remember him to have been more than fifty years ago, when in the prime of his manhood and the vigor of his faculties, he would address us while sitting under the trees during the pleasant days of summer.

The happiness which those of the same faith felt when they happened to meet in the wilderness is well illustrated by the account given above of the interview between Elders Dillahunty and McConnico. And it is altogether unlike what is felt in densely populated sections at the present day. Their loneliness and isolation caused a thrill of joy at meeting more easily imagined than described.

Who shall describe the deep feeling of brotherly love among the few men and women who met in Severn's Valley, ninety years ago, under the branches of a primeval sugar maple, to organize the first Baptist church ever constituted in the state of Kentucky? The men were clothed in hunting shirts, leggings, and moccasins all made of the skins of wild beasts, and wearing hats made of buffalo hair rolled round oaken splits. The women wore garments of the same materials. Their descendants who now worship in costly temples have little conception of the Christian affection that filled the hearts of these strangers meeting thus in a strange land.

CHAPTER XVI.

I took occasion after your grandfather had reached the vicinity of Port Royal, where he remained a few months, to call your attention to various subjects which I thought would interest you, viz., the character of the people he found there, a brief description of the country in which he was henceforth to labor, and a notice of some of the Baptist preachers with whom he was associated after his arrival in this country, the Red River Association, and some of the usages or customs of the Baptists.

It is now time to inform you that in the winter of 1808 he removed seven or eight miles nearer Clarksville, and went into a cabin more comfortable than the one we had left, belonging to an old gentleman named Christopher Owens, who with his wife were prominent members of the Baptist Church. They were in good circumstances, owning land and negroes. They had everything plentiful around them, and abounded in milk, butter, and wild honey; that is, honey found in hollow trees growing in the woods, and called on that account Bee-trees. The old lady was very kind to your twin aunts and myself, and when she saw us playing at a distance would often send for us and give us a feast on milk, butter, and honey, and made a life-long friend of me by the way in which she encouraged me to eat. Butter at our table in those times

153

was rather a rarity, and I had been taught to help myself to it rather sparingly. Aunt Owens, however, as we came to call her, would set out large platefuls, and noticing that from the effects of education I took but little, told me to eat just as much as I wanted,—the more the better. So soon as I became satisfied that she was in earnest, I did full justice to her kindness and hospitality, and thought things were beginning to look something like what I had expected to see when we reached Cumberland.

The old gentleman, though probably as kindly disposed as his wife, we did not like so well, on account of his rough manner. Whenever he saw us out of place or in mischief of any kind he would say: "You little heifers, what are you doing there?" This word heifers we thought had some bad meaning,—though what we could not tell,—and always took to our heels when we heard it.

This year your grandfather raised a crop of corn. He labored in the field every day except Saturday and Sunday, which he devoted to preaching. The crop he raised here was very fine, and the luxuriance of its growth and abundance of its yield delighted him very much.

We children had rather a pleasant time while living here. Our cabin was near the river-bank, which was fringed with reeds, whose evergreen leaves looked pretty in winter, especially when sprinkled over with snow. In spring the trees nearer the river put forth their light-green leaves very early, forming a beautiful border, contrasting finely with those further from the water. Here we first saw flocks of Paroquets, called by Ornithologists "Carolina Parrots," a little larger than the common tame pigeon, and whose plumage was very beautiful. The prevailing color "a bright-yellowish silky green with light-

blue reflections." Their notes, though, are harsh and dis-
cordant. These birds of bright plumage we children never
tired of looking at. We were told by some one that they
slept at night suspended by their crooked bills from the
branches of the forest trees. I think they have for many
years past left our country.

I can but regard it as very singular that after so many
changes of residence I am now living almost in sight of
where this cabin once stood. This spot seems indeed the
centre of a charmed circle, from which it is impossible to
escape. All things around it are now greatly changed
except one,—the beautiful stream of water, which, like
that described by one of the poets,

"Flows and flows, and will forever flow!"

A few years before his death your grandfather, while
on a visit to me, proposed very unexpectedly that we
should ride over and look at the place. I say unexpectedly, because I knew he never liked to visit a place after
he had left it. On the way he was quite chatty and more
cheerful than usual. When he reached the place, however,
a change soon came over him. The shadows of long vanished years no doubt began to pass before him. He sat
on his horse and looked around a few moments, and then
proposed that we should return; few words were spoken
on our way home. I regretted I had not dissuaded him
from going when he proposed it. So depressing was the
effect upon him.

During this year (1808), the Spring Creek Church was
constituted. Their meeting-house was near Spring Creek,
a tributary of the West Fork of Red River and in Montgomery County, Tennessee, a short distance south of the

State Line, and took its name from the pretty stream of water near which it stood; it was on the north of the stream, and only a short distance above its mouth, near what was long known as the Brumfield place, from an old gentleman who lived on it many years ago. A road leads from the south side of the creek to what are known as Cobb's and Peacher's Mills; soon after crossing the creek it passes near the old site which is a few yards only to the right. Several graves, very indistinct some years ago, marked the spot where it stood.

North of the church there was a grove of heavy timber owned at one time by your uncle Charles N. Meriwether, and south of it the limpid stream in which so many were baptized in early times, nearly all of whom have since passed away. In looking over the mutilated records of the old church now before me, among others I see in faded characters three names—Sister Barbara Barker, Sister Mary Meriwether and Sister Mary D. Barker. The first your maternal grandmother; the second her sister, the friend of your childhood; the third the friend of your beloved mother.

This meeting-house was built of large poplar logs hewn on two sides, and the openings between them in some places were large enough for a small boy to crawl through. No ceiling intervened between the rough floor and the naked rafters. The pulpit, such as it was, stood on the north side of the room, and the door fronted it in the south side. It was a bleak place as you may well suppose in winter—*"domus ventorum,"*—*a temple of the winds.* In summer, though, airy and pleasant, open to every passing breeze.

It was built about the year 1804, three or four years

before we came to the country, and at first had no chimney or fire-place as appears from the following extract from the journal before referred to.

" Saturday, October 3d, 1807. The church met in order. Brother Todevine chosen Moderator. On motion, it is ordered that there be a chimney erected to this meeting-house."

I remember to have seen, even after a chimney had been built, large fires made on the ground near the house in very cold weather for the people to warm themselves by before going in to hear the sermon.

The members who worshipped at this meeting-house before being organized into a church were fourteen in number all of whose names may still be seen in the journal. Before the Red River Church received its name it was called the Fort Meeting-house Church, and the fourteen members who worshipped at Spring Creek Meeting house were what was called an arm, or wing, or *branch* of the Fort Meeting-house Church. These arms, wings, or branches were under the supervision and care of the mother church until regularly constituted, when they set up for themselves, and managed their affairs in their own way.

The Spring Creek wing in 1807 concluded they would like to organize, and petitioned the mother church to give them permission to undergo the necessary transformation, which was granted by the kind old mother; a presbytery, consisting of Elders Jesse Brooks, Josiah Horn, Josiah Fort, and others, was sent down when the wing, or arm, was organized into a regular body, or church. This was done on Saturday, April 2, 1808.

In the month of June following, an order was passed

8

that it should be called "The Spring Creek Church of the West Fork," which name it still bears. On the same day petition was made for admission into the Red River Baptist Association. This is a brief history of the origin of this old mother of churches.

About the same time they made a church covenant, in which they pledged themselves to watch over each other for good, to maintain the discipline of the church, and to try in the most brotherly and affectionate manner to reclaim those whom they saw falling away and neglecting their religious duties.

They also agreed on certain rules of decorum, by which they were to be governed while transacting the business of the church. Many of these rules indicate no small degree of wisdom and forethought. Your grandfather was upon all the committees that arranged these instruments. When finished they were spread upon their journal, and frequently ordered to be read by the Clerk that they might be retained fresh in the memories of their members.

They next began to think of choosing a pastor. Accordingly, on Saturday before the first Lord's Day in September, 1809, on motion, they agreed to take into consideration the expediency of calling a pastor.

On Saturday before the first Lord's Day in October, 1809, the church appointed Saturday before the next meeting as a day of fasting and prayer, before entering upon this important business.

On Saturday before the first Lord's Day in November, 1809, the reference respecting the choosing of a pastor for the church was taken up, and it was agreed that it should be done by private vote. Whereupon Elder Reuben Ross was chosen. On motion, it was agreed that Brother

Ross should have some time to consult his own mind, and report whether he was willing to take upon himself that office.

On Saturday before the first Lord's Day in March, 1810, on motion, Brother Reuben Ross is called upon to give the church an answer whether or not he will take the pastoral care of this church in conformity with their former call. Whereupon he answered in the affirmative, with this consideration, that both church and pastor shall be at liberty to separate, either from the other, whenever they may deem it to be to their spiritual advantage. Thus reads the old record. Here, then, we see that in the month of March, 1810, your grandfather was chosen Pastor of Spring Creek Church. This connexion lasted, I think, about twenty-nine years, and seems to have been an unusually happy one.

The preceding account will give you some idea of the simple course the Baptists have followed from the days of the renowned Roger Williams—whose name has been forever rescued from oblivion by our distinguished historian Bancroft—down to the present time.

Your grandfather was now becoming one of the most popular and influential preachers of the times. He was deeply interested in the work before him. He sympathized with all in distress, especially with those who were in trouble on account of their sins. He commenced about this time his work of preaching funeral sermons more extensively, of which he did so much in the course of his life. On these occasions he was sure to say something to soothe the troubled spirits of those who had lost their loved ones, and to turn their thoughts for a few brief moments, at least, from this land of shadows and of death to that brighter world beyond the stars where all will meet again, and sin and sorrow be seen and felt no more.

The youths and maidens were pleased to have him unite them in marriage, and to hear him pray that theirs might be a long and happy union ; and those who had repented of their sins and believed in Christ desired him to lead them down into the baptismal waters. In a word he seemed to be just suited to the people and the times, and his influence began to be felt to an extent by no means inconsiderable.

Our rude old meeting-house in the course of years became a center of great attraction, and drew to it all classes of people both far and near. It seemed to have an attraction also for the preachers who did not live at too great a distance. Here might often be seen and heard Elder Moore dealing heavy blows on Arminianism, against which he waged ceaseless warfare. Here Elder Todevine, with his full round face and large black eyes, seldom failed to attend, and here were seen the mild attractive features of Elders Fort and Brooks. Still later, now and then a distinguished preacher from a distance might be seen there.

I remember on one occasion, on a cold dark day in autumn, while the wind was sweeping through the large open cracks between the logs of our old meeting-house; and each one, with his neck drawn down, and his coat collar raised as high as he could get it, sat waiting for preaching to commence—a dark, thick set, substantial looking man, with black eyes and hair, with saddle-bags on his arm and umbrella in his hand, entered the door-way, and walked across the room to the pulpit.

On reaching it he spoke a few words to your grandfather (introducing himself no doubt), whose countenance at this expressed great delight, and a warm greeting ensued. The stranger then entered the pulpit, and took his seat.

By this time we lookers on, as you may readily suppose, had our curiosity raised to an uncomfortable height. After singing and prayer by your grandfather, in which I fear we did not join as heartily as we ought for thinking of the stranger in the pulpit, the latter rose up and read from his Bible these words: "If any man love not the Lord Jesus Christ let him be Anathema Maran-atha," and preached a sermon that was long remembered by those who heard it. When he came to tell us what it was to be accursed at the coming of the Lord, his discourse bordered on the sublime and terrible, and many from that day, as was said, dated the commencement of a better life.

The stranger proved to be the celebrated Elder Isaac Hodgen from Kentucky, who afterwards with Elders Warder and Vardeman occasionally visited the southern portions of the state.

CHAPTER XVII.

SCENES AT THE OLD CHURCH.

THE first Saturday and Sunday in every month were the days for preaching at the old Spring Creek Church for many years. For some reasons the May and June meetings were much better attended than any others. On these occasions the people from all the country around might be seen moving towards it, as to a common centre.

Buggies, carriages, and vehicles of every sort are now associated in our minds with big meetings. But as far back as 1812 and 1815 these were seldom to be seen. The first thing I remember in the way of a pleasure carriage was a small vehicle without top or springs, called a Jersey Wagon, or Carryall. When one of these was first seen rattling along—people—especially children and negroes, would stand and look at it till out of sight.

The next improvement was the gig, with only two wheels, and drawn by one horse in shafts. I first saw elderly ladies riding in these with a man-servant on horseback leading the one attached to it by the bridle. My conclusion was that none but very rich people could afford to ride in this style. The first carriage I ever saw in this country, fitted up for two horses and an outside seat for a driver, with handsome top cushions and silver-mounted harness, belonged to two or three maiden sisters, who came, I think, from Virginia and settled near us in the Barrens. This was considered by us juveniles as a marvel of elegance and splendor, and after the ladies would leave it and go into church, rustling in their silks, we would stand around at a respectful distance and admire its beauty. But this was long after the time of which we are speaking.

You would see *pater-familias* on his way to church on horseback, with the baby before him on a pillow, and another little fellow riding behind him. His wife, perhaps, on a mare with a young colt, with one child in her lap, and another behind her also, jogging along after him. Most of the horses would have two persons on them.

The beau might be seen with a large bunch of pinks or roses in his button-hole—the larger the better—riding beside his young lady, holding her parasol or umbrella over her fair face to protect it from the sun or rain. It was also his duty to raise any branches of trees that extended across the narrow road, that she might pass without inconvenience. Some were more expert in these matters than others, and gained credit in proportion.

There was a practice the beaux had which they called " cutting out." This was when a young lady and gentleman were riding along cosily together, and anything happened to throw them a little apart, for another gentleman who was riding close behind to slip in between them and leave the first out in the cold. This, I think, was a very ugly practice, but by common consent considered "fair play," if it could be done without jostling the young lady. When she happened to be a sort of belle there was quite a scramble for her in this way. It was considered unladylike for her to show any preference on such occasions, however much she might feel.

It was the duty of these knights to see that their ladies did not suffer from thirst during the long hot days, and they might be seen at all times passing through the crowd carrying them fresh water from the spring which they often drank from a gourd. These gourds were sometimes very pretty, and many thought water from them tasted sweeter and fresher than from anything else.

Almost every mother carried her baby with her to meeting, and at the big meetings they would be in great force. These little fellows on account of the heat and the restraint would sometimes become furious, and make their little fat legs fly about at a wild rate; and when a number of them would join in concert, they would almost drown the voice of the preacher. After the mother had done all she could to pacify the babe and failed, she would hand it over to its father, who, if after trying in a very motherly way to soothe it did not succeed, would take it on his shoulder, and walk off under some shady tree, where perhaps soon after both might be found fast asleep.

The dress of these belles some years later was very striking. They had two appendages attached to them called sleeves, about the size of large pillows, which had the effect to make them look like birds with enormous wings, beyond all proportion to the body. The head was ornamented with a Leghorn hat, or flat, with a brim of prodigious size. Its only trimming was a broad bright ribbon which passed round the crown, with long ends which hung down behind a yard or more.

These hats were costly, selling sometimes for thirty-five or forty dollars, or even higher. They were greatly prized by the girls. The effect of these hats with the broad brims and these large sleeves was to diminish the stature; and a lady, a little below the medium height, sailing along under one of them, was a queer-looking object. Yet a kind word or approving smile from one of these beauties, was as much prized as when arrayed in the beautiful costumes of later times—those of 1871 and 1872 excepted, which in hideousness excel all ever known before; causing them to look as if their backs were broken.

There were several families in the vicinity of this church whose custom it was to take people home with them to dine after preaching. The more company they could engage the more delighted they seemed. They would often come to you before getting off your horse and make you promise beforehand to go home with them.

I and my set usually went home with an old gentleman named Buckner Killebrew. On reaching the house, after helping their sweethearts off their horses, each young man would take off his saddle, bridle, and blanket, and lay them by themselves. Then he would turn his horse into a large enclosure, where would be a number of troughs filled with corn and pumpkins, and racks full of sweet blades of fodder stripped from the stalks of Indian corn. Here the horses would fight, and eat all the evening. If one was whipped off from his trough, he would go and drive another from his, take his place, and so on all round.

On going into the house all would be invited to "take something." What they called something at this place, was commonly old peach or apple brandy and honey. All from the old men and preachers down to the boys, would help themselves to some of this. You must not be surprised, for besides the belief that something of this kind was conducive to health, we were every one old Calvinistic Baptists at that time, all of whom are supposed *by nature*

8*

to like something good to drink. And Temperance societies and everything of that sort were no more dreamed of than railroads, telegraphs, or ocean cables.

After this preliminary movement we were invited to a dinner that it would do any one's heart good to look at. The table would be literally covered with good things, so that there was not room enough on it for another plate or dish. But the most interesting thing of all was the pleasure it gave our old friend and his wife to see us eat. They watched us closely, and when they saw one about to quit were really distressed. This may seem like exaggeration, but I could mention some that even you can remember who were sorely troubled if their friends did not eat heartily of their bountiful tables.

After the first course was ended no one was permitted to leave his seat until the *debris* of the first battle were swept away, and pies, cakes, and tarts brought on. These were of various flavors—some very sweet, some quite acid, and others less so. The shapes also differed : some were round like the full moon, some like the half moon, and others again crescent-shaped, interspersed with pitchers of cider, and cold sweet milk not with the cream all taken off, as is often done " in these degenerate days."

At length the feast ended, as everything good and beautiful must in this world. After this we would have some pleasant chat, in which the host and hostess took part. Then some one of the company would say, " The sun-is getting low" which was, alas, too true, and a slight shade of sadness might be seen stealing over our faces, and our party would break up and all start for home, sad, to think another long month must pass before we should meet again.

I will only add that the last time I passed the place where this hospitable mansion stood—it had fallen into decay and ruins, and all around it looked sad and lonely. "Sic transit."

Such are some of the recollections, still fresh in my memory, connected with this old church in the bygone times.

In process of time when the wants of the community required it, the members, assisted by their neighbors and friends, decided to build a more commodious house of worship. Accordingly on the opposite side of the same creek, a few miles distant and to the east of the old site, near what was known as Booth Malone's spring, another was built retaining the same name. This also in course of time, after the country became more densely populated, was found to be too small and inconvenient, and another was erected still farther to the east, on the road leading from Clarksville, Tennessee to Trenton, Kentucky. It is a very pretty country church, and among its members may be seen on meeting days many of the descendants of those who met at the old log meeting-house first built. Some time after the first house had been abandoned an elderly lady, distinguished for her piety and deep religious feeling, remembering the happy days she had spent within its walls, had it removed and rebuilt at her own cost near her own residence, hoping that some of her old brethren in the ministry would continue to preach there occasionally. But its glory-had departed, and it soon ceased to be known as a place of worship altogether. It stood on the right side of the road leading down the creek from where your grandfather lived, on the land owned at present, I think, by the Hackney family.

CHAPTER XVIII.

LIFE IN STEWART COUNTY.

WE must now return again to your grandfather, whom we left at the "Owens' Place" on Red River in 1808, where he made a crop of corn.

In the fall of that year a land-owner, or land-agent, called on him and told him of some valuable land he had for sale in Stewart County, near the Cumberland River, on Saline Creek, and advised him to go and look at it. He did so, and was so well pleased that he made a purchase. I do not remember either the number of acres he bought or the price he paid for it.

His brother, Nathan Ross, who had moved to this country this year, also purchased land and settled in the same neighborhood, at which your grandfather was very much gratified. With this purchase he was well pleased, and hoped he had now found a home and resting-place for himself and family, and that his wanderings were at last ended.

On returning home he gathered his crop of corn, and sold it to a man named Duval, who soon afterwards failed, and the money he expected to receive for it was lost. This man Duval built the first brick court-house in Clarksville, which stood so many years on the public square, and was long considered the chief ornament of the place. The crop, I think, amounted to a hundred barrels, and the price was one dollar per barrel. I need not say that this was a heavy loss to your grandfather at this time, when the price of the corn was so much needed. He soon after removed to Stewart County, into the neighborhood of his land, and went into a cabin where a man named Outlaw had been killed a short time before by lightning, while standing on the hearth near the fire. The place where the lightning entered through the roof was still visible. We children begged hard not to be carried into a place of such evil omen, but there was no help for it, as the weather was bitterly cold, and there were no improvements at all on our land. We always felt ill at ease in this house, and often looked up at the roof with a shudder.

The winter of 1808 and 9 was so cold and inclement that but little out-door work could be done. The most important enterprise we undertook at that time was preparing a sugar camp. There were a great many sugar maples on our land, and your grandfather wished to make a supply of sugar from them for his family.

The old pioneer arrangement for making sugar was very simple. A rude shelter was made with boards for protection from rain and snow; under this a trench was dug in the ground as a sort of furnace, and over it boilers of every kind which could be obtained were placed so that a hot fire could be made under them. A sort of pocket-shaped notch was then cut in the tree to catch the sap, which was conducted off through reeds or pieces of elder-stalk into small wooden troughs made for that purpose.

When sap enough had collected, it was put into the boilers and boiled down to a certain consistence, and then set off to cool slowly and in order to make cake sugar;

but if the intention was to make granulated sugar, it was stirred while cooling.

In this way families often made more sugar than they needed for their own use. While the sugar-making was going on, every one, the children and negroes especially, was in high spirits. New Orleans sugar, when they could get it, was preferred by elderly people for coffee, but for all ordinary purposes the tree sugar answered well enough. The syrup made of it was then, as now, highly esteemed, for its peculiarly rich and delicate flavor.

It was often necessary at these camps to sit up all night and keep fires under the boilers. This I never liked. To stand near the bright fires and look out into the "blackness of darkness" that surrounded us was a little unpleasant, especially when, as was often the case, the wolves were howling and the owls hooting in the distance. The owls I disliked more than the wolves. They sometimes broke out into something like a fiendish laugh, which I abhorred. I had often heard that Indians would imitate owls when signaling each other at night on their murderous expeditions.

On one occasion, when several hours before day, your grandfather and I were sitting up attending to the boilers, a wild beast, seemingly of the larger kind, commenced a sort of wailing cry a little way from our camp, passing round it all the while at apparently the same distance. Your grandfather stood and listened for some time, and then said, "We had better get on our shelter." I went up first, and, after handing me his axe, he came up himself. The animal continued its circuit round the camp for some time afterwards. Your grandfather struck the board of our shed violently several times with his axe, which made quite a loud noise, but it did not seem to be heeded. Finally the creature went off in a straight direction, uttering its wail as far as we could hear it. We thought it was a panther, attracted and confused probably by our fires. I may here add that we made abundance of sugar that winter to supply us till the next season.

You must remember we were now on the very extreme limits of the white settlements. At this time, on the west bank of the Tennessee River the Indian territory began, and extended to the Mississippi River, an extensive country occupied by the Chickasaw Indians and wild beasts for many years until it was purchased by General Jackson, settled by white people, and known afterwards as "Jackson's Purchase."

When the weather was unfavorable for sugar-making, and not too inclement for out-door work, your grandfather was busily engaged in cutting logs and making boards for building a cabin. He generally took me with him when thus employed for company, and that I might be able to amuse myself, he gave me a hatchet to fell small trees with near where he was at work in the woods.

One day when a tree on which he had been chopping for some time began to fall, on looking round he saw me standing immediately under it. He gave the alarm, and I sprung behind a tree near by for protection. Had it not been there, I must have been killed by the broken limbs, which fell with a crash all around me. The shock produced by this disqualified him for doing any more work that day, and he went home, taking me with him. As we walked along together he spoke of the uncertainty of human life, and of the importance of always being prepared for death. He praised me also for my presence of mind in sheltering myself as I did behind the tree. My situation was indeed a perilous one, and my escape little less than a miracle.

As soon as his timbers were ready his neighbors assisted him in raising his cabin, and when we moved into it all were happy in having a home and resting-place of our own, although it was one of the rudest description, built with a view of using it as a shelter only until one more comfortable could be erected, as were most of the cabins of the pioneer settlers. The floor was made of logs, split open and laid down with the smooth side uppermost, and then dressed off a little with an adze.

Your grandfather was every day more and more pleased with the tract of land he had purchased. The growth upon it indicated great fertility. Besides the larger trees, such as the poplar, ash, walnut, and sugar-maple, there were also the buckeye, hackberry, papaw, redbud, spice-wood, and grapevines of enormous size, reaching to the tops of the tallest trees.

When spring had fairly opened, and the forest was decked in its gay attire, its beauty was not to be easily described. The poplar with its tulip-like blossoms, the dogwood with its gay white petals, the redbud with its delicate purple bloom, and the blackhaw with its snow-white clusters mingled with the light green leaves of early spring, made a picture of surpassing beauty.

Our cabin was near the right bank of a small stream, a tributary of Saline Creek, that wound along its gravelly bed, and whose water was so clear that one could see the smallest fish playing at the bottom, even where it was deepest. On its margin at that time grew many flowers —bluebells, wild pinks, a delicate little iris of singular fragrance and beauty, and a tiny white one, which I suppose was a variety of the anemone, or wind-flower.

This year we cleared off a few acres of land, and had the first log-rolling I had ever seen. This was to my mind a grand affair—six or eight strong men on each side of a heavy log, carrying it along with measured tread to the heap where it was to be burned. Yet we did not get our little field ready for a crop of corn this season, but had to rent one. This lay immediately opposite where the Saline Creek Baptist Church now stands, as I learn, in a little bottom near a small spring which breaks out under the bluff. This spring attracted our attention several times while we were living near it. It was observed, that when the creek was high, and the water flowing a little flush from the spring, great numbers of fine black perch would come out from under the bluff and flutter along down the little branch to the creek which was near. Many, when this was known, went with bags and baskets, and filled them with fish which they took out of the shallow water with their hands.

At this time, though living in the plainest way one can well imagine, as regards both food and raiment, we were very cheerful and happy, the demon of discontent not as yet being awakened among us by seeing others better off than ourselves. To this our pretty wild frontier home, in which we all felt so great an interest, in no small degree contributed. But alas, all our pleasing anticipations were destined soon to be blighted.

Your grandfather now learned, when too late, that the individual of whom he had purchased the land had no legal title to it, and consequently could make him none; and that it, with the little improvements he had made or

it and the money he had paid—which was about all he
had—was lost without any recourse whatever. This was
a cruel blow, and one from which he did not recover for
many long years. I remember well how unhappy he appeared to be, but there was no help for it. He immediately rented a small place in the neighborhood, and we
bade adieu to our pretty home, where for a short time we
had been so hopeful and happy. I do not remember that
I was ever at the place afterwards, though we lived some
two years near it. None of us, I believe, wanted to see
or think of it again.

Notwithstanding all these disappointments and misfortunes, your grandfather, during the whole time he lived
in Stewart County, which was nearly four years, kept up
his regular courses of preaching two days in every week
in the different settlements within his reach. These days
were Saturday and Sunday. Besides these he often
preached on other occasions, funeral sermons mostly.

Although until late in life he gave much of his time to
this kind of preaching, I think he never had any particular partiality for it. But as on these occasions he generally had large and attentive audiences, he considered
them as opportunities for doing much good, and availed
himself of them to direct the thoughts of the people to
the importance of being prepared when they too should
be called to stand in the presence of the Great Judge, and
give an account of the deeds done in the body.

As the death of many whose funeral sermons he preached were not hopeful, he did not dwell long on the life and
character of the dead, unless there were peculiar circumstances connected with them which could be turned to the
advantage of his hearers. But after making a few re-

marks suitable to the occasion, he would proceed to preach a discourse after his usual manner, first to invite attention to what the Bible and our own experience teaches us in regard to our being in a state of irreconciliation with our Creator, and the necessity of coming to love and serve him before we can be adopted into the heavenly family and become heirs of salvation.

He would then explain the great and glorious provision made for our salvation by the sufferings and death of Christ, and then exhort us to flee from the wrath to come by every consideration,—the uncertainty of life, the certainty of death, and after death the judgment when all must appear in the presence of God to give an account of the deeds done in the body, whether they be good or whether they be evil. He warned us not to neglect this great salvation, but while we had time and opportunity to seek the Lord while he may be found, and call upon him while he is near, since, as the Bible teaches and the poet sings,

> " There are no acts of pardon past
> In the cold grave to which we haste ;
> But darkness, death, and long despair
> Reign in eternal silence there ! "

In preaching funeral sermons of little children, which he was often called to do, he would give expression to many beautiful thoughts calculated to soothe the bitterness of parental grief. It was generally believed, he would say, that one-half at least of the human race die before reaching the age of accountability, and consequently, all had safely reached the mansions of eternal rest, were numbered among the happy spirits, and safe forevermore. Add to these the myriads of holy men and women who had come up out of great tribulation, and entered through the gates into the city, and we are not surprised to hear John declare in his glorious vision: "I beheld, and lo, a great multitude that no man could number, of all nations, and kindred, and peoples, and tongues, stood before the throne and before the Lamb, clothed with white robes, and palms in their hands." This was a theme on which he loved to dwell.

While living in this county he travelled and preached much with a minister named Dudley Williams. He possessed fine talents, and for many years was much esteemed on account of his zeal and Christian character. As a preacher he was eloquent and impressive, and your grandfather loved and admired him. He seems, though, to have had a turn for trade and speculation, and finally became involved in debt. Hoping to extricate himself from his embarrassments, he left home and went down into what was then called the Attakapas country in the southeastern part of Louisiana, and commenced trading in beef cattle for the New Orleans market. Here he remained for several years, but failed in his expectations of mending his fortunes. On returning home he commenced preaching again, but seems to have lost prestige as a minister, and suffered to some extent in his reputation, the particulars of which I do not remember. After some years he died, and his sun, which in early manhood had shone brightly, finally set under a cloud. Your grandfather never thought of him afterwards but with deep regret and sorrow. He was often at our house, and I remember him well.

All the time he lived in Stewart County, your grandfather preached for the Spring Creek Church as its pastor, though distant about thirty miles. It was his custom to leave home on Friday, and reach the neighborhood of his church in the evening of the same day, preach on Saturday and Sunday, and return home on Monday.

One morning soon after leaving home to attend his meeting he returned, and told some of the neighbors where he had just seen a bear, and then went on again. The whole settlement soon collected together mounted on horseback with dogs and guns. On going to the place where the bear had been seen they soon found him. After a long and exciting chase bruin was brought to bay and killed. Late in the evening the hunters in triumph came by where your Aunt Polly and Aunt Nannie were setting on the fence awaiting their return. They stopped a few moments, and showed us the great paws of the bear, which they had cut off and brought home as a trophy. We were almost afraid to look at them, they seemed so formidable. This gave us something to talk and think about long afterwards, and checked our rambling about in the woods so far from home, lest we might fall in with others like him.

To me the few years we lived in Stewart County were by far the most interesting of my boyhood, and I am not a little surprised at the distinctness with which long forgotten scenes and incidents re-appear even now when I think of those early times. Memory is, indeed, a wonderful faculty, the great store-house where countless forms of beauty and loveliness repose, but, alas, where also, side by side with these, are many dark shadows of grief and sorrow, from which, were it possible, we would gladly turn away. And here, had I a turn for moralizing, which I have not, I would say, let every one consider well what he says and does in this life, since memory will not always linger alone on what is bright and beautiful in the past.

CHAPTER XIX.

CUSTOMS AND SCENES IN STEWART COUNTY.

WHEN we first moved to Stewart County in the winter of 1808, nearly all that portion of it lying immediately on the Cumberland River, from near Dover to the mouth of Saline Creek, was a wild, uninhabited district, which had not yet attracted the attention of settlers, and was almost precisely in the same state it had been in for ages. Its hills, valleys, and streams were as nature had left them; and no one at present passing over it would have any conception of the difference wrought in its appearance. Perhaps no one standing on the site of the little cabin we built there could believe it was the spot I have described.

There was a wild, rugged district lying west of us between the Cumberland and Tennessee Rivers, about twelve miles in width, an almost unbroken solitude, after which, as already stated, commenced the Indian territory, extending to the Mississippi River, since known as the Tennessee and Kentucky Purchases.

Soon after we moved there, however, a great change took place in our district. Settlers came in very rapidly. Many cabins were built along the streams or creeks, and small fields were cleared up and planted in corn and pumpkins, which grew with amazing luxuriance. I will not risk what claims I may have to veracity by telling you how thickly I have seen these pumpkins lying on the ground, or the size to which they sometimes grew.

Soon the cow with her tinkling bell was seen grazing on the rich pea-vines among the hills, and swine feeding on the mast or acorns, which in many places covered the ground. The little tub mill soon followed, near which the still-house—the never-failing sign of a dawning civilization—might be seen with its lazy wheel raising water from the creek by means of cows' horns fitted to its rim.

These still-houses followed in the wake of "Boyd's Red-heifer," at Nashville, where, in 1787, when a *run* was made, a horn was blown to convey the glad tidings to all the thirsty souls in the city; and Paton's "Buffalo Bull," near Clarksville, to or from or by which the County Court ordered so many roads to be made at a still later period. This seems, indeed, to have been a famous watering place in its day, though after diligent inquiry I have not been able to learn its exact locality.

Many of the comforts and conveniences of life at this time were not easily procured. Salt was very scarce, and consequently dear. It was made near Shawneetown, in Illinois, and brought down the Ohio River in crafts called pirogues,—a French name, I think. These were made of great trees, dug out after the manner of common canoes. When two of these were lashed together they could carry a considerable amount of freight. Bringing down salt in these in former times was attended with danger. There were many bad Indians, and worse white men, infesting the banks of the Ohio, who used to kill those in charge of the pirogues and rob them of their freight, whatever it might be. And long afterwards, when the Indians had passed away, men in their trading boats were murdered and their goods carried off. Many, no doubt, remember the murders and robberies that used to be committed at and near Ford's Ferry on the Ohio River in later times.

When the pirogues would land at the mouth of Saline Creek with salt, people went with horses and bags a considerable distance to get small supplies of it. I went once with your grandfather, and saw quite a crowd at the landing. I think he gave three dollars and fifty cents per bushel, of fifty pounds, for what he got then.

An old gentleman, named Hubbard, had brought down this salt, and I heard him relate some of his experiences while engaged in this business in former times. He said that he would keep his pirogues out in the middle of the river when he saw or heard anything suspicious on shore, and lie down in them, holding the rudder in his hand, occasionally raising his head an instant to see if he was going right, and then ducking it down quickly before an Indian could shoot him.

Of coffee, for the first few years, there was little or none. The same might be said of imported tea. A substitute for the latter was made of sassafras, spice wood, and sage, sweetened with maple sugar. Young people and children liked these beverages very well, but elderly people did not regard them with much favor.

Several years, I think, passed without any flour in our house. At length some was obtained, and we had hot biscuit on Sunday mornings for breakfast, which we children considered high living. Your grandmother would also sometimes permit us to put some in our pockets to eat during the day. Considering the quality of the flour of which they were made, I can but wonder that we should have liked them so well. It has been my good fortune since to eat as good biscuits as were ever made, I suppose; but these remain still embalmed in my memory.

The wheat sowed in our settlement was in little patches, and was reaped as in the days of Boaz and Ruth with a sickle. I doubt if you have ever seen one of these implements of husbandry. The wheat was gathered in the left hand and cut off with the sickle held in the right, and then dropped in little handfuls on the ground. Old Hussey's reaper was then no more dreamed of than some great invention which shall come to light centuries hence. A dozen or more men all abreast and about half bent, reaping in this way, made a pretty sight.

The manner of getting out the wheat was no less primitive. As in ancient times the sheaves were laid down and the grain beaten out with flails; but more frequently many of these were laid on a yard made smooth and level by careful preparation, and a number of horses with boys on them made to trot round and round upon the sheaves until all the grain left the heads, after which the straw was taken off. Then, as even wheat fans had not come into use among us, on some windy day a man would stand on an elevated place and pour the wheat slowly from a pail or basket until the dust and chaff, or at least a part of them, were carried off by the wind. A sack of this wheat would then be sent to one of the little mills, and perhaps ground immediately after a sack of corn. Consequently a large amount of corn meal was mixed with the flour. It was then put into a hopper, and run through a bolting cloth stretched on a frame and turned by hand with a crank, like a grindstone. It was the business of each mill boy to bolt his own flour. This part of the business was our abhorrence, and I shall never forget

9

having to sit on a platform and turn this miserable crank by the hour. Your grandmother tried once to make light bread of this flour, but without success, though for biscuit and batter-cakes we thought it answered very well.

It was the business of the husband to provide his family with food. This was easily done if he had a small piece of rich bottom land cleared and fenced in, and was the owner of a few cattle and hogs. The former could live during the winter on very little besides the cane which had not yet disappeared, and the latter on the beech mast and acorns which were very plentiful. Then almost every man had his rifle, with which he could furnish for his family supplies of wild turkeys, venison, and other game. The graceful and sprightly squirrel, whose home is in the forest, was also to be had. These sometimes appeared in such numbers as to be regarded as pests. To destroy them our settlers often turned out in companies with their rifles, and sometimes rewards were offered to those who brought in the greatest number of scalps within a specified time. They often emigrated in vast numbers, swimming across the Ohio, Tennessee, and Cumberland Rivers, and people would stand on the banks and kill them with sticks as they came ashore. One woman, while washing her clothes on the river bank, was reported to have killed several hundred in one day. Goldsmith tells us, if I remember rightly, that these little animals often get on pieces of dry bark, hoist their tails for a sail, and in this way cross rivers and lakes. I do not remember, however, that any were ever seen crossing our rivers in this fanciful way. Wild pigeons, too, at certain seasons of the year, were to be seen in countless numbers, extending from one side of the horizon to the other, darkening the heavens while passing over. All these things combined give a charm to frontier life, which causes the pioneer to remember it with pleasure, though often at the same time surrounded by dangers and privations.

It was the business of the wife and mother to provide clothing for her family, and to aid her in this every settler had his little cotton or flax patch, or both. When the balls opened the cotton was picked out, and after being dried in the sun a few days was stowed away. As there were no cotton gins in our part of the country, the seeds were picked out by the fingers instead.

At night, during the winter months, after a large fire had been made and the hearth swept, your grandmother would put a little parcel of this cotton down before it for each one of us to pick before going to bed. In each one of these was enough to keep us busy an hour or so. It was placed thus before the fire, because, when heated, the seeds could be taken out much more easily. After grumbling a good deal about the size of our respective piles, and getting her to take some from one and put it on another to equalize them, we went to work, plying our fingers nimbly till our tasks were done. When finished and all put together it made quite a pretty show.

This was a famous time for talking about ghosts, witches, bears, panthers, and Indians. We knew many stories of the heroic men and women of still earlier times, who had to contend with the cruel Indians. We often found ourselves, without knowing how we got there, far away under other skies in the land of Gideon, Samson, David, and Goliath. Our father and mother were generally seated a little apart from us, she sewing or knitting, and he reading or meditating, though one would think to little advantage, considering the noise around him. Many times we would all be telling the same story at the same time, each in a prodigious hurry lest another should get before him in the narrative. Our mother would occasionally help us on with our story when at fault. In reading the Old Testament she took great delight, and was consequently specially able to keep us right in our Bible stories.

After the tasks were done, the stories finished, and a little time allowed us to compose ourselves, the evening devotion followed, consisting of the reading of a chapter from the Bible, the singing of a hymn, and prayers. In your grandfather's prayers there was a peculiarity I never observed in those of any other person. No two of these had the least resemblance as regarded set words and phrases. He seemed filled with the very spirit of prayers which found utterance in no set form of words whatever, and even when a child I used to admire their beauty.

There was an evening hymn which was a special favorite of his about this time, and we all joined with him in singing it.

> " The day is past and gone,
>   The evening shades appear,
>   Oh, may we all remember well,
>   The night of death is near!
>
>   We lay our garments by,
>   Upon our beds to rest,
>   So death will soon disrobe us all
>   Of what we now possess."

He invariably read out two lines of the hymn, and after singing these, two more. This had the advantage of keeping us all well together, and preventing the dis-

cord which is apt to arise when this is not done.   In large
congregations this enabled all to sing.   And when the air
was a familiar one, and the couplets tastefully read out,
the swell and volume of sacred melody in those old times
was often grand and beautiful.   For congregational singing, I think no other method can compare with this.

Many families cultivated the indigo plant in those days
(which I think very much resembled our common
penny-royal), and manufactured their own indigo, thus
saving the expense of buying, which was an important
consideration with us.   Your grandmother and I were
famous indigo makers.

Dressed buckskin was with the settler an important
article of clothing.   A young fellow with hunting shirt
and trousers made of it was considered as provided for in
the way of clothes for an indefinite period of time. I never
heard any one estimate their probable duration.   I have
myself seen a boy wear a pair of these trousers until they
would descend but little below the knee though long
enough when first made; but it must be remembered that
while the boy was growing taller the buckskin was inclined
to shrink.   Dressed buckskin when new is soft and vel-
vety, and of a rich buff color, but time would tell upon it
more or less, as upon other things.   In its last stages it
became blackish and almost as sleek as glass.   If a boy
on a cold frosty morning put on a pair of these trousers in
this state without drawers, as was often the case for the
best of reasons, a considerable clattering of teeth might
be heard.   But then what could be better to have on
when one climbed a tree with rough bark or ran through a
patch of briers ?   The hunting shirt made of this material came down to the hips, and was confined at the waist

by a belt. It generally had a small cape notched round
the edge to give it a pretty finish. The bottom of the
shirt was ornamented in the same way. When a boy my
heart's desire was to have one of these suits, but that happiness never fell to my lot.

Besides cotton cloth and buckskin a good deal of linen
was also made. The flax plant was pretty while growing,
especially when its tiny pale blue blossoms were out. When
prepared, it was spun on a small wheel turned by a crank
kept in motion by the foot. Elderly ladies used these
mostly, and in the course of a day would spin a large
amount of thread on them. Cloth made of this constituted a large portion of the clothing of the men and boys
in summer. It was used also for towels, napkins, and
table-cloths.

Many persons tanned their own leather and made their
own shoes. A large tree was cut down, and made into
a trough. The hides were prepared and put into these
troughs and oak bark laid between the folds. They
would at length imbibe enough of the tannin from the
bark to be converted into leather. This was made into
shoes sometimes by a member of the family, and at others
by an itinerant, who went from house to house for that
purpose. Your grandfather sometimes made shoes for us
children, and was thought by us to be a wonderful genius on that account. For many years he kept a set of
shoemaker's tools in the house for that purpose.

Nothing was more valued by the settlers than good
axes. The unskilful blacksmith often failed to temper
them properly, and they would then bend or break on the
edge, and consequently much time was lost in carrying
them to the shops. One of the fine Collin's axes that

afterwards came into use would then have been considered a great treasure.

Bells to put on horses and cattle were at this time considered of great value, but less so than some years earlier, when 640 acres of land near Nashville, on what is now the Lebanon Pike, sold for "three axes and two cow bells," and a faithful rifle, and a clear toned bell were traded for another tract. Of all the bells ever made, perhaps no two ever sounded exactly alike. The practiced ear could detect the difference, and each person could go to his own bell though many might be sounding in the distance at the same time, and thereby find his own stock. Cattle and horses, too, knew their own bell, and in this way kept together.

Their attachment to it was often so great that they would follow it almost any where. While at New Madrid many years ago I heard the story of a mule drover who being asked what he considered an exorbitant price by the ferryman to set his mules across the Mississippi River, said he would not give it. And taking his bell off his leader got into a skiff, and as he was rowed across rang it loud and distinctly. His large drove all came down to the water's edge—stopped, listened a moment and then plunged into the mighty stream. For some time their heads and long ears could be seen by those standing on shore, but at last owing to the distance they disappeared and all seemed to have gone down to rise no more. At length one was seen to emerge on the other shore near the man who rang the bell, and then another and then another until finally all were seen standing together among the cotton trees on the opposite bank near their bell.

A blacksmith who could make a good bell found it very

profitable, since nothing was more sought after in those times. For most of the settlers being scarce of feed for their work animals after the day's work was done turned them out to graze at night, and had to collect them again in the morning, which was easily done when they had bells on them.

It should have been mentioned sooner that every family had its spinning wheels, cards, and loom. All the girls were taught to spin, card rolls, and weave. I used to think they appeared to great advantages while spinning. Their light and graceful movements and handsome forms had an effect altogether pleasing. I doubt if any female employment ever showed them off to a greater advantage or was more conducive to health.

A wonderful story was told of a young lady who could spin a thread so fine that the wool required to make a piece of cloth of average width could be drawn through her finger ring. If this were so, it is well she did not live in the days of the envious Minerva, or like poor Arachne, she too might have been turned into a spider for rivalling that goddess in her favorite art.

When the thread was spun very fine and even, then dyed blue, and woven into strips or checks tastefully shaded it made very pretty dresses for ladies. The dyeing was done mostly by old women, whose hands while thus engaged were of a deep blue color. The process of dyeing, for some unknown cause, often proved a failure as did that of soap-making likewise. With both these operations many supposed witchcraft had something to do.

All amusements were conducted with an eye to something useful. The young people had their cotton-pickings, and at these there would be a good deal of mirth and gayety, but a large quantity of cotton picked also. At the quiltings they would have a lively time, chatting, joking, and courting; but there was a pretty quilt to show when all was over. House-raising and log-rolling involved so much hard work, that one would think they could not have been regarded as holidays, but they were nevertheless.

The corn-shucking was a favorite pastime. At these, about dusk, the hands would assemble and a pole be laid across the corn-pile to divide it into two equal parts. Then two men would be chosen called captains, after the manner of school-boys preparing for a game; each, one after the other, chose his man, and the corn-crib was uncovered to receive the ears as the shuck was pulled off. Each captain took his men on his side the pole, the darkies raised the corn-song, and the contest began. In a few hours the large corn-heap would melt away, and the dividing pole fall on the side of the victors. They would often then seize their captain and bear him off in triumph on their shoulders. The darkies had a variety of corn-songs and a name for each. " I'm gwine way down the river," "The nigger-trader bought me," and " Fare you well, Miss Sarah," were very fashionable. The airs, and what little of sentiment there was, generally had a tone of sadness in them, and the rich mellow voices of the singers, when heard far away during the stillness of the night, had a very pleasing effect. After supper all returned home to meet again in a few nights at the house of another neighbor, and thus go on till the shucking season ended.

Boys were kept pretty well to business during the week, but on Sundays they literally ran wild. Robert

9*

Raikes and Sunday-schools had not been heard of then. After breakfast in summer we would repair to our play-ground in some secluded place under the shady trees and spend several hours, running races, jumping, wrestling, and playing at ball and marbles. The black boys were permitted to join us on terms of perfect equality.

After amusing ourselves in this way till satisfied, we often took our bows and arrows, which we had carried with us, and went to the creek, pulled off our trousers, wound them round our necks, and waded up and down in the shallow water to shoot fish with only one garment on, and sometimes not even that. When we came to water of sufficient depth we all plunged in, diving, swimming, and splashing the water about like dolphins.

In autumn we roamed the forests in search of nuts, wild grapes, persimmons, papaw apples, and black haws. The latter was a fruit we highly prized. It grew on a dwarf tree about the height of the common dogwood, with smooth glossy leaves.

In our rambles we sometimes passed by the solitary cabin of an old hunter named McCulloch. It stood on the bank of a stream called Hays' Fork, in a grove of beech trees. The stream, if I remember correctly, was a tributary of Saline Creek. His cabin was one of the rudest kind, very low and small, and the cracks between the logs were large. There was a fire-place in one end, and a chimney about breast high, across which sticks were laid for the purpose of drying or curing his venison.

He was a good deal past the middle age, tall, spare, and sinewy, with a florid complexion. He had a beautiful rifle, mounted with silver, and kept in the most perfect order. No living thing—not even a dog, the usual companion of the pioneer hunter—was to be seen about the place. He was, I think, one of the last of the old hunters that had lingered in our settlement—one of the Leather-stocking type. It was said he would leave home some-times for weeks together—gone perhaps on a distant hunt. He killed a great many deer, as was reported, for their hams and skins, which he used to sell. It was supposed he had money secreted in the woods somewhere near where he lived.

His method of approaching the deer, of which he killed so many, was very singular. He took care to get the deer between himself and the wind, so that it could not scent him. When the deer's head was up he stood per-fectly still, and when it was down grazing and could not see him he walked towards it till it was about to raise its head again, and then stopped. He knew when it was going to raise its head, because before doing so it always shook its tail. In this way he could approach as near his game as he desired—so near as never to fail to bring it down when he fired.

I heard that he used to say all or nearly all the tales told about the killing of people by wolves were untrue, as he had never known but one person killed by them. A negro man, who had been sent to help a neighbor to kill his hogs, and was on his way home after night with fresh meat in a basket, had been attacked by a gang of them and devoured, together with the meat he was carrying. When he did not return as expected, his master, on going to look for him, found nothing but a piece of his hat and his shoes to show where he had been killed.

An account he gave of an unwelcome visit he once had from a panther was quite thrilling. He had observed that for several nights in succession some of the venison he had placed over his chimney to dry was carried off, and concluded to lie down and cover himself with skins and keep awake to see what was going on. He did not wait long before he heard something jump up on his scaffold. Almost at the same instant scaffold, meat, and a large panther fell down together into his cabin. He had never, before nor afterwards, been in such deadly peril. For although the panther is a great coward naturally, yet when hemmed in or wounded he knew it to be the most dangerous wild beast of the forest. His first impulse was to reach out for his rifle to shoot it, but he was afraid it would notice this and tear him to pieces. The creature at first seemed greatly astonished at what had happened, and stood still for some time looking round the cabin. As good fortune would have it the door had been left partly open, and on seeing this his visitor passed out into the dark and left him, greatly to his satisfaction and comfort.

As the settlement increased in population, and game became more and more scarce, the old hunter at length left his cabin and never returned. Whither he directed his steps, I think no one ever knew. Perhaps still farther towards the setting sun.

The first school in our settlement was taught by a gentleman named Ferrell, which name sounded so much like ferule as to be suggestive. His curriculum, or course of studies, was spelling, reading, and arithmetic. As regards his proficiency in these branches I can only testify as to his penmanship, which was simply marvellous for its beauty.

This school, at least while I attended it, was quite large. It was composed of girls and boys, and I think in some respects deserves notice.   In the first place, it could boast of only one arithmetic, which belonged to the master. When a boy wanted a sum to work.upon he carried his slate to him, and had one set down suited to his age and advancement. He took his slate out under the trees, and was allowed his own time to report progress. He might take a week if it suited his convenience.   After trying it a few days, if he could not work it himself, he generally, carried it to some boy more advanced, and had it done. He then took it to the master, who, if on examination it was found correct, ordered him to set it down in his cypher-ing-book in which each scholar was required to enter in full every sum he worked or rather *had* worked for him. These cyphering-books consisted of about one quire of common cap paper stitched together and placed between a covering made of pasteboard.   These were preserved with great care, and generally ornamented with some of the elegant penmanship of the master.   After writing down his sum the master set down another on his slate, and he went out into the woods as before.

Another peculiarity of this school was the absence of everything like classification. So soon as the master took his seat in the morning the head scholar came forward made a bow, and spelt or read his lesson.   Before he could reach his seat the next in order would come up, recite, and go back ; and this went on all day, no two reciting together.

No scholar was permitted to study upon his lesson to himself, but was required to spell or read it out in a loud tone of voice with his book held up before his face so that he could not look about.   The louder they read and the more noise they made, the better the master was pleased, and

when they were in full blast the din was simply tremendous. On seeing some gentlemen riding by one day he
told us to let them have it, and they got it sure enough.
He liked people to hear us when preparing our lessons.
The boys soon learned that, provided they did it in a proper
tone of voice, they could talk on any subject they desired
without being detected.

Our teacher believed in the virtue of the rod, and kept
three or four very pretty specimens by him on nails driven
in the wall near where he sat. I think he must have had
a good eye for things of that sort as in my rambles in the
woods I never saw any so tapering and shapely as his were,
and have no doubt that when passing about if he saw one
of these beauties he secured it for our benefit. I think
he preferred the black hickory, though, to the time-honored
birch.

These he not only used in individual cases, but sometimes made a general application of them, as when he
noticed a sort of languor in the school, he would go round
and whip the whole concern. If a boy who was conning
over his lesson at the time complained of being whipped
unjustly, he would be told that a chap who failed to get
a whipping ten times when he deserved it had no right to
complain if he got one now and then when he did not.
As a general thing we took our whippings as a part of our
schooling, without making much ado about them, and
thought if we did not get more than one or two a day we
were doing pretty well.

But our teacher had one practice which we all considered
"dog-mean," to use our phrase. He kept a little stick
about eighteen inches long lying on his table, and when on
looking round he saw a good many not attending to their

lessons he would throw this stick out into the middle of the
floor, and order all that were idle to pick it up and bring
it to him. Whereupon, half a dozen little fellows would
be seen to rise slowly from their seats, on which they left
their spelling books; pick up the miserable stick with their
little brown hands; march up with it " slowly and sadly,"
as if they were carrying the last friend they had in the world
to his grave ; receive their whipping; and return to their
seats again.

The day of deliverance at length dawned. The larger
scholars decided to strike for a holiday. Consequently,
one day when the master went to his dinner they barred
up the door securely. On returning he inquired, " What
it meant." He was told we wanted holiday, and he could not
come in till he agreed to let us have it. He replied that he
would go and cut an armful of switches, and if the door
was not unbarred when he returned, we would be sorry
we had ever heard of such a thing as holiday. Then he
started off to get them as we supposed. All now became
terribly frightened, and not waiting to unbar the door ran
up the chimney which was low, jumped down upon the
ground and ran home. This broke up the school for the
present. I think he taught there afterwards; but your
grandfather never sent me to him.

Here I think it but just to state, that though this teacher
did a good deal of flogging, he never whipped us cruelly,
and seemed to do it rather as a duty than from ill temper. I
remember him well. He had red hair, a long narrow
face, and fair complexion.

You will perhaps hardly believe it when I tell you we
had an Exhibition while I was going to this school ; but
it is true. This was considered a wonderful event in our

settlement, and excited it from centre to circumference. What we called a stage was made before the school-house door and raised some distance from the ground. A part of this was concealed from public view by counterpanes tacked together for a curtain. The speakers and actors issued from behind this, and came out on the boards in full view of the spectators, who stood or sat on the ground. There were many speeches spoken and dialogues acted to the great delight of the people.

The great event was the killing of Cæsar by the Roman conspirators. He came out first on the stage—then one, and then another of the assassins. While they were standing and talking together in a very friendly way, one of the conspirators drew his dagger and struck at Cæsar. The rest joined in, and while he was defending himself as best he could, Brutus drew his dagger and struck the mortal blow. Cæsar then folded his robe around him, and fell pouring out at the same time some red paint prepared for the occasion, which trickled down like blood. It was a terrible spectacle, and many who witnessed it turned pale. Few present had seen anything of the kind before, and it made a deep impression on their minds. I think even now, all things considered, the acting was very good. Thus you see, though nearly out of the world, we were already enjoying some of its entertainments.

Our old school-house, I think, stood across the creek in a southeasterly direction from the present Saline Creek Church, distant from it, perhaps, three-quarters of a mile. I think it was used as a meeting-house before the present one was built. The last time I saw it I was in company with your grandfather and Elder Fort, who held a meeting there "long time ago."

As I have told you a fish story I will now tell you one about a snake and then bid a final adieu to the old school-house with all its pleasant and unpleasant memories.

A schoolmate and I were going to the spring for water and we saw a flock of partridges just before us. As he was very expert at throwing stones, he threw one at them and killed one partridge. We were very proud of the feat, and after looking at it some time laid it on an old log, intending to get it on our return, and show it to the boys when we got back to the school-house. We loitered some time at the spring, but when on our return we came to look for the bird behold, it was no where to be found! We walked around and around wondering what could have become of it, when on looking down, wonderful to tell, there lay a rattlesnake almost under our feet. I need not tell you he was in size a monster, for in snake stories they are always so. This fellow had just swallowed our bird, as we found afterwards. Why he had not bitten us it would be hard to tell.

An old hunter who lived near Greysville, Todd County, Kentucky, was standing near a tree waiting for his dogs to bring by him a deer which they were pursuing; on looking down saw a prodigious rattlesnake coiled up almost under his feet, and at one bound placed himself at a safe distance. As the snake had behaved so well toward him, he hesitated for some time about killing it. After thinking the matter over he concluded that, though a good snake himself, he belonged to a bad family and killed it. We came to the same conclusion concerning our snake, and did likewise. He was an ugly-looking rascal and we thought he had poison enough in him to kill a dozen boys had he bitten them.

CHAPTER XX.

WAR—INDIANS—COMETS—EARTHQUAKES.

THE year 1811 was an eventful one, both for our settlement and for our country. " Coming events " were beginning to " cast their shadows before," and to fill the public mind with forebodings of trouble.

The English Government claimed and exercised the right to search American vessels on the high seas, and to take from them all they thought or pretended to think were British subjects, and to put them on board their own vessels of war. All foresaw that this would make war inevitable, if persisted in, as no proud, high-spirited people could brook so great an indignity.

It was known, too, that nearly all the Indian tribes were more or less disaffected and hostile, and that in the event of a war with England an alliance would be formed among them, and that the tomahawk and scalping knife would again be used to perform their bloody work.

It was well known, also, that Tecumseh, the famous Indian chief, was busily engaged in forming an extensive confederacy of all the surrounding Indian tribes, the object of which was to exterminate the white race, and to prevent all further encroachments on what they considered their territory.

This celebrated chief is said to have been one of three brothers, born at the same time, on the banks of the Scioto

River, near Chillicothe, Ohio. His father was the famous Shawnee chief, Cornstalk, who commanded the Indian warriors in the battle of Kanawha, or Point Pleasant, in 1774, where but for the vigilance of Robertson and Sevier, it seems that the army under General Lewis must have met with a bloody defeat. His mother is variously stated to have been a Shawnee, a Creek, and a Cherokee Indian. "His enmity to the whites was constant and bitter. In all the terrible incursions of the savages by which the first settlers of Kentucky were harassed, he was conspicuous, but rarely appropriated to his own use any of the booty thus obtained. The love of glory and his desire of sating vengeance on the whites were his predominant passions."

"In person he was about five feet ten inches high, with handsome features, a symmetrical and powerful frame, and an air of dignity and defiance." As a warrior, politician, and hunter, he had no equal in his tribe. Of his skill in hunting it is narrated that, being challenged to a contest by the best hunters of his tribe, he returned, at the end of three days, with thirty deerskins, while none of his competitors brought in more than twelve.

After inspiring the northern tribes with deadly hostility to the whites, he passed through the Chickasaw and Choctaw nations, on his way to the Creeks and Cherokees. When he set out on this journey he left his brother, Elskatawa known as the Shawnee Prophet, in command of his northern warriors, with strict orders to strike no blow until his return. But he, becoming impatient, attacked General Harrison, November 7th, 1811, at Tippecanoe, where he was defeated in a bloody battle, and the Indian war fully inaugurated.

This disobedience of orders on the part of the Prophet well nigh ruined all the splendid schemes Tecumseh had been forming for years. He did not succeed, it is true, in bringing our Indians, the Chickasaws and Choctaws, into his league. Had he done this all our settlements on the Cumberland must have been broken up. But as our people could not know certainly how matters stood, they were constantly harassed by alarming rumors. At one time a report came that they were killing people at the Mouth of Sandy, on the Tennessee River, and that they might be expected in our settlement any hour. The report reached us about dusk, when your grandfather was from home. As soon as it was quite dark, your grandmother took us all, and went over to the house of Uncle Nathan Ross. She forbade us to speak a word or make any noise whatever on the way. We moved along, like so many silent spectres, in the darkness. On reaching his house, we learned that he had already collected a number of men, and had gone to see what the Indians were doing on the Tennessee. Returning in a day or two, he reported that only one family had been frightened from home, after which the bed-ticks had been ripped open and carried off, and the feathers left scattered about the house and yard, but by whom this had been done, I think, was never known.

Although Tecumseh did not succeed in turning our Indian neighbors against us, it was different with the Creek Indians, and the massacre at Fort Mimms, in what is now the State of Alabama, one of the bloodiest in the annals of Indian warfare, soon followed. The flame there kindled by him among the southern Indians continued to blaze, until it was finally quenched in their blood, during the wars waged against them, by the heroic Jackson. I may here state that after Tecumseh returned from his southern tour, he collected together the warriors left after the battle of Tippecanoe, and joined the British army in Canada, was made a brigadier general, and distinguished himself for courage and conduct, until he fell in the battle of the Thames in 1812, while gallantly leading his warriors to the charge.*

To add to the causes of uneasiness already mentioned, the great comet of 1811 made its appearance at this time. It was a splendid affair; having a tail long enough, it was said, to have coiled round our planet five thousand times; a comet of tremendous magnitude. I remember well when we first saw it, at your grandfather's. A stranger had died in the neighborhood, and his remains had been brought to our place to be buried. It so happened that the interment had not been completed till after dark; and while the grave was being filled up, some of the bystanders happening to look to the northwest, saw the terrible stranger on the verge of the distant horizon. I need not say its appearance caused a deep sensation in a crowd, all of whom had been taught to look upon comets as harbingers of impending calamity. To add to our misfortunes still further, the northern lights were particularly showy and beautiful this season. And when they would change rapidly from one part of the heavens to another, and sometimes assume a dark red hue, many thought that the movements of armies and bloodshed were portended, and lost heart altogether. But the worst was not yet. On the 16th of December, 1811, the severe

* For what has been said of Tecumseh see *Cyclopedia Americana* and *Putnam's Annals.*

shock of an earthquake was felt about two o'clock in the morning. This produced the greatest consternation. Many of the neighbors, while it was yet dark, left home, and came to learn of your grandfather what it was, and what was the cause of it. He told them it was an earthquake, and that earthquakes were supposed to be caused by great fires raging in the bowels of the earth. And when he added that not only single houses, but great towns and cities had often been shaken down by them, and thousands of people buried in the ruins, all thought they had made a merciful escape, and about daylight started home happy, and it is to be hoped, thankful, that they had escaped so well, not doubting that all danger was now over. But about sunrise, a noise like distant subterranean thunder, far away to the southwest, began to be heard. As it approached nearer and nearer, and grew louder and louder, the ground began to tremble. When it reached us the noise for a moment was terrific, and the vibrations of the earth violent. Then the rumbling sound gradually rolled away to the northwest till it became inaudible.

The feeling produced was sublime and awful. Even dumb animals seemed to be awed by it. They looked pensive and dejected, as though something strange and mysterious was going on. We are familiar with the rumbling noise of thunder in the air. It appears to be in its place there, but when the same sound is heard deep down in the earth, it seems strange and unnatural.

I was in bed, asleep, when the first shock was felt, and of course knew nothing about it, till all was over; and when I heard them telling how the ground shook, furniture, plates, and dishes rattled and clattered ; and the house itself seemed ready to fall, I regretted that I had not been awake to see and hear it all. But I was soon to be more than gratified. Your grandfather, like the rest, supposing all was over, had sent me out into the field early in the morning after his horse, when the second shock—much more violent than the first—came on. When I heard the rumbling noise and felt the ground shaking under my feet, I threw away my bridle, turned, and fled to the house with all speed, which I reached in a badly demoralized condition. About the same time, the neighbors who had just left, and many besides, came pouring in, a pitiable and terror-stricken crowd, and remained in and about the house and yard all day, expecting another shock every moment. A few who lived nearest went home for something to eat, but were soon back again. Toward evening their uneasiness seemed to increase, and it was soon apparent they intended to stay all night and have your grandfather preach for them. Erasmus was right when he exclaimed: "*Quam religiosus nos afflictio facit!*" *How religious affliction makes us!*

The weather was quite cold, and large fires necessary. The stout young fellows took their axes, and soon provided a good supply of wood, by splitting up some large logs, that lay in the way, near the house. All seemed serious and thoughtful, and very much disposed to huddle together. The thought of the long dark night that lay before them, and of what might befall them, before another sun arose, awakened feelings of anxiety and apprehension. That night many knees bent in prayer that had, perhaps, never bent in that way before. All, without exception, from the least to the greatest, might be seen in that humble attitude, so becoming those who appear, as it were, in the

presence of the Deity, to implore his favor and protection,
in times of perplexity and danger. There are few things
more impressive, than to behold a whole congregation at
once upon their knees.

In his discourse that night, your grandfather told us
of the ancient Ninevites, who had become so wicked that
a prophet was sent to warn them of the judgments about
to fall upon them and their doomed city. And how, after all, from the king on his throne, to the beggar in the
street, had repented of their sins in sackcloth and in
ashes, they were saved from the impending destruction.
Then he exhorted us to do likewise, as the Heavenly
Father was merciful, and did not desire the death of the
wicked, but that all might repent and live. He added,
that with repentance toward God, and faith in Christ, we
had the promise of the life that now is and of that
which is to come, and would then be ready to meet death,
whether he should come in "sunshine or in storm," in the
earthquake or in "the pestilence that wasteth at noonday."

These were words of encouragement, which led many of
those present to repent of their sins, reform their lives,
make a profession of religion, and honor the professic
they made, by a pious walk and godly conversation.
Others again who seemed to have started well, faltered by
the way, and as the earth became more and more steady,
their faith became more and more unsteady. These were
called "earthquake Christians," to distinguish them from
those who held out faithful to the end.

During this winter, night-meetings were held, more or
less frequently, at the houses of the settlers in our neighborhood. And as the different groups who attended
them, were seen approaching with torches after dark, from

various points, some nearer, and others more distant, the scene was both wild and beautiful. These torches were made of dry poplar rails, split up into small pieces. The light they made was very brilliant, when seen among the forest trees, during the darkness.

Besides the religious benefit which the settlement received from your grandfather, he rendered it valuable service in other respects. When the spring of 1812 opened, slight shocks of the earthquake still continued to be felt frequently, and some believed the earth to be in a constant vibratory motion, because, as they affirmed, any one laying his hand on the top rails of a common fence, could perceive a constant movement of the rails. On account of these things many became very despondent, and were little disposed to make preparation for a crop. He showed them them how unwise a course like this would be, since if they were spared by the earthquake, they might yet be subjected to the greatest suffering for want of supplies for themselves and families. He made them more hopeful, too, by informing them that there were many instances on record, where after the earth had been violently agitated for a time, no great calamity had been suffered by the people where it had occurred.

Although the earthquakes were very alarming to us on the Cumberland, they were much more so at New Madrid in southeastern Missouri.

In the journal of the famous Lorenzo Dow, who attracted much attention in the early part of the present century, and who will appear hereafter in our narrative, may be found a letter written to him, by a lady of that place, giving a graphic description of the earthquake there. In the autumn of 1836, I had occasion to visit New Madrid,

10

and in riding over the surrounding country, even then the
effects of the terrible earthquake were everywhere to be
seen. In places, the surface of the earth was covered
over with great heaps of white sand ; and great fissures,
where the earth had opened and thrown up volumes of
water and sand to a great height, were visible in all directions. The little knoll to which the terror-stricken crowd
fled in despair was pointed out to me. This being the
highest spot, they thought it would be the last to disappear, when the earth sank down, and the waves of the
great river overwhelmed them.

A gentleman who lived near New Madrid, with whom
I stayed all night, entertained me with a good many
amusing anecdotes, one or two of which I will repeat.
They were connected with the earthquakes, or what he
called the " *Shakes*."

He said there was at that time, and had been for some
years previous, near New Madrid, a Frenchman, somewhat advanced in years, who had no fixed home, but lived,
sometimes with one family, and then with another. All
were glad to have him with them, as, besides being
very entertaining, he was a fine hunter and angler, and
kept the family with which he stayed bountifully
supplied with game and fish of the best quality. He
seemed to have been finely educated, in fact, " to know
every thing," rather solitary in his habits, very religious,
and a Roman Catholic. No one knew anything of his
history, but the conclusion was, that he had been a person of rank in his own country, and probably compelled to
leave it on account of political troubles, and that he had
come to New Madrid, perhaps because a great many people were there of French extraction, and speaking the
French language.

After the first shake which had alarmed them all greatly, they came to the conclusion, as we did on the Cumberland, that all danger was over, and began to think about other matters. About sunrise, or a little before, he being then a lad, was sent to look after some cattle in the cane-brake, near the river, and the Frenchman concluded to accompany him. They had nearly reached the place to which they were going, when the terrible noise, deep under their feet, began to be heard. Soon the tops of the tallest trees were seen to bow down to the ground, yawning chasms to open and close, with a noise resembling the report of artillery, and the waters of the Mississippi in great waves to roll up stream, in a most frightful manner, carrying with them the boats, and all other craft that were cabled to the shore.

These terrific sights and sounds, as he said, frightened him so badly that somehow the thought came into his head to get down upon his knees and pray, and accordingly down he went. The Frenchman, who happened to be standing near by, leaning on his rife, asked him " What he meant?" "Going to pray to God to have mercy on me," was the reply.—" Ever pray to God before, or thank him for any of his blessings?" " Never thought of such a thing before in my life." " Well, you mean, piti- ful, cowardly fellow, you shan't do it now. If you attempt it, I'll kill you on the spot." And throwing his rifle into the hollow of his left arm, he sprung the trigger, and looked as if he would rather do what he said than not.

There he was between the earthquake and the French- man, hardly knowing which was the worse. He knew after- wards that the man's intention was to teach a good lesson —not to put off praying till the last moment. But he never fully forgave him for it, and thought no one that wanted to pray as badly as he did at that time ought to be prevented, even if he were scared into it.

He related also an anecdote of an old woman, who lived on the bank of the Mississippi. Her husband and children all died from the unhealthiness of the country, and she was left poor and lonely. Going down the river bank one day for water, in a very disconsolate mood, she thought while there she would say her prayers. Going to a place where the bank hung over a little, she got down upon her knees and prayed that, if it was the Lord's will, she might be taken from this world of sin and sorrow, to another and a better, where her troubles would end, and she could be at rest. While thus engaged in prayer, a slight shock of the earthquake occurred, and a small slide of earth took place, some of which fell upon her back. Springing up to her feet and brushing the sand from her shoulders, she said: "Well! I declare! what is this world a-comin' to? I would like to know? Everything anybody says now-a-days is taken for *yearnest!*" And she hurried off, as if highly offended. My host seemed to enjoy this joke greatly, and could mimic the old lady finely.

Peter Cartwright, the famous old circuit-rider, who could preach sermons, scare up sinners, whip rowdies, and tell good stories with any one, says in substance, that he was in Nashville when the first severe shock of the earthquake was felt, and saw a negro woman start to the spring for water, with an empty pail on her head. When the earth began to shake, and the chimneys and scaffolding around the new buildings to tumble down, she raised a shout, and said: "The Lord is coming in the clouds of heaven! The day of judgment! The day of judgment!"

Her two young mistresses hearing this, came running out of the house, dreadfully frightened, and begged her to stop and pray for them. She said: "I can't stop to pray for you now. I told you how it would be. He is coming! He is coming! I must go to meet him. Farewell! Hallelujah! Glory, hallelujah!" and went on clapping her hands and shouting.

Old Brother Valentine Cook (he adds), a man of "precious memory," and his wife Tabitha, were living at that time near Russellville, Kentucky. They were in bed when the earth began to shake and tremble. He sprang out, threw open the door, raised a shout, and with nothing on but his night clothes, steered his course easterly, shouting, every jump, as he went: "My Lord is coming! My Lord is coming!" His wife took after him, also in her night-dress, crying at the top of her voice: "Oh, Mr. Cook, don't leave me! don't leave me!" "Oh, Tabby," he said, "my Lord is coming. I can't wait for you, Tabby." And hurried on, shouting, as he went: "My Lord is coming! I can't wait for you, Tabby."

There were but few deaths reported from the effects of the earthquakes. One poor woman at New Madrid was said to have been so overcome with terror, that she swooned away and never recovered. In one of the boats that broke loose from its moorings, and which was wrecked, it was reported, a woman and six children perished. The most considerable change effected in the face of the country was the formation of what is called Reelfoot Lake, on the opposite side of the river from New Madrid. Here a tract of country, some eighteen or twenty miles long, and five or six wide, sank down, and was covered over with water, in some places to a considerable depth; it is said also that the tops of tall trees may still be seen under the water, by those passing over the lake in canoes. The beautiful country around New Madrid was much damaged by the earthquake, and the people so much alarmed and discouraged, that our government kindly agreed to take back the land it had sold them, and granted them the privilege of removing and finding new homes on government lands elsewhere. Many moved away. Others sold their claims to speculators, and for several years there was a lively trade in these claims, which were known as "floats," if I remember rightly.

Not only did the earthquakes alarm the whites, but many of the Indians, who had been removed west of the Mississippi by our government, deserted their new country, and came back, supposing the Great Spirit was angry with them for having deserted the bones of their chiefs, their warriors, and their forefathers, and signified his displeasure by making the ground tremble under their feet.*

Before leaving the settlements on the Cumberland, an account of which will be given in our next chapter, I will remark, that in the year 1810, as already observed, the Red River Association met at our old Spring Creek Church, from whose minutes of that date I will make a few extracts, thinking they may be of some interest to you.

"First.—The introductory sermon was preached by Elder Josiah Horn, from John 5: 39—'Search the Scriptures.'"

"Secondly.—The Association met for business. Prayer by Elder Lewis Moore. Brother Anthony New chosen Moderator, Brother William Aingall, Clerk, and Elder Reuben Ross, Assistant Clerk."

"The number baptized in all the churches this Associational year was 78. The number received 118. The number dismissed by letter also

* See Putnam's *Annals.*

118. Excommunicated, 39. Died, 9. Total number of members 1,020
Money in the treasury, $35.37."

"Six churches petitioned for admittance, and on being found *ortho-dox* were received."

"Received with much pleasure and gratitude correspondence from Cumberland, Green River, and Wabash Associations: to wit, from Cumberland, Elders Gaines, McConico, White, and Turner. From Green River, Collins and Lamars. From Wabash, Isaac McCoy."

"Appointed Elders Reuben Ross, J. Benbrooks, I. French, and Anthony New a committee of arrangement.

"Appointed Elders White, McConico, Turner, and Moore, to preach to-morrow, and to begin at ten o'clock, A. M."

"Appointed Elder Sugg Fort, and Brother Wells, and Grey, to write corresponding letters to Cumberland, Green River, and *Kehukee* Associations."

"*Resolved*, To allow Elder Reuben Ross five dollars for his services as messenger to Cumberland Association. Elder John Benbrooks one dollar and fifty cents for his services to Green River Association, and Brother Aingell six dollars for his services as Clerk.

"*Resolved*, That Elder Sugg Fort write the next circular letter and choose his own subject."

"*Resolved*, That Elder D. Brown, preach Introductory Sermon to the next Association, and in case of failure, Elder Reuben Ross.

"*Resolved*, That next Association be held at Blooming Grove, Montgomery County, Tennessee, on Saturday before the second Sabbath in Aug., 1811."

"After prayer by Elder D. Brown, the Association was adjourned to the next time and place mentioned! Anthony New, Moderator, William Aingell, Clerk."

I make an abstract from the circular letter on prayer:

"With regard to prayer, it appears to be the desire or breathing of the soul to the great God, and is held forth in Scripture, by drawing near to God—lifting up our souls to him—pouring out our hearts to him. It is said by some that the English word prayer is too strait: for that properly signifies petition, or request; whereas, humble adoration and thanksgiving to God are as necessary as any other part of it; if so, it consists in adoration, thanksgiving, and supplication. That it is our duty to adore him, as he is a Being transcendently glorious, self-existent and independent, infinite and eternal, appears plain, from both Scripture and reason."

CHAPTER XXI.

A NEW HOME IN MONTGOMERY COUNTY.

From the time when he lost his house on Saline Creek, in Stewart County, your grandfather was restless and uneasy until he procured another. Early in the year 1812, he purchased on credit of Mr. Needham Whitfield,* about three hundred acres of land, lying in Montgomery County, Tenn., eight or nine miles north-west of Clarksville, immediately on the State line, something less than two miles west of where the turnpike road from Clarksville to Hopkinsville, Kentucky, crosses it. Of this tract, the State line formed the northern boundary. I think he agreed to pay about twelve hundred dollars for it, in such sums as he could spare, annually, after supporting his family.

Mr. Whitfield acted in a very liberal and friendly manner in this transaction. He never pressed your grandfather for any of the purchase money; but was satisfied with the payments he was able to make, from time to time. I think it was seven or eight years before he was able to pay principal and interest, and get his deed. I had the pleasure of helping a little towards making his last payment.

Soon after the purchase was made, leaving me, then about eleven years old, to stay with your grandmother and the children, he took his axe and went on his place. I

* Then, and until his death, living on Spring Creek, in Montgomery County.

212

think he cut all the logs to build his house with his own hands. He took great pains, as he always did in everything, to select those that were straight and pretty. His nearest neighbor, with whom he boarded, was a kind old gentleman named Rogers, a member of his church, whose family consisted of a wife and an only son. I hardly need say that they all became very much attached to each other.

When ready to bring his timbers together, he made an arrangement with his old neighbor and his son, Joel, to assist him, promising to aid them, in turn, in housing their crop of corn. At length, having everything ready, he collected the neighbors together, and his house was raised. It had two rooms, and a passage between them, as was very common at that time, and even much later. He worked hard, in order to get one room ready for his family before cold weather set in, only coming home now and then to see us, and let us know how he was getting on, and to answer our questions about the new place.

When one room was habitable, he came for us, and we all moved up to it. We regretted leaving our old friends and neighbors on the Cumberland, to whom we had become much attached, on account of the common dangers and hardships we had experienced while living together there; but were glad to remove farther from the Indians and earthquakes, our new home being about twenty-five miles farther east. I always intended revisiting the old neighborhood but put it off until it is now too late. I shall never forget how wild and beautiful all things appeared to me the first spring we lived near Saline Creek.

It was late in the fall when we reached our new home.

10 *

There was not the slightest improvement on the place besides the unfinished house. All around looked sad and dreary, especially, when the wind swept over the dry and withered grass, or rustled among the dead leaves of the post-oak and black-jack trees. None who ever witnessed the desolate appearance of the Kentucky Barrens in early times, during the winter season, can forget the feeling they produced. Far as the eye could reach, it seemed one barren, cheerless waste.

Seen at this season of the year by the early explorers, it is not strange that they called them the Barrens, or the barren lands. The pioneer hunters had no conception of their fertility, and very naturally supposed that there were only a few stunted trees in these wide prairies, because the ground was so poor. No greater mistake could have been made. During this winter I first saw the tremendous fires caused by the burning of the dry grass. In many places, this grass was very thick and tall; and when perfectly dry, should it get on fire, the wind being high, the spectacle became truly sublime, especially at night. The country around far and wide, would then be illuminated by a lurid light, reflected from the clouds of black smoke in the upper regions of the atmosphere. The flames, when the wind blew strong, would move with such rapidity that animals of all kinds had to hurry forward to avoid perishing in them. They would sometimes burn the leaves on trees, twenty, or thirty feet in height. Sometimes they would consume all the fencing around the farm, in spite of all that could be done to save it.

No one who ever witnessed one of these great fires would ever afterward be at a loss to account for the scarcity of timber in the Barrens, as trees of all kinds, when small, were destroyed by them. Should a little twig or bush put up from the ground one season, it was sure to be burned the next. The Indians, in early times, used to set this grass on fire, when hunting, and killed great quantities of game as it fled before the flames.

But if, in winter, the barrens looked cheerless and dreary, it was far otherwise in spring and early summer. It would be difficult to imagine anything more beautiful. Far as the eye could reach, they seemed one vast deep-green meadow, adorned with countless numbers of bright flowers springing up in all directions. At that time of the year I was sometimes sent to Hopkinsville—then called " Christian Court-house "—distant sixteen or eighteen miles. The whole distance was a scene of unvarying loveliness and beauty; only a few clumps of trees and now and then a solitary post-oak were to be seen, far as the eye could reach. Here I first saw the prairie bird, or barren-hen, as we called it, which I afterwards met with in such vast numbers on the great prairies of Illinois. Here the wild strawberries grew in such profusion as to stain the horse's hoofs a deep red color.

It is not strange that Daniel Boone, Finley, Clark, Henderson, and others, who saw Kentucky in its virgin beauty, gazed upon it with admiration and delight. Nor is it strange that the red man contended, so long and so obstinately, for an inheritance so rich and so beautiful.

Only a few years before we moved into the Barrens, their fertility began to be known. Before that time immigrants usually settled along the water courses, where they found timber and water more abundant, though land much inferior in quality. But when their fertility was known, settlers were attracted in great numbers; the want of timber and water, however, were two great draw-backs.

Sometimes three or four families were compelled to haul water for several miles, from the same spring, causing much loss of time and no little trouble. Many deep wells were dug, at considerable risk and expense. Cisterns would have remedied the evil, but they were then unknown, and did not come into use till many years later.

I remember to have heard a good deal of a man whom all considered very lucky. He was the owner of a valua-ble tract of land in the Barrens, on which there was no water. After digging a number of wells, and failing to reach water, he began to think of selling it. About this time he was visited by a friend from a distance, to whom he told his troubles, and in the course of conversation, happened to observe that he had seen a muskrat at a certain place a few days before. His friend told him there was always water within a few yards of the spot where this animal was seen. On going to the place, and bending down the tall grass, they found just below the surface a beautiful cave-spring.

After having hauled water for several years, as others in the neighborhood did, and becoming heartily tired, your grandfather determined he would dig a well, though it by no means suited him to incur the expense it involved. There were men who professed to be able to divine the presence of water and its depth below the surface of the ground, called water-witches, though it seems they should have been called water-wizards.

He had little faith in these pretensions, but to obtain water was of such great importance, that he determined to-avail himself of all the chances, and rode some distance to find one of reputation in this art, thinking " if it did no good it would do no harm."

When the diviner came, he went to a peach tree growing in the yard, and cut from it a branch with two prongs; taking one in each hand, he walked around some time. At length the end of the rod bent down toward the earth. Here, he said, a fine bold stream of water would be found, by digging about sixty feet. A stake was driven down, to mark the spot; a well-digger employed, a windlass and bucket provided, the work commenced. This went on with many alternations of hope and fear, until the depth of ninety feet was reached, when it became too dangerous to proceed farther, and the well was abandoned. Another sad disappointment. When I last saw the place a mound of red earth was still visible to mark the spot where so much labor had been in vain expended.

As no land was cleared on our new place, we were compelled for several years to rent, preparing three or four acres of our own land for cultivation every season. Your grandfather did much of this work with his own hands, being employed in this way all the time he was not out preaching. Many of his neighbors, being in good circumstances, helped him. Sometimes they sent two or three hands to assist in making rails, and doing other heavy work, and at length there was no need of renting, which relieved him greatly.

Among his kindest neighbors were Dr. John T. Gilmer, and his brother Nicholas, who removed from Georgia, and brought their young families and servants w.th them. They and their families soon seemed to regard us, very much as near relatives, and perhaps there have been few instances, where a greater degree of harmony, good-will, and love subsisted among those not related. They belonged to the Methodist Episcopal Church, we to the Baptist, yet this never seemed to have been thought of by either; but regarding each other as Christians and followers of the same Divine Master, all else seemed to be forgotten.

These excellent men are now no more. Dr. Gilmer came to prefer a *free state ;* sold his old Kentucky home; removed to Illinois; and died there many years ago. His brother Nicholas remained in Kentucky until his death, which took place about the same time as that of your grandfather. I remember well, when he drove up, within less than a mile of us, and pitched his tents among the grass and wild flowers, and remained encamped, until temporary houses were built. Your grandmother sent your aunt Polly, aunt Nannie, and myself, to their encampment, with butter, milk, eggs, and a basket of dried fruit, supposing these acceptable after their long journey, and thus our acquaintance began. All who had milk cows abounded in milk and butter at this season of the year.

Among our other kind neighbors was a Mr. James Lockert, a relation of the Lockert's still living in Montgomery County, who removed to or near Little Rock, Arkansas. We were sorry when he left us, as his children were our playmates, and together we hunted wild grapes, strawberries, and hazlenuts in the barrens.

Mr. Hinton and his family, kind and agreeable people, who belonged to the Presbyterian Church, were as regular in attending your grandfather's meetings, as any of his own denomination. Mr. John Hinton, a graduate of the University of North Carolina, and long one of the most distinguished teachers in the country, was a member of this family. Mrs. Hinton, the mother, was very kind and attentive in times of sickness, of which we had a great deal while living at this place, and very much endeared herself to your grandmother. Whenever I was sent to her house on errands, she had a little table set out with milk, butter, light bread, and preserves for me to eat before I left. In my estimation she was one of the saints, for whose canonization, I would have voted any day.

The neighbor who used to entertain me most, was an elderly gentleman, Captain Thomas Rivers. He was a man of property; owned many negroes, and a valuable farm, near what is now called Mansion's Spring which then supplied many families with water. He was the grandfather of the distinguished Methodist Episcopal preacher, I think, of Louisville, Kentucky. Captain Rivers, though a kind-hearted gentleman, was rough, boisterous, and, as some thought, overbearing in his disposition. I became acquainted with his boys at school, and was often invited home with them to spend the night, where I used to hear him relate many amusing incidents and anecdotes of his life. He said one of his neighbors permitted his large flock of sheep to run on his pastures most of the time, not troubling himselve to keep them at home, whom, he told one day, to let them remain as long as he thought proper, they should be treated just as if they were his own. He told how he killed a fine mutton every week for a long time, until the owner accidentally found it out, and when he complained, asked him if he did not remember his saying they should be treated just as his own. The sheep did not trouble him any more.

He had a number of pretty daughters, and it was said

when idle young fellows would go to see them and stay longer than he thought necessary, he would make out a little bill, charging them so much a day for themselves and horses,—hand it to them and get on his horse and ride over his farm. On returning he generally found his house was his own ; none of them ever returned, except those who meant business.

War was declared against Great Britain on the 20th of June, 1812, and no period in our country's history, before our great civil war, was shrouded in deeper gloom than the first two or three years after our removal from the Cumberland, back to Montgomery County. Especially may this be said of the western people, during the last few months of 1814. Portentous rumors were then afloat, of a vast armament, that was being fitted out in the West Indies, whose destination was the capture of New Orleans, and the mouth of the Mississippi. And there was perhaps not a well informed man in all the country who believed these important places could be successfully defended.

Should the British effect the permanent occupancy of New Orleans and the Mississippi River, they thought the ruin of the South and West would be the result, as it would give them possession of our other great rivers—enable them to turn all the surrounding tribes of Indians against us, and probably succeed in driving us again beyond the Allegheny Mountains. These apprehensions induced Kentucky and Tennessee to put forth all their strength in aiding the heroic Jackson to defend these vital points.

In the month of December, 1814, a number of volunteers were encamped upon the bleak, snow-clad hills

around Clarksville, awaiting transportation to New Orleans, where it was reported, an army of fourteen thousand men were about to be landed by the enemy.   These
volunteers sent a request to your grandfather to come and
preach for them, as often as he could, while they were in
camp.   This request was promptly complied with, and he
spent much of his time with them.   These soldiers belonged to families in the surrounding counties, with many
of whom he had become acquainted in his frequent tours
of preaching, and he came to feel a deep interest in their
welfare, both temporal and spiritual.   When speaking of
them to your grandmother, after having visited them, he
would tell her what noble-looking young men they were,
and how his heart misgave him, that their manly forms
would be seen no more among us after their departure.   It
is well known that in those days, when a call for volunteers was made, it was answered first, by the best material—the flower of manhood of the country.

At length he bade them adieu ; and they embarked on
their perilous voyage, down the great rivers in the dead
of winter, on the crowded and uncomfortable flat-boats,
but his heart still followed them, and they were long remembered in the evening prayer.   When the news of the
great, and on our part almost bloodless, victory reached us,
he was more moved than I had ever seen him on any joyous occasion.   He understood the crisis, and knew better
than we, the greatness of our deliverance, and the lustre
it shed upon our arms.   Above all, he rejoiced to think
that so many he never expected to see would return home.
Of this victory I well remember, we at first heard a vague
rumor as if floating in the air.   None could tell whence it
came.   The whole community seemed to be struck with a

kind of awe, and repeated what they had heard almost in whispers. The feeling was much like that produced by the first uncertain news of General Taylor's victories over Santa Anna in Mexico, but more intense. Could it be that the course of victory which had so long followed the arms of England had been checked? Could it be, that our beautiful country, south and west of the great mountains, was to remain our own? Many suns rose and set, many were the alternations of hope and fear, before the news was fully confirmed. When it was, no bonfires were kindled, no cannon heard to boom in honor of the great event; but I doubt whether a greater load of apprehension and dread was ever removed from any people. You must remember it was not war, but Indian-war, that was so much dreaded by our people, war upon helpless age, women, and children. Hope revived; cheerfulness and gayety returned; and many songs that grew out of the events of the war became very fashionable. Especially those recounting our brilliant naval victories on the lakes and high seas. One called "The Races," which referred to achievements on land, was a great favorite. Of this, I remember several stanzas, though not in their proper order, as follows:

> " Ross came to Baltimore and swore,
>   More than a match they'd find him,
> So swift he ran, from boy and man,
>   He left the world behind him.

> " When Harrison, the battle won
>   On Thames, from bloody Proctor,
> Poor Proctor's speed, none could exceed
>   Not e'en his aid and doctor.

> " When Packingham, to Orleans came
>   Full sure of easy victory,
> Resolved forthwith to try the pith
>   And mettle of old Hickory.

"Great was the stake he wished to take,
 'Twas beauty, sir ! and booty,
And much the wag did boast and brag,
 But Jackson knew his duty.

"He won alas ! a fatal race,
 He ran till out of breath, sir :
His booty was a burial place,
 His beauty, wounds and death, sir!"

The war of 1812, lasting about three years, was a period
of anxiety and trouble. Our extended sea-board was ex·
posed to British vessels of war, from Maine to New
Orleans ; our Atlantic towns and cities destroyed, and
the National Capital laid in ashes. During these years,
your grandfather preached much of his time, his labors
greatly lessened by being nearer his church. The Baptist
churches in those days were often in trouble, less on account of doctrine than of order and discipline A member would do something supposed to be improper ; some
would be for, and others against him. Then one of the
sister churches was requested to send what were called
"helps," that is discreet, unprejudiced men, who after
hearing both sides, would advise a certain course, which
was usually, though not always, agreed to. Your grandfather, being very persuasive and free from all suspicion
of partiality, was in great request, and had great weight
in settling these troubles. One little church, called "Cub
Creek," was nearly always in "hot water." Deputation,
after deputation would come up for him, to go down to
help them. Their case had become chronic. At one
time he was so often with them, that when brethren would
ride up to our gate and inquire of me where he was, I,
(for mischief,) would tell them I expected they would find
him down about Cub Creek meeting house.

CHAPTER XXII.

OUR SCHOOL—BASCOM—MORRIS—CARTWRIGHT.

FOR several years, during the war and after its close, I occasionally attended a school in our neighborhood. Near what was at first called River's Spring, but afterward Manson's, was built a school-house and a little log meeting house also, called Bethel, for the use of the Methodists of whom several families were living in the neighborhood This church still bears its old name.

This was considered a high school at that time, as in it were taught the Latin and Greek languages, and the mathematics to some extent. Classical learning was held in high estimation among us in those days, and almost every one who could afford it, had his boys studying Greek and Latin, so that many who had but little knowledge of the English branches could translate Virgil and Horace, Xenophon and Homer, with ease and elegance. A thorough knowledge of the grammars, and a rigid application of their rules were required.

The education of the distinguished men of Kentucky and Tennessee then began and ended pretty much with the Classics, It is not strange that a thorough course of Classical studies has always been held in high estimation by those who are capable of appreciating their value, since it exercises and develops every faculty of the mind,— memory, reason, taste, judgment, and imagination. Besides this a habit of patient application is formed, which is of priceless value, since it enables the individual to investigate and master with comparative ease, any subject to which he may turn his attention Most of the great philosophers, poets, orators, historians, divines, jurists, and physicians of Europe and America owe their renown to the mental training derived from a thorough study of Classical literature. And as these noble studies seem at this time to be on the decline, might it not be well for the friends of learning and progress, to awake to a sense of their importance and value?

Mr. Davis, a young teacher from East Tennessee, taught at this place for some time, and was much esteemed by all who knew him. Valentine Barry, son of Daniel Barry, one of the finest classical scholars in the West then, or perhaps since, succeeded him. He had been educated in Ireland, his native country, taught a school near Bardstown, Kentucky, before he came among us, and numbered among his pupils there Judge Rowan and Judge W. T. Barry, as I have heard. These were among Kentucky's great men.

He left two sons, Henry and Valentine, whom he had educated with great care. Henry died young, and was lamented by our whole community, as he was highly esteemed, and of bright promise. Some years after his death, which occurred in or near Louisville, some young friends and myself went to the burying ground to seek for his grave, but after spending several hours reading the inscriptions on the grave-stones, we failed to find his name.

His elder brother, Valentine, our teacher, afterward studied law, and was appointed Judge of one of the courts of Tennessee, but has now been dead many years. There

were several sisters, two of whom, Mrs. M. I. Killebrew
and Mrs. N. Johnson, taught schools also. The former of
these, (I think) is still living in Mississippi. The latter is
dead.

While in occasional attendance at this school, I saw
several ministers of the Methodist Episcopal Church, who
afterwards became famous in the West, to wit: Bascom,
Morris, and Cartwright. All of these I heard preach in
our little church, Bethel.

Dr. Bascom was then young, handsome, and very prepossessing in the pulpit; of a fresh and ruddy complexion, fine head, hair, and eyes, well formed, and of good
size. I only heard him once. The impression left on my
mind is that he described to us the garden of Eden, its
beautiful trees, fruits, and flowers; its green hills, shady
valleys, and crystal waters. He told us how our first parents, for disobedience, were driven away from this fair inheritance, and never again permitted to behold its matchless beauty. But, he added, there was a fairer Eden, in a
still brighter clime, prepared for those who were willing
to become the followers of Christ, and "by patient continuance in well-doing, seek for glory, honor, and immortality." His language was highly poetical and beautiful.
None of his printed sermons can compare with this, according to my recollection, in beauty of style and splendor of diction. He became a star of the first magnitude
in his church, which still honors his memory.

Bishop Morris, I heard preach two or three times. He
was rather below medium height, with black eyes, black
hair, and rather dark complexion. His expression was
solemn though pleasant and engaging. Your grandfather
spoke in very high terms of him, as if he had formerly

made his acquaintance.   I am not certain whether he was a circuit preacher or a presiding elder when in our part of the country, but believe he was the latter.   I heard him preach from the text " Pay that which thou hast vowed."   He alluded to our proneness, in times of afflic- tion and danger, to make vows of repentance and reforma- tion, and to forget all these promises of amendment when the danger is over.   He asked what we could expect, when afflictions again came, and we implored divine assist- ance, but the solemn declaration :   " I will laugh at your calamity.   I will mock when your fear cometh.   When your fear cometh as desolation, and your destruction, as a whirlwind.   When distress and anguish cometh upon you.   Then shall they call upon me, but I will not an- swer.   They shall seek me early, but shall not find me."

This discourse made a deep impression on those who heard it.   His manner in the pulpit reminded me of your grandfather.

Elder Morris rose high in his church.   In 1817, he was a travelling preacher in Ohio, Kentucky, and Ten- nessee.   In 1836, he was elected bishop, by the General Conference.

Peter Cartwright, I also heard preach in our little church.   He was slightly above medium height, well formed and muscular, with a well-shaped head and face, large mouth and healthy complexion.   He was born in Virginia, 1785, and consequently was about nine years younger than your grandfather.   In his autobiography, he gives a thrilling account of his father's removal to Ken- tucky :

" After we struck the wilderness, we hardly travelled a day (he says) but we passed some white persons murdered and scalped by the Indians, while going to, or returning from Kentucky," "In the Fall of 1793, my father," he adds, "determined to move to what was then called the Green River country, in the southern part of the State of Kentucky. He did so. And settled in Logan County, nine miles south of Russellville, and within one mile of the state line."

We thought we had managed to get pretty much out of the world, when your grandfather moved upon the Cumberland, but times were a little harder with the Cartwrights, according to the statements of Peter Cartwright-

"When my father settled in Logan County, there was not a newspaper printed south of Green River, no mill short of forty miles, and no schools worth the name. Sunday was a day set apart for hunting, fishing, horse-racing, card-playing, balls, dances, and all kinds of jollity and mirth. We killed our meat out of the woods, wild, and beat our meal and hominy with a pestle and mortar. We stretched a deer skin over a hoop, burned holes in it with the prongs of a fork, sifted our meal, baked our bread, ate it, and it was good eating too. We raised or gathered out of the woods our own tea. We had sage, bohea, crossvine, spice, and sassafras teas in abundance. As for coffee, I am not sure that I ever smelled it in ten years.

"There were two large caves on my father's farm, and another about half a mile off, where was a great quantity of material for making saltpetre. We soon learned the art of making it, and our class-leader was a great powder-maker. When a considerable quantity of powder had been made, they concluded to take it to Fort Massick, a military post on the Ohio River, some distance above its mouth, and barter it for such articles as they most needed. A large poplar tree was cut down, and made into a pirogue, which was launched into tho Red River, the powder put on board, and proclamation made to the surrounding country, to bring in their bills of what each wanted, how much, and names duly signed. Some sent for a quarter of a pound of coffee, some for one yard of ribbon, for a butcher knife, or a tin cup.

"When all things were ready, the class-leader went on board, descended Red River to the Cumberland, the Cumberland to the Ohio, and up the Ohio to the Fort; made satisfactory exchanges, returned, and for weeks they had a time of great rejoicing at the success of the enterprise."

Peter was what would now be called a "*fast* boy;" at sixteen, his father gave him a race-horse and a deck of cards. He was the old man's only son, who, no doubt, rejoiced at his precocious boyhood. But Peter's mother, a pious woman, shed many bitter tears, when she saw the course he was taking. It seems, though, his career was suddenly stopped. He and his father had been invited to a wedding, where they had a lively time. After his return home, Peter began to feel very badly. The blood seemed to flow to his head, his heart to palpitate, and his eyesight to fail. He thought his hour had come, rose from his bed, got down on his knees, and began to pray. His mother sprang out of her bed, kneeled down beside him, prayed and exhorted him to look to the Saviour for help. He did so, "and then and there promised, if the Lord would spare his life, he would serve him the rest of his days," which promise he had never fully broken. He now gave his race-horse back to his father, and requested that he should be sold, brought out his pack of cards, handed them to his mother, who laid them on the fire.

It was long ere he was relieved of his burden of sin and guilt. Once he retired to a cave on his father's land to pray, and to bewail in secret his unhappy condition, when, suddenly, such a fear of the devil fell upon him, that he seemed to be personally present, to seize and drag him down to the bottomless pit. With terror he sprang to his feet and ran home to his mother. The neighbors thought Peter had gone crazy, and his father released him from all business on the farm. At length, during the progress of the great revival of 1800, at the old Red River Church, in your vicinity, where eighty or ninety were

11

converted, Peter raised the shout of victory, and rejoiced in the hope of eternal life. There is reason to believe that Elder Finis Ewing, one of the founders and ornaments of the Cumberland Presbyterian Church, was converted at the same time and place. The Rev. James McGready, an able Presbyterian minister, seems to have been the leading spirit in these great meetings.

Soon after his conversion, Peter began to be heard in the class-meeting and love-feast, then as an exhorter, and, after that, as a circuit-rider, in which capacity his name became familiar in Tennessee, Kentucky, Ohio, Indiana, and Illinois. When disposed, he could preach a scary sermon. He once gave us a glimpse of the bottomless pit and what might be seen in it. He leaned over from the pulpit, as if he saw it, and it was a dismal place indeed; old Dante, in his vision, never saw anything more horrible. It was away down, down, almost out of sight. As the fiery billows rolled along, one after another, he could see lost sinners floating upon them, like wrecks upon a troubled sea, and behold their agony. Here he saw an infidel, who used to be so flippant when talking about hell; there, a scoffer at religion; yonder, a murderer; and yonder again, a miserable drunkard, that had brought his broken-hearted wife and little children to beggary and ruin. But the greater number he saw were a pack of miserable sinners, fools, that had blundered along like so many idiots, just as if there had been no God, heaven, or hell in the universe, until they dropped into hell, and the devil got them. Over the dreadful abyss, he would describe a sinner as hanging by a single hair, and cutting as many antics as a monkey, having no more idea of his danger than a brute beast, until the hair snapped, and down he went. One would suppose these extravagant and frightful pictures would have had no good effect. But they sometimes took such hold on the imagination of thought-less and wicked men, as to wake them up, lead them to repent of their wickedness, reform their lives, and become exemplary Christians. It seems that a real bad scare is now and then not without its use, especially if nobler mo-tives fail of success.

Elder Cartwright belonged to the church *militant*, fought gallantly for his religious dogmas, and, according to his own account, had the rare good fortune to conquer in all his battles. Baptists, Reformers, Unitarians, New Lights, Universalists, Mormons, and Shakers, all fell under the blows of his ponderous battle-axe. Nor did it fare better with the blackguards, ruffians, and rowdies that hung around his camp-meetings. They too, sooner or later, were doomed to come to grief.

He did not see the necessity of theological schools, and an educated ministry, since, to use his own words, " God, when he wants a great and learned man, can easily over-take some learned sinner, shake him awhile over hell, as he did Saul of Tarsus, knock the scales from his eyes, and, without any previous theological training, send him to preach Christ and the Resurrection." " A powerful con-viction and a sound conversion" were held in high estima-tion by him, and these might be begun and finished in a few hours, where the good work was progressing, with energy and power.

For many years it seems to have been his chief delight, at his great camp-meetings, " to ride the whirlwind and direct the storm," " to see men," according to his own ex-pression, " fall around him, as if slain in mighty battle."

By day, the scene was picturesque and striking, but at night it became wild and weird beyond description.

To stand apart and listen to the groans and lamentations, the prayers and exhortations, the shouts and hallelujahs, of the vast crowd, mingled with the voices of the preachers, in the dimly illuminated encampments, would produce impressions never to be forgotten.

At the close of the sketch of his eventful life, written by himself, when far from his " old Kentucky home," and the old church where he was converted ; he begs his brethren of the Methodist Episcopal Church " not to let camp-meetings die out." And says in his pathetic language : " He wants to see their revival before he descends from the walls of Zion and goes hence."

At the time of which we are speaking, the great revival of 1800 was still felt by the people of the West,—and especially by the Methodist and Presbyterian communities. From the latter of these a new denomination arose, destined to rank high as a religious organization—the Cumberland Presbyterian Church. Elder Cartwright saw the beginning and the end, and was a chief actor in the wonderful drama.

As this was an important event in the times of your grandfather, I propose giving you a short account of it in our next chapter.

CHAPTER XXIII.

In the year 1799, several ministers of the Presbyterian Church, Elders McGready, Hoge, and Rankin, and one belonging to the Methodist Episcopal Church, Elder John McGee, held a sacramental meeting, at the old Red River Church, which stood on or near the same site as the church of that name now does. The meeting drew together a large congregation, considering the thinly settled country.

On Sunday Elder Hoge preached and, as he was often heard to say afterwards, addressed the assemblage with a freedom and power, never before felt. The hearers though riveted in their attention, remained silent and quiet. As he closed his discourse, Elder John McGee rose, singing,

> Come, Holy Spirit, Heavenly Dove,
>> With all thy quickening powers,
> Kindle a flame of sacred love,
>> In these cold hearts of ours.

He had not sung more than the verse quoted, when an aged lady, Mrs. Pacely, sitting quite across the congregation to the left, and Mrs. Clark, also advanced in years, seated to the right, began in rather suppressed but distinct tones, to hold a sort of dialogue with each other, and to reciprocate sentiments of praise and thanksgiving to the Most High, for his grace in redemption. Still the preacher sang on, and the venerable ladies praised God,

233

in louder tones. The preacher, still singing came down from the pulpit, intending to take the hands of these two happy old sisters; shaking hands, however, as he passed along, with all those within his reach. Suddenly persons began to fall as he passed through the crowd – some as dead; some most piteously crying for mercy ; and a few, here and there, lifting their voices high, in the praise of the Redeemer. Among these last was Elder William McGee, who fell to the floor, and, though shouting praises, was for some time so overpowered as to be unable to rise. The other ministers, McGready, Hoge, and Rankin, were so surprised and astonished at this apparent confusion in the house of the Lord, that they made their way out of the door, and stood asking each other in whispers, " what is to be done." Elder Hoge looking in at the door, and see- ing all on the floor, praising or praying, said, " We can do nothing. If this be of Satan, it will soon come to an end; but if it is of God, our efforts and fears are in vain. I think it is of God, and will join in ascribing glory to his name."

He walked into the house where the others presently followed. Rapidly those who had fallen to the floor mourning and crying for mercy, arose, two or more at a time, shouting praise, for the evidences felt in their own souls, of sins forgiven—for " redeeming grace and dying love." So there remained no more place that day, for preaching or administering the Supper. From thirty to forty, that evening, professed to be converted.

Thus began that wonderful religious movement, which not only pervaded Kentucky, Tennessee, and Ohio, but crossed the mountains, and spread over many of the states on the Atlantic seaboard. On account of the strange bodily agitations attending it, it was considered the most wonderful event of the times.

" The next appointment was for the Saturday and Sunday following, at what is to this day called the Beach Meeting House, situated a little south of the Cumberland Ridge, ten miles west of Gallatin, Sumner County, Tennessee." Here a vast crowd assembled, and scenes similar to those at Red River Meeting house transpired. But the most wonderful meeting was at Muddy River Church, a few miles north of Russellville, Kentucky, the Sunday after. " The people came in from the two states twenty, thirty, fifty, and even a hundred miles. Some came in tented wagons, some in open wagons, some in carts, some on horse back, and many on foot."

The meeting house, hours before preaching commenced, could not seat the third part of those on the ground. And still they came by dozens, fifties, and hundreds. A temporary pulpit was quickly erected under the shady trees, and seats made of large trees felled and laid upon the ground. The preaching commenced, and soon the presence of the all-pervading Power was felt, throughout the vast assembly.

" As night came on it was apparent the crowd did not intend to disperse. What was to be done? Some took wagons, and hurried to bring in straw from barns and treading-yards. Some fell to sewing the wagon sheets together, and others to cutting forks and poles, on which to spread them. Counterpanes, coverlets, and sheets were also fastened together, to make tents or camps. Others were dispatched to town and to the nearest houses to collect bacon, meal, flour, with cooking utensils to prepare food for the multitude. In a few hours it was n sight to see how much was gathered together for the encampment."

"Fires were made, cooking begun; and by dark, candles lighted, and fixed to a hundred trees; and here was the first, and perhaps the most beautiful camp ground the world ever saw." (See Smith's *Legends of the War of the Revolution.*)

Barton W. Stone, at that time in the fellowship of the Presbyterian Church, and Pastor of the Cane Ridge and Concord congregations, in Bourbon County, Kentucky, heard of the mighty work going on in southern Kentucky, and determined to go down and see for himself. He seems to have been a man of fine talents, respectable learning, spotless character, and childlike simplicity; but easily attracted by what was strange and marvelous. Early in the spring of 1801, he set out for Logan County, to attend one of the great camp meetings.

"On arriving," he writes, "I found the multitude assembled on the edge of a prairie, where they continued encamped many successive days and nights, during all which time, worship was being conducted in some parts of the encampment. The scene to me was passing strange. It baffles description. Many, very many, fell down, as men slain in battle, and continued, for hours together, in a comparatively breathless and motionless state. Sometimes for a few moments reviving and exhibiting symptoms of life, by a deep groan, or piercing shriek, or by a prayer for mercy most fervently uttered. After lying thus for hours, they obtained deliverance. The gloomy cloud that had covered their faces, seemed gradually and visibly to disappear; and hope, in smiles, to brighten into joy. They would then arise, shouting deliverance, and address the surrounding multitude in language truly eloquent and impressive. With astonishment did I hear women and children declaring the wonderful works of God and the glorious mysteries of the gospel. Their appeals were solemn, heart-rending, bold, and free. Under such addresses, many others would fall down in the same state, from which the speakers had just been delivered.

"Two or three of my particular acquaintances from a distance, were struck down. I sat patiently by one of them, whom I knew to be a careless sinner, for hours, and observed with critical attention, every

thing that passed, from the beginning to the end. I noticed the momen-
tary revivings as from death, the humble confession, the fervent prayer,
and ultimate deliverance; then, the solemn thanks and praise to God,
the affectionate exhortation to companions and to the people round to
repent and come to Jesus. I was astonished at the knowledge of gospel
truth displayed in these exhortations. The effect was that several sank
down into the same appearance of death. After attending to many such
cases, my conviction was complete, that it was a good work, nor has my
mind wavered since on the subject."

Elder Stone, in chapter sixth of his book, enumerates six
kinds of bodily agitations during this great excitement.
The falling exercise; the jerks; the dancing exercise; the
barking exercise; the laughing exercise; and the singing
exercise.

"The falling exercise," he says, " was very common among all classes,
both saints and sinners of every age, and every grade, from the philosopher to the clown. The subject of this exercise, would generally, with
a piercing scream, fall, like a log, on the floor, earth, or mud, and appear
as dead.

"The jerks cannot be so easily described. Sometimes, the subject of
the jerks would be affected in the whole system. When the head alone
was affected, it would be jerked backward and forward, or from side to
side, so quickly that the features of the face could not be distinguished.
When the whole system was affected, I have seen a person stand in one
place, and jerk backwards and forward, in quick succession, their hands
nearly touching the floor behind and before. All classes, saints as well
as sinners, strong as well as weak, were thus affected. They could not
account for it, but some have told me, these were among the happiest
moments of their lives.

"The dancing exercise generally began with the jerks, and was peculiar to professors of religion. The subject, after jerking awhile, began
to dance, and then the jerks would cease. Such dancing was indeed
heavenly to the spectators. There was nothing in it like levity, or calculated to excite levity in beholders. The smile of heaven shone in the
countenance of the subject, and assimilated to angels, appeared the
whole person. [Rather highly colored!]

"The barking, as opposers contemptuously called it, was nothing but
the jerks. A person afflicted with the jerks, especially in the head,
11*

would often make a grunt or a bark, (if you please) from the suddenness of the jerk. This name "barking," seems to have had its origin from an old Presbyterian preacher of East Tennessee. He had gone into the fields for private devotion, and was seized with the jerks. Standing near a sapling, he caught hold of it, to prevent his falling, and as his head jerked back, he uttered a grunt, or kind of noise similar to a bark, his face being turned upward. Some wag discovered him in this position, and reported that he found him barking up a tree.

"The laughing exercise was frequent, confined solely to the religious. It was a loud, hearty laughter, but one *sui generis*. It excited laughter in no one else. The subject appeared rapturously solemn, and his laughter excited solemnity in saint and sinner. It was truly indescribable.

"The running exercise, was nothing more than that persons, feeling something of these bodily agitations, through fear attempted to run away, and thus escape from them, but it commonly happened that they ran not far before they fell or became so greatly agitated, they could proceed no farther.

"The singing exercise is more unaccountable than anything I ever saw. The subject, in a very happy state of mind, would sing most melodiously, not from the mouth or nose, but from the breast entirely, the sound issuing thence. Such music silenced everything and attracted the attention of all. It was most heavenly. None could ever be tired of hearing it. Dr. J. P. Campbell and myself, were together at a meeting, and were attending to a pious lady thus exercised, and concluded it to be something beyond anything we had ever known in nature."

This is, in part, what Elder Stone saw and heard, when he visited Southern Kentucky, in 1801, at the commencement of these strange exercises, expressed in his *naive*, or artless way. Lorenzo Dow, while on a tour of preaching in 1804, says:

"I passed by a meeting house, where I observed the undergrowth had been cut down for a camp-meeting, and from fifty to one hundred saplings cut off about breast high, and on inquiring about it, learned that they had been left for the people to jerk by.

This excited his curiosity, and on going round, he "found where the people had laid hold of them and jerked so powerfully that, they had kicked up the earth, like horses in fly-time"! He believed the jerking was "entirely involuntary, and not to be accounted for, on any known principle."

Peter Cartwright, in his book, speaks of the strange bodily exercises of the times, and seems to have been rather amused at what he sometimes saw.

"Just in the midst of our controversies on the subject of the powerful exercises among the people under preaching, a new exercise broke out among us called the *jerks*, which was overwhelming in its effects upon the bodies and minds of the people. No matter whether they were saints or sinners, they would be taken under a warm song or sermon and seized with a convulsive jerking all over, which they could not by any possibility avoid. And the more they resisted, the more violently they jerked. If they would not strive against it and pray in good earnest, it would usually abate. I have seen more than five hundred persons jerking at once in my large congregations. Most usually, persons taken with the jerks, to obtain relief, as they said, would rise up and dance—some would run, but could not get away—some would resist,—on such the jerks were most severe.

"To see those proud young gentlemen and ladies, dressed in their silks, jewelry, and prunella from top to toe, take the jerks, would often excite my risibility. The first jerk or two you would see their fine bonnets, caps, and combs fly, and their long, loose hair crack almost as loud as a wagoner's whip."

He tells an amusing story of two young men who brought their sisters to meeting one day, each armed with a horsewhip, and told the crowd that if Cartwright gave their sisters the jerks, they intended to horse-whip him. The girls went in, took their seats, and the youngsters stood at the door. Being a little unwell that day, and having a vial of peppermint in his pocket, just as he rose to commence preaching he drank a little of it. The young fellows, keeping their eyes on him steadily, saw this.

While in the midst of his sermon the girls fell to jerking
violently. When he had finished, and came down from
the pulpit, he was told by a friend to be on his guard, as
there were some fellows at the door who intended to whip
him. On hearing this, he went to them, and asked why
they were going to whip him ? They answered, because
he had given their sisters the jerks. He told them he
had not given them the jerks. They replied he had,
for they saw him with the medicine he carried about with
him for that purpose. He then said, if he had given the
girls the jerks he reckoned he could give it to them too,
and commenced taking his peppermint out. At this the
young fellows wheeled, took to their heels, and he saw no
more of them.

Elder Stone tells us he had never seen anyone injured
by the jerks; but Elder Cartwright says:

"During a camp-meeting, at a place called the Ridge, in William Mc-
Gee's congregation, there was a very large, drinking man, cursing the
jerks and all religion together. Soon he commenced jerking himself and
started to run, but could not get away. He then took out his bottle of
whisky and swore he would drink the jerks to death, but jerked so violently he could not get the bottle to his mouth, though he tried very
hard to do so. At length he fetched a very violent jerk, snapped his
neck, fell, and soon expired, surrounded by a very large crowd."

After Elder Stone had spent some time in Southern
Kentucky, he returned to Cane Ridge, and related the
strange things he had seen and heard. The people seemed
to be solemnly impressed, and much feeling was manifested. During the second sermon he preached, after his
return, two little girls were struck down, and the most
intense excitement ensued, which overspread the whole
country. At some of the great camp-meetings that fol-

lowed, it was thought that from twenty to twenty-five thousand people were present, and bodily exercises of the most wonderful character were there likewise.

Thus far, no one, in public, had ventured to say aught against these strange phenomena, every one being as it were overawed by what they saw and heard. But at length, during a great camp-meeting near Paris, Kentucky, a Presbyterian minister arose and in the strongest terms denounced what he saw as extravagant and monstrous. A party took ground against it immediately. A bitter opposition arose, and from that day the wonderful movement began sensibly to decline.

B. W. Stone, Richard McNamar, John Dunlavy, John Thomson, Robert Marshall, and David Purviance, the leading spirits of the revival, finally seceded from the mother church and formed a new organization called the Springfield Presbytery. A year or two after, they abandoned this enterprise and Presbyterianism likewise, and formed a new body which they called the " Christian Church," but which others called New Lights, if I remember rightly.

This body held many of the views which characterized Elder Campbell's Reformation; and Elder Stone intimates pretty clearly, in his book, that they had adopted his views, or stolen his thunder, especially the famous dogma, " baptism for the remission of sins."

The Shakers came along, however, and took off two of his preachers, Dunlavy and McNamar. Marshall and Thomson went back to the Presbyterians and Elders Stone and Purviance united with the Reformers ; and thus the old " Christian Church " finally disappeared in Elder Campbell's Reformation, which has adopted the old name again, " Christian Church."

CHAPTER XXIV.

CUMBERLAND PRESBYTERIANS.

The Cumberland Presbyterian Church, so called because it was organized in the valley of the Cumberland, arose out of the great religious movement at this time.

The revival of 1800 extended from Logan County, Kentucky, into the border counties of Tennessee, and many were added to the Presbyterian Churches. Many more ministers were needed to organize churches and administer the ordinances. Although there were a number of able and pious preachers among them, the mother church would not ordain them, since their education was not such as the rules of the church required; and, in addition, they were considered rather unsound in their faith in regard to Election and Predestination, and altogether too noisy in their meetings and worship. The celebrated Gideon Blackburn expressed the sentiments of the old order when he told Elder Barnett that "noise and nonsense never converted anybody, or the world would have been converted by thunder long ago."

After much dissatisfaction and contention, these determined to withdraw from the mother church and organize an independent presbytery, which was effected in 1810 by Elders Finis Ewing, Samuel King, and Samuel McAdoo, in Dixon County, Tennessee. This is now a large and flourishing body of Christians, and spread over the great

Valley of the Mississippi, south and west. As to their doctrinal views, they occupy a sort of middle ground between Calvinists and Arminians. Their church government is similar to that of the Presbyterian, from which they separated.

The leading spirit in this movement was the celebrated Finis Ewing, a man of marked ability and great influence. Though he had been a member of the Presbyterian Church for several years, he was not truly converted, according to Dr. Cassett, his biographer, until the great revival at old Red River Church. He was a very able preacher and a great revivalist. I heard him, when a boy, preach the funeral discourse of Mr. James Jeffries, one of our neighbors. He compared human life to a narrow isthmus lying between two shoreless oceans, and human beings as emerging from one of these, hurrying swiftly across the narrow slip of land, and then plunging into the other, no more to be seen forever. Yet, during this brief transit, we had to decide the momentous question of endless happiness or endless woe!

He organized a very flourishing church near Trenton, Todd County, Kentucky, near which he lived for many years. This place was famous for camp-meetings. All the marvelous bodily exercises and agitations, before described, were seen there as late as 1816 or 1817, and people from far and near were attracted.

At length, land in that part of Kentucky was found to be eminently suited to the growth and culture of tobacco, and accordingly rose in value. The first settlers, who mostly composed the membership of the Lebanon Church, tempted by the rise in the price of land, began to sell their farms to immigrants from Virginia, and to remove to Missouri. Elder Ewing, who said, " the country was destined to be occupied by tobacco-makers and Baptists," determined to go with his flock to Missouri; and in May, 1820, he bade adieu to old Lebanon, " the mother of churches, and glory of Southern Kentucky," as Dr. Cassett fondly terms it, and turned his face toward the distant Missouri, far from the theater of his early life and fame. He settled in Cooper County, Missouri, where he soon built up a flourishing church, which from a fond recollection of the old one he had left in Kentucky, he named New Lebanon. To this a camp-ground was added. He lived in this state till 1841, when his pilgrimage ended.

Dr. Cassett says: "The Baptist influence was promoted here, by the instrumentality of two pious and devoted Baptist ministers—Elders Tandy and Bourne, who preached in the demonstration of the Spirit, and in power; a blessed work of grace ensued, and flourishing Baptist churches were collected, on the very ground, once occupied by the Lebanon congregation."

So far as I have learned, the great religious excitement of the times, was hardly felt by the Baptists. I think it never or very rarely appeared at their meetings, in the shape of any bodily agitations, which fact seems to give plausibility to the opinion that they seldom appear to any great extent where they are not encouraged.

I have witnessed but one instance of the kind at a Baptist meeting. While we were living near Port Royal, when your grandfather was preaching, a Miss McFadin was taken with the jerks. Could it have been possible, the poor woman would have been stared out of countenance. I watched her closely and expected to see her fall to the floor every moment. But she did not, and when preaching was over went to her horse, and was helped on it, still jerking. I did not think it possible for her to keep her seat in the saddle, but as far as we could see, her, she held on, still jerking. The expression of her countenance was both unnatural and unpleasant, altogether unlike the heavenly beauty witnessed by Elder Stone. I think she never spoke after the jerks came on, but looked like one who was weary and needed rest.

It was supposed by many, that the strange manifestations seen during this and other great excitements, in the history of the Christian church, were the effects of divine power, and to be considered in the light of miracles, attesting the truth of religion, as those on the day of Pentecost. Others again considered them as caused by Satanic influence, and intended by the evil one to discredit religion generally, and camp-meetings and revivals in particular, which he feared would convert the world, and destroy his power. They are, perhaps, to be considered as neither, but only the effects of natural causes.

The imagination is one of the mental faculties, which operates directly on the nervous system, by means of the images it creates. And the sensations produced, partake of the nature or character of the images presented. If they are pleasing and attractive, the sensations are pleasing and attractive also, just as the contemplation of a beautiful picture will draw forth expressions of delight and satisfaction.

So when the preacher presents to view a picture, or description of the joys of heaven, the glories of the upper world, and an eternal deliverance from all the sufferings and sorrows of this mortal state, it is so delightful that in a congregation where these manifestations are allowed and

encouraged, some will clap their hands and shout on account of the beautiful vision. These feelings are not
caused by any supernatural power, any more than the delight caused by the contemplation of a beautiful landscape,
but are alike in every particular.

On the other hand, should the preacher, instead of holding up to view a picture of loveliness and beauty, present
one of dread and horror, the sensation corresponding to
the character of the picture might produce groans and
trembling, instead of shouts of joyous gladness. All this
would be simply the effect of a frightful impression on the
nervous system, nothing more. When we remember that
the shock produced on the human frame 'by fear is often
so great as to cause death, we should not wonder that men
and women become convulsed, and fall, or exhibit some
other strange bodily affections under it. Nay, sometimes
a flood of joy produces the same effect. As when an aged
father recently met his long-absent son in Philadelphia,
and expired with happiness too great to be borne.

But it will be asked, why were lookers-on, who were not
moved by joy or fear, often affected in the same way ?

To this it may be answered, that this was the effect of
sympathy, something which no one seems to understand,
but with which all are familiar. It may be defined as an
involuntary inclination to do or act as we see others doing
or acting. You will see, for instance, a man at work, and
a little child looking on, going through the same motions
with its little hands, and even exhibiting the same contor-
tions of face. A number of persons may be sitting together ; one gapes or yawns, and every one goes through
the same performance. Your friend is in deep distress,—
the tears flowing down his cheeks,—and your eyes will

immediately fill, likewise. Why, then, may not one who gazes at others jerking, fall to jerking too ? This appears strange because it is uncommon.

Perhaps many good Christians felt these strange agitations, and honestly believed them to be the effects of divine power. But this does not show that they were such, or had anything supernatural about them. These singular affections were not by any means peculiar to the times of which we are now speaking, since history informs us that in times of great excitement they have appeared in other ages and in other countries.

In the days of Whitefield and the Wesleys they were common and remarkable for their violence. These great and good men believed they were from God, and accordingly encouraged them. But wherever they have been discouraged, they have prevailed very slightly, or not at all—an important fact.

Although nothing ever rejoiced the heart of your grandfather more than a revival of religion, he was in no sense of the word a modern revivalist. No one ever saw him descend from the pulpit, pass through the crowd, shaking their hands, and leading them to the " mourners' bench " or "anxious seat."

Under proclamation of the great and solemn truths of the gospel, to see a deep interest in religion pervade a community, to see men troubled on account of their sins, repenting of their wickedness and folly, reforming their lives, turning to God, confessing him before men, going down into the baptismal waters, and crowding into the churches, full of deep religious emotions, but free from all noise and confusion,—such was his ideal of a religious revival !

CHAPTER XXV.

LORENZO DOW.

About the year 1814, after the excitement growing out of the great revival had nearly subsided, the famous Lorenzo Dow made his appearance among us. He preached at Clarksville, Palmyra, Hopkinsville, Russellville, and other places in our vicinity. Many went to hear the strange old man, but many more to see him of whom so many anecdotes were related.

I was nearly crazy to see and hear him, but for some reason, now forgotten, never had the pleasure.

He was, without doubt, partially deranged. But like many others in that unhappy condition was an exceedingly sharp observer of men, and quick to detect their characters, motives, and weaknesses. Among other anecdotes related of him, I remember the following.

One of his brother preachers, at the close of every discourse, would give a description of the day of judgment, when at the sound of Gabriel's trumpet, the Son of man would appear in the clouds of heaven, with all his holy angels to judge the quick and the dead, uniformly adding a description of the alarm and terror that would overwhelm the impenitent sinner, but saying what a glorious day it would be for the righteous, of whom he humbly hoped he was one. Lorenzo becoming disgusted with his repetition, resolved to put a stop to it, and engaged a boy famous for his skill in blowing the trumpet, to climb a tree near the church that night, and when the preacher got to the day of judgment and Gabriel's trumpet, and how his heart would rejoice that the day of deliverance had come, to blow a loud terrible blast. All worked well, the preacher gave an animated discourse and at its close, as usual, brought in Gabriel and his trumpet. At this the boy from his trumpet uttered such an awful peal, that every one's heart died within him, and leaving hat, saddle-bags, and umbrella, the preacher cleared the pulpit at one leap, rushed to the door and took to the woods, followed by his terror-stricken hearers. Henceforth the preacher gave Gabriel and his trumpet a wide berth.

In the beginning of his ministry, it was said, he made a vow never to accept anything for his preaching more than just enough to enable him to continue his labors. When this was known, many would ostentatiously offer him costly presents knowing they would not be accepted. He determined to put a stop to this. Accordingly when a pompous young fellow in a large crowd, offered him a costly gold watch and begged his acceptance, he thanked him for his kindness and deliberately put the watch in his pocket, and went his way. The young fellow was nearly broken-hearted, but there was no help for it. Presents were not offered after that, for the sake of showing off.

One of the most characteristic anecdotes of him is the following: While travelling on foot, one day he saw a man sitting by the way side, disconsolate at the loss of a fine axe, which was his chief dependance for a living, but which had been stolen. Dow told him to cheer up, and come with him to the preaching, the thief would probably be there and he could get the axe.

The wood-chopper was greatly surprised to see him get up to preach. "Thou shalt not steal" was the text, and keeping his sharp eyes on the crowd, he made stealing appear to the last degree odious and detestable. During his discourse he noticed that one person winced and appeared very uncomfortable, whenever he gave thieves a hard blow. Before dismissing his audience, he related the circumstance of the stolen axe, adding that the thief was sitting just before him, and he intended to hit him with his hymn book, and raised his arm. The thief dodged, and on being questioned, told the wood-chopper where to find his axe.

Many such anecdotes caused numbers to believe he was no ordinary mortal, but could divine the thoughts of men.

This singular but interesting old man was born, as we learn from his journal, in Tolland County, Connecticut, 1777. He was a very delicate child, and during most of his life suffered severely from asthma, often for months being unable to lie down and sleep from difficulty of breathing. This affection had been caused by drinking too much cold water when overheated. His parents were tender of their children, and endeavored to educate them both in religion and common learning.

His early religious experience bears a striking resemblance to those of the olden times. There was first an awakening, a deep repentance and sorrow for sin, troubled dreams and gloomy apprehensions : then, in many cases, some text of Scripture containing a blessed promise, heard as if distinctly spoken to them, a thrill of joy unspeakable, followed by a hope, bright and clear, that their sins were forgiven, the Holy Spirit bearing witness with their spirits that they were born of God. Dow gives the following account of his awakening :

"When past the age of thirteen years, and about the time John Wesley died, it pleased God to awaken my mind by a dream of the night, which was this: An old man came to me at mid day with a staff in his hand, and said, 'Do you ever pray?' I told him 'No.' Said he, 'You must,' and then went away, but soon returned, and the conversation was repeated."

Soon after this dream he began to be distressed on account of his sins, and it is sad to hear him tell the story of his troubles, heightened evidently by the deranged state of his mind. He prayed and fasted, as his delicate frame could endure, slept but little for fear he might die before he awoke and find himself in the lake that burns with fire and brimstone. At length, at the words, " Son, thy sins which are many are forgiven thee,—thy faith hath saved thee," the burden of sin and guilt fell from his shoulders, and he could rejoice in the hope of a blessed immortality beyond the grave. From reading his journal, one will perceive he considered himself under the immediate guidance of the Holy Spirit, and when the Spirit pointed out the way, it was his duty to obey implicitly, notwithstanding all dangers and difficulties. This will account for most of the wildness and extravagance of his conduct.

There was a singular family likeness in most of the conversions we hear of in old times. This was considered very desirable, since it indicated that all were led in the same way, by the same Spirit. When bordering on the supernatural and terrible, they were listened to with great attention.

After his conversion he attached himself to the Methodist connection, and it was impressed on his mind that he ought to preach the gospel; for being alone in a solitary place, kneeling in prayer, these words came to him : " Go

ye into all the world and preach the gospel to every creature." At first he thought this must be a temptation of
Satan; but, finding that the more he resisted, the more
unhappy he felt,—clasping his hands together, he said:
" Lord, I submit to go and preach thy gospel; only grant
that my peaceful hours return, and open the door for me."

It was usual among the Methodists of that day, when
an individual of their church expressed a desire to preach,
to permit him to go around with a circuit preacher, and if
he showed some aptitude for praying in public and exhortation, to give him permission to do so. And if he
appeared to improve and to promise well, then to allow
him to preach from a text and to become a circuit-rider.
From a beginning like this, have arisen many of the able
men of that flourishing denomination.

Lorenzo's preacher, after giving him a trial, advised
him to give up all idea of preaching and go home. He
was then only about eighteen years old. Another preacher,
after a trial, ordered him to go home. This nearly broke
his heart. "Two or three handkerchiefs were soon wet
with tears, for the worth of immortal souls lay heavy on
his conscience."

But, notwithstanding so many discouragements, and so
many " buffetings of Satan," sometimes on foot, sometimes
on horseback, sometimes almost without money or clothes,
he continued trying to preach. So strong was the impression that it was his duty. At length he began to
show unmistakable signs of no ordinary ability. And,
though his addresses were often below mediocrity, they
were frequently remarkable for their power and effect.
From reading his journal, one would infer that this was
characteristic of his preaching all his life.

Hoping they might now make him useful, his church tried hard to make him do steady work, but in vain. He would, if put on a circuit, leave it, if he had an impression that he ought to go somewhere else, and would soon be heard from, perhaps, a hundred miles away. Finding it impossible to make him submit to the discipline of the church, they finally ceased to consider him as belonging to it or to their jurisdiction at all.

He now flew from place to place and from state to state. In 1799 he crossed the Atlantic, and went to Ireland to preach to the people there, and became really a *Cosmopolite*, as he now called himself. While there, he preached in the prisons, in the barracks to the soldiers—in the towns and cities—sometimes in churches, then in the streets and in private houses, and at length became known as Crazy Dow, or the Crazy Preacher.

On going to a strange place, he would put up a number of little hand bills, which he carried about with him; soon a large crowd would be collected, and he would preach them a sermon none would ever forget. He had a plan of bringing the people into a "covenant." When he perceived they had been much moved by his discourse, he would invite them to come forward and give him; their names, and if they would agree to join him, promised to pray for them at a certain hour every day for a month or more, wherever he might be. When all their names were written down, he would call God to witness the covenant, fold up the paper, put it in his pocket, bid them an affectionate farewell, and perhaps never be seen by them again. By this simple device many were led to pray, and to commence a better life, having been drawn into this promise when their hearts were tender and easily influenced.

12

In controversy, it was said few could equal him; his knowledge of the Scripture was so great and his logic so powerful. Unconditional election and reprobation, he was much opposed to, and used to tell the high Calvinists that their doctrine simply amounted to this: "You can and you can't; You shall and you sha'n't; You will and you won't; You're damned if you do, and you're damned if you don't." Atheism, deism, and infidelity, generally fared badly when they encountered him. It appeared strange to see one so uncouth, in appearance, argue his points with so much force and clearness.

Many liberal donations made by those who pitied his hard life and destitution, were not accepted. Some, though, in taking leave of him in a crowd, would put money in his hand, and disappear before he could return it; or would drop money in his coat pockets. On pouring out some crackers put up for him, he found a sum of money among them. His wants were sometimes supplied so opportunely and unexpectedly, that he could but think himself in the care of a special providence.

Arriving one day at a ferry without money, or anything to pawn, to pay his fare, he saw something shining in the sand, and on picking it up, found it to be a *York shilling*, just the sum needed. At another time when he needed money for the same purpose, two strangers put each a half dollar in his hand. So many incidents of the same kind, constantly occurring, gave him confidence, and he would venture on long and distant journeys, believing, to use his own expression, that "the door would be opened." The speed with which he travelled seems almost incredible. In one day he rode twenty-five miles, preached five times, and addressed three "classes."

He says, in order to do this, "I had to be in earnest."

"I entered a meeting house on one occasion, having on an old borrowed great-coat, and with two hats on my head. Some were alarmed, some blushed, some laughed, and all were excited."

"On the 17th of June, I rode thirty-five miles, and preached five times. On the 18th, I rode fifty-five miles, preached five times, and spoke to two classes. On the 19th, I preached six times, and rode twenty-five miles."

In two months he rode 1,500 miles and preached 180 sermons.

He would often send on his appointments to preach, more than twelve months before, and nothing that could be overcome by human exertion, would prevent his being in the place punctual to the time. Mountains and rivers storms of hail and sleet, swollen streams, cold, and hunger were unheeded by him.

Strange as it may seem, Lorenzo Dow, just like other men, thought he must have a wife; and hearing of a young woman who had said: if she ever married at all she would rather marry a travelling preacher than any one else, he called on her and inquired if this were so? She said, it was. He then asked her, if she thought she could accept of such a looking object as himself for a husband?

At this she became frightened and left the room. Soon after this he called on her again and told her he was going South, and would not return under eighteen months. In the meantime, if she saw no one she liked better than him, and he saw no one he liked better than her, on his return, if she were willing, they would be married. But he gave her distinctly to understand that she must never, never interfere with him in regard to preaching. For if she did, he would pray to God to take her away, and he believed he would do it!

At the appointed time he returned, on the third of February, 1804, he and Peggy, poor thing, were married. She seems to have been a sweet-tempered, gentle, uncomplaining creature, content to ramble over the world with him—sometimes walking by his side, sometimes riding on horseback, or in a rude vehicle. Occasionally he would deposit her in some cabin by the wayside, to remain until called for.

In England, where she followed him after her marriage, she gave birth to a little daughter, who died soon afterwards. She being prostrated by a long and dangerous illness, it was taken away to be cared for until her recovery. She saw it once again before it sickened and died, while she was in a state of utter prostration.

Just before leaving England to return to America, in her artless but interesting journal she writes:

"I stayed in the town of Warrington a few weeks, and frequently visited the little chapel where my sweet little infant's remains were deposited ; and often felt a pleasure of the sweetest kind in contemplating that my child had escaped all the dangers and vanities of this uncertain world, for the never-fading glories of Paradise, where I hoped, when life should end, I should meet her, to part no more."

Dow's strange life and restless wanderings at last ended. He died in Georgetown, in the District of Columbia, in 1834, in the 57th year of his age. On the front leaves of his journal are two quaint pictures of himself and Peggy. Above them is written: "The morning of life is gone—the evening shades appear." And below: "We are journeying to the land from whence there is no return."

CHAPTER XXVI.

CLARKSVILLE AND ITS RECOLLECTIONS.

CLARKSVILLE, our country town, was a place in whose spiritual and temporal welfare your grandfather ever felt a deep interest, on account of the many kind friends he made there, and because, too, he first carried there Baptist influence, and planted a Baptist church. It therefore deserves a special notice in our narrative.

Like most of the towns and cities of the South, its growth has been slow. It is a point of considerable importance, however, on account of its valuable agricultural productions, among which is its fine tobacco, known in almost every part of the world. The first notice we have of its locality, is as far back as the Spring of 1780, about twenty-seven years before your grandfather came to the country. At that time the celebrated Col. John Donelson, of Virginia, with his toil-worn voyagers, from the distant Holston, having descended the Tennessee and ascended the Ohio, and Cumberland Rivers, on their dangerous and difficult voyage to the spot, where Nashville now stands, "reached the mouth of a small river emptying into the Cumberland on its north side, which, Moses Renfroe, one of his companions, called Red River, up which he intended to settle." See Putnam's *Annals of Middle Tennessee*.

There is no event in the history of Tennessee, of deeper or more thrilling interest, than this voyage of Col. Donel-

son and his party. He was the father of the beautiful
Rachel Donelson, wife of our heroic Jackson, more beloved
and prized by him, than all the honors heaped upon him,
by his admiring countrymen.   Few, perhaps, without drop-
ping a tear have read the account of her father's tragic
death—killed almost in sight of home, returning from a
distant journey.

It would seem the hills, above and below the mouth of
this little river, were attractive, even then, for by the middle of the next year, the number of settlers amounted to
more than twenty, whose sad fate has not been forgotten.
Learning that a band of savages were approaching to destroy their settlement, they gathered up a few of their effects
and started in haste, hoping to reach the stations near
Nashville before they were overtaken.   But at night, while
encamped on the banks of a little stream that flows into
what is called Sycamore Creek, in Cheatham County, they
were attacked by the Indians, and all—men, women, and
children—murdered, except one poor woman, who made
her escape, and reached a station next day, twenty miles
distant, with her clothing all torn off by the brush and
canebrakes through which she passed in her lonely flight·
The little stream, the scene of this tragedy, is still known
as Battle Creek, though in truth there was no battle, but
a cruel massacre.

Here, too, Col. Valentine Sevier, brother of General
John Sevier, one of the heroes of King's Mountain, who
attempted a settlement at the mouth of Red River, lost
three of his sons. They had started to Nashville in a
pirogue, were fired upon by a band of Indians concealed
in the cane on the banks of the Cumberland, a short distance above where Clarksville now stands, and all three

were killed and scalped—a terrible blow to their aged parents, who, in these perilous times, so much needed the strong arms and brave hearts of their gallant sons. The struggle for this locality, and the beautiful country stretching to the west, north and east of it, was long and persistent, but the white man finally prevailed here, as elsewhere, and the Indian disappeared forever.

Thomas Reasons and wife, and a Miss Betsy Roberts, in the year 1796, were the last victims of savage cruelty near Clarksville. For some slight cause, the little party which was to be at Mr. Reasons' that night did not take place, or many others would have been killed. This, if the dates are correct, took place about eleven years before your grandfather came to the country. Seldom, we presume, do the citizens of Clarksville and New Providence call to mind the perils of those who won these places from the savages.

In the spring of 1808 I first saw this place. Your grandfather had occasion to go there to make some little purchases, and took me with him. We crossed Red River in a ferry-boat some distance below the present bridge. Mr. William Farrier, who put us across, was one of your grandfather's highly-esteemed brethren, and owned the ferry and farm adjoining.

If I remember rightly, the whole distance from the ferry to the public square was a forest of tall and beautiful trees, at least two miles in extent. This was principally owned by a son of the Emerald Isle, Hon. James B. Reynolds, called Count Reynolds, at one time a member of Congress, who named his fine property, Grattan's Grove, in honor of his illustrious countryman. But its glory has long since departed, and the ground where the stately forest once stood is now almost covered by the shanties of " American citizens of African descent."

Clarksville was then quite a small place ; there was the Public Square, called the "Public Lot," by the first County Court held in 1791, and which it ordered to be " cleared up," like any other piece of woodland, " and put in order." Around this were a few unpretending houses, thrown in the shade by the new brick court-house standing in the middle of the square. I think there were as many houses down near the river as on the hills—in all very few.

The next time I saw Clarksville, which was after our return from Stewart County to the Barrens, it was very much improved. The dry goods stores of Messrs. McClure & Elder and of John H. Paxton were doing a good business. There were lawyers, doctors, tailors, blacksmiths, etc. The flatboats were being loaded with corn, pork, flour, whisky, and tobacco, at various points at or near the town, to descend to New Orleans. Our town had taken quite a start in the world.

The occasion of my visit to town was to see a lion, which some one had brought there for exhibition. I had read of lions in the Bible, and formed most extravagant ideas of their size, power, and ferocity, and was nearly crazy to see one. I wanted especially to hear one roar, shake the panes of glass out of the windows, and terrify not only man but all the beasts of the field. The price for seeing him was a silver dollar. But alas, how great was my disappointment. Instead of the terrific monster I expected, with fire flashing from his eyes, lashing his sides with his tail, and bending the iron bars of his cage in his efforts to break them, I saw what seemed to be little more than a large brindled dog, quiet and respectful in behavior, and little "like the lion roused by the swelling of Jordan," mentioned in the Bible.

Before the building of the brick court-house, Clarksville had no place set apart for public worship. After this was built, any of the religious denominations used it that chose, and from what I have heard, the old preachers often had some hard cases to deal with there.

It was here, according to tradition, that parson N., a good old Methodist brother had his feelings so much outraged. While describing the lower regions in the most dismal colors, and exhorting his hearers in the most earnest and affectionate manner to repent of their sins, and reform their lives, in order to escape it, a half drunken fellow arose and said : "Parson, I don't think there is any such place as that, or some body would have heard of it before." This sounded so droll and unexpected, that the audience could not help laughing. The parson soon brought his remarks to a close, and as he passed the door was observed to move his feet slightly, as if to shake the dust from them, and never preached there again, but left them to be convinced, when too late, that there is such a place, or ought to be.

In former times, the court house and public square used to be lively places on public days. Nearly all the men and boys from the country would be there. It was a time to settle accounts, swap horses, drink whisky, listen to lawyers and candidates, hear the news, and see something of the world. My greatest delight was to hear the lawyers trying their cases ; They would sometimes, as in my simplicity I thought, become "fighting mad," and I would expect to see a fight, so soon as court was adjourned for

12*

dinner. But instead of this, they would walk off arm in arm to the tavern, like brothers, much to my amazement, after saying so many hard things of each other. They were to me a great mystery.

The horse swapping was very amusing. Sometimes they would swap even—horse, saddle, bridle, and martingale,— again boot would be given, and generally one would have to treat. When the fever for swapping was high, the same horse would perhaps have half a dozen owners in the course of the day.

The drinking was managed rather differently from what it is now. So soon as one came to town, he dismounted, hitched his horse securely,—there were no livery stables then, or until long afterwards—went into a tavern,— no saloons then in Clarksville, at least none bearing that name —and bought a half pint, pint, or quart of whiskey or brandy. Each one received in a bottle the quantity called for, from the barkeeper, took a drink, and set his bottle on a shelf provided for that purpose, and then went out to attend to his business, if he happened to have any. And whenever in the course of the day he felt his thirst coming on, he would go in and help himself, sometimes accompanied by a friend. When his bottle gave out, he would have it filled again, if he thought it necessary to his comfort. A long row of these little bottles, side by side, on their shelves, looked very showy. Any one living near town would see men, after one of these gala-days, riding home in a variety of strange ways, sometimes leaning forward, or on one side or the other. Some would camp out all night, and not get in until next day, often minus hat or saddlebags. One old gentleman whom I knew, before leaving home would carefully divest himself of everything that could be lost, and his family could always tell by this what was on his mind.

For many years, most of the change, or fractional currency used in Clarksville, was made by cutting silver coins into smaller pieces. Before this, mankind understood that no one thing could have more than four quarters, but now found they were mistaken, for skillful manipulations demonstrated that, by the aid of a mallet or cold chisel, a Spanish dollar often contained five or six quarters. This discovery was quite profitable. The people at first grumbled at this, but, as the silver was very pure and the change convenient, by common consent it passed freely among them.

Sometimes the angles of this fractional currency were so sharp that one had to be careful when handling it. It was not safe to thrust one's hand incautiously into one's pocket.

Judge Humphreys used to hold the courts in Clarksville at the time of which we are now speaking. He was a mild and pleasant gentleman, of whom I stood in great awe, on account of the deference and respect every one paid him, and the vast amount of wisdom and learning I supposed him to possess. He was, I think, a Carolinian by birth, and held in such estimation as to give his name to one of the counties of his adopted state. Your grandfather used to speak of him after his death, as one of his particular friends of the lower part of the county, where he often preached and married the young people.

The most distinguished lawyer in Clarksville was William L. Brown, a small, delicate-looking man, with fine, black eyes, dark complexion, and low, massive forehead. As a speaker he was bold, confident, and vehement. Young as I was, I could perceive his superiority to the other lawyers, and his greater influence with the court and juries.

While sitting one day in the court-house, watching the proceedings, I thought I observed him look towards me several times. At length he rose up from where he was sitting within the bar, passed out of it, took a few turns in the room, and then coming where I was, leant against the wall near me, and entered into conversation; in the course of which he asked me my name. When I told him who I was, he said : " Is that so ? " seemed to be pleased, and told me he and my father were great friends. He next asked how old I was ? If I was going to school ? If I thought I should like to be a lawyer when I grew up to be a man ?

After chatting with me a short time in a very pleasant manner, he said that he was going up to his office, and if I would go with him he would give me some books. On entering the office, he went to the library and brought out a Latin dictionary, well bound and covered with buckskin ; a fine Delphine Virgil, and Wettenhall's Greek Grammar, and made me a present of them, saying the dictionary was the one he used when he studied Latin. He advised me, in conclusion, by all means, to make myself well acquainted with the Latin and Greek, adding he would talk with me again some day about being a lawyer. I hardly need say I was very much pleased with my books, and at being thus noticed by the great lawyer.

After this he removed to Nashville, where he became famous on account of his legal abilities, and was appointed by the Federal Government one of the Commissioners to settle the long-vexed question of boundary between Kentucky and Tennessee.

Your grandfather saw him at Nashville several times afterwards, and said he always made many kind inquiries about me. He died comparatively young. Had he lived, he would have ranked high among the great men of the West. On account of his knowledge of the law and his high moral character, General Jackson had intended to place him on the bench of the Supreme Court, which place was filled after his death by Judge Catron of Tennessee. Judge Brown was twice married, and his children by both marriages died when young. On the banks of the Cumberland, a stream which he loved from his boyhood, is his residence, called " Ross Cliff;" and there, in a cluster of beautiful cedars, I saw the handsome tomb which marks his last resting-place.

Among the truest friends of your grandfather, in Clarksville, not belonging to any church, was the Hon. Cave Johnson. His appearance, in the prime of life, was truly noble and striking—tall, handsome, and of. a commanding presence—a fine specimen of the young Tennesseeans who fought under Jackson in the Indian wars. He had, as a lawyer, politician, and sagacious man of the world, few equals; he rose to high distinction, was fourteen years a member of Congress, and four years a member of the Cabinet during President Polk's administration. In his palmiest days he never forgot an old friend, or failed to meet him with a pleasant smile and kindly greeting. Even when a young man, he manifested great esteem and regard for your grandfather, called on him whenever he was in town,—and, when he had business in court, as guardian, always attended to it for him free of charge. Many years later, as you remember, when it was desired by his friends to get your brother Reuben appointed a cadet in the Military Academy at West Point, he took the business in hand and arranged it all in the most satisfactory manner.

There is an incident of his life both pleasing and romantic, which throws light upon his character. While living in the family of Judge Humphreys studying law, which he commenced full of hope, never doubting of success, he became acquainted with Miss Elizabeth Dortch, then in all the freshness of her early beauty, fell in love, addressed her, and was rejected. At this he was deeply mortified and resolved never to marry. But, instead of moping about, as many love-sick swains do on such occasions, and neglecting his studies, he applied himself with renewed energy, obtained license to practice law, rose in his profession, was appointed States Attorney by the legislature of Tennessee, without ever having applied for it, or knowing when it was done,—was elected to Congress again and again against the most determined opposition. Time rolls on. Miss Dortch marries, and becomes a widow with three children. His old love revives ; he again proposes, is accepted, and they were married by your grandfather in 1838, and spent many happy years together, including those during which he was a member of the Cabinet, amid the gayeties and pleasures of Washington society.

He, too, has passed away, with nearly all the men of that shining period ; but had the happinesss to live in what will, perhaps, be remembered hereafter as the golden age of his country's history.

One, at first, will be apt to think it strange that your grandfather, who never turned aside to seek the friendship of any man, but always accepted it frankly, when offered, should have had so many true and lasting friends among those who never manifested any very decided interest in the great subject to which he devoted his life. But it is probable, that all men have an ideal of a good man, and when they meet one who corresponds to this ideal instinctively love and esteem him.

I am not able to say when your grandfather first preached in Clarksville; whether he did so by request of the citizens, or sent an appointment of his own accord.

His audience was at first very small, one account made it only two ladies—Mrs. McClure and Mrs. Elder—and one gentleman, who took their seats in the court house, though a good many stood near the door outside. He sang a hymn, prayed, and delivered a short address, and at the close told his little audience, that there was a good promise on record, when two or three were gathered together in his name. After this his audience steadily increased, became large and attentive, and an impression was made in the place, favorable to religion and Baptist sentiments.

By reference to the journals of the old Spring Creek Church, of July 1831, an order was passed for the organization of the Clarksville Church. Isham Watkins, Jesse Ely, William Killebrew, Joshua Brown, and others being petitioners for the same. Previous to this time, it had been an arm, or branch, of Spring Creek Church. Your grandfather acted as one of the presbyters on that occasion, and was its first pastor.

It is now (1870) a large and flourishing church, under the pastoral care of Elder A. D. Sears, D. D., with a new and handsome house of worship.

To the building of this church, S. A. Sawyer, formerly

a merchant of Clarksville, but now of Brooklyn, New York, contributed most liberally, showing that though far away, his heart is still with his brethren of former times.

The religious sentiment has been well developed in Clarksville. And in this respect it will compare favorably with any of the towns and cities of the South and West. In it, the Baptists have one church; the Methodists, one; the old Presbyterians, one; the Cumberland Presbyterians, one; the Episcopalians, two; the Reformers or Christian Church, one; and the Catholics, one. At all these large and attentive congregations meet for worship.

The population of the city of Clarksville is now about seven thousand. For morality, intelligence, and refinement, it will compare favorably with any town or city of the West. The South-western University, under the management of the Presbyterian Church, and a flourishing female college under that of the Methodist Episcopal Church are here located.

CHAPTER XXVII.

FAMILY AFFLICTIONS.

Of all the years of your grandfather's pilgrimage, 1815 was the most sorrowful. In less than one month, during this year, he lost four of his little children—Thomas, Martin, Reuben, and Maria, the last of whom was about nine years old; the others, younger. Two of these were dead in the house at the same time. At this great affliction, our family was struck with awe and astonishment, and our kind neighbors almost as much so as ourselves.

It will not be easy for those who have never experienced a like affliction to imagine the feelings of a family that has lost so many of its inmates in so short a time. Your grandmother was almost heart-broken, and for days together sat with her head covered. and mourned the loss of her loved ones. Your grandfather was silent as men will sometimes be who, in deep distress, are afraid to speak, lest in doing so they should lose control of themselves. We children who were left moved noiselessly about the house on which a dark shadow seemed to rest. It no longer appeared the same home; too many little voices were hushed forever which were wont to make it so cheerful and pleasant.

Your grandfather selected a place not far from the house for a burying-ground, and made their little graves. The wild cherry tree was always a favorite with him, and

269

he went into the woods and collected a number of these
which he planted around the graves, so as to form a little
grove.   They grew very thriftily, and their spreading
branches, and green leaves soon made a pretty shade.   It
was a pleasant spot when I last saw it, long years ago;
here your aunt Polly was buried the next year, and your
uncle Garrard, who died of erysipelas, October 5th, 1823,
in the sixteenth year of his age.   You will no doubt ask
the cause of this unusual mortality. An unusual quantity
of rain had fallen in the early part of the year, and all
the low places in the barrens were covered with water,
and much vegetation was either killed or in a dying condition ; so that when the hot suns of August and September
came, a malaria was produced, that brought on ague, chills,
and bilious fever. Large families were often so prostrated,
that there was not one left able to hand another a cup of
water. Neighbors less unfortunate would render all the assistance they could to each other, by going themselves or
sending their servants to wait upon them.   The little
children in our family were reduced to mere shadows, but
might have recovered had not the whooping-cough
supervened.   Then nothing could save them.   No doubt
many are still living besides myself who remember but too
well those unhappy seasons.   During the next winter, your
grandfather went down to Woodville, a little town in Mississippi, near the Louisiana line.

He had some years before, formed the acquaintance of
Col. Charles Stewart, the first proprietor of what is known
as the Peacher's Mill property, situated in Montgomery
County, Tennessee. This, together with the large body
of valuable land connected with it, was a fine estate, but
being full of enterprise, and fond of making money he sold

it to your grandfather Barker, and removed south in 1813, believing, that cotton planting there would prove more profitable than any business he could follow in this country. His brother, Duncan Stewart, had settled near Woodville the year before.

Although making no pretensions to religion himself, Colonel Stewart had formed a great friendship for your grandfather, and persuaded him to leave this country, as he had done, and go to Southern Mississippi, and settle near him, offering him at the same time considerable inducements to do so; telling him of the mild and pleasant climate, the ease with which he could make a support for his family, and hinting at the good he might do there by preaching to a people almost entirely destitute of religious instruction.

Fearing that the place on which he now lived was unhealthy, and having but little hope of getting a supply of water by sinking a well, he concluded to go and look at the country first, and then decide whether, all things considered, it was likely to be an advantageous move for himself and family.

Major John Nevill, being about to take a boat-load of produce down to New Orleans, invited him to take passage on his boat to some point on the river near where Colonel Stewart lived. This invitation was thankfully accepted, and he accordingly went and was absent from home about three months. His voyage was tedious, and attended with much danger, on account of fogs, sawyers, and floating ice.

At length, however, he landed, bade adieu to his companions, and soon arrived at the hospitable mansion of his friend, who received him with great cordiality and treated

him with the kindness of a brother. Here he remained
some time looking at the country, which was already
clothed in the beauty of early spring. After seeing a good
deal of it, he decided not to move his family there. The
manners and customs of the people seemed strange to him,
and their thoughts so full of cotton, sugar, and money-
making, that he did not think the voiçe of the preacher
was likely to be heard by them to much advantage.

I may mention here that Colonel Stewart had two twin-
brothers—Duncan, already mentioned, who removed to
Mississippi in 1812, and James, who remained in Tennessee till 1818. The latter at all times felt that singular
attachment for his brother which is characteristic of the
Scottish race, and especially desired to be buried by his
side when he died; and as age and infirmity increased,
this desire increased also. Finally, he determined to leave
his home (a few miles from Clarksville, and long known as
the Stewart Place), and descend the Mississippi to where
his brother lived. He had a substantial coffin made, and
what the people persisted in calling his funeral sermon
preached. After which, placing as much of his effects on
board a boat as he thought he should need, together with
the coffin, he finally reached his destination; and after his
death, according to his wish, was buried by the side of his
brother.

It was long before the community ceased talking of this
strange transaction. But, no doubt, the coffin was provided in case he should die on the journey, and the preaching was intended to bring his friends and neighbors together that he might give them a hospitable entertainment
before bidding them adieu. An old lady, with whom you
are well acquainted, told me lately that she was at what

was called the funeral, and thinks your grandfather preached on the occasion.

These Stewarts were said to have been of the royal family of Scotland, and from a description given me by your grandfather of Mary Stewart, a daughter of James Stewart, she must have been little less beautiful and lovely than the renowned Scottish Queen herself whose name she bore.

While considering in what way he should come home, your grandfather had the good fortune to meet with an old Kentucky friend, Dr. Walker, who was about to return by land, through the Indian nation. He immediately procured a horse, and taking leave of his kind friends there, whom he now saw for the last time, turned his face homeward. He followed what was then called the Old Natchez Trace, through the country occupied by the Chickasaw Indians. This was the road usually travelled by boatmen and traders on their way home, by land, from New Orleans.

This journey home proved to be one of great entertainment to him; and was a subject of conversation long afterwards. On it he saw the Indians engaged in one of their famous Ball Plays, in which they displayed wonderful agility; he also heard them uttering their lamentations for the dead.

For a certain length of time it was their custom he said to go out twice a day, after they had lost one of their family, and raise a wail or lamentation that could be heard to a great distance, and fell sadly on the ears of those passing by. When the mourners were too few to produce an imposing effect they would hire others to assist them. He also first heard, while travelling among the Choctaw Indians on his way home, the following interesting legend connected with their early settlement in the country they then occupied.

"Their tribe came originally from the distant regions of the West, and when they commenced their journey had two guides—a long straight pole and a large dog, In crossing the Mississippi their faithful dog was drowned and henceforth they had to depend on their pole alone. Every evening this was set up in their encampment perpendicularly. In the morning they observed carefully which way it leaned and journeyed in that direction This they continued to do till they came to the bank of a beautiful river. Here on setting up their pole they saw with the pleasure only known to those who are weary from long travelling, that it remained perpendicular for several days; hence they named the river *Alabama*, which in their soft and musical language means; 'Here we rest.'

"But their wanderings were not yet ended, for again they perceived their pole leaning in a certain direction and again they travelled on until they reached the place known as the Chickasaw Old Towns, where when the pole was set, it stood erect permanently and here the tribe remained ever afterwards."

On this old trace which your grandfather travelled stands the lonely Monument of Governor Merriwether Lewis, a striking and startling object when first seen by those who still occasionally pass by this wild sequestered spot. After his exploration beyond the Rocky Mountains, in 1803, to the distant Oregon, then a " terra incognita," he was appointed Governor of Louisiana, by President Jefferson, and being on his way from New Orleans, in a violent attack of hypochondria, to which he was liable, he put an end to his life, as is generally supposed, though many thought he came to his end by other hands than his own. It would be hard to find a more beautiful tribute to the memory of any one than that penned by Mr. Jefferson, for his young and gifted friend, as it may be seen in the *Encyclopedia Americana.*

After his return from Mississippi, your grandfather devoted himself more than usual to preaching. His long absence from his people seems to have endeared them to him more than ever, and they too were happy to learn he had abandoned all thought of leaving them.

In 1816, the Bethel Church was constituted. This church and their pastor, Elder William Tandy, were greatly beloved by him, and he often preached for them in those early times. I well remember the little log meeting-house, near the salubrious springs, where the people used to meet before the present church was built; and the pleasant rides with your grandfather along the narrow path, bordered with flowers, through the beautiful prairie we crossed on our way to it.

In the month of August of this year your aunt Polly died, and our house again became a house of mourning. I still retain a vivid recollection of her last illness and death. She had been ailing for several days, and the family physician, Dr. Gilmer, had been called in to see her. After prescribing some simple remedies for the irritation of her stomach, of which she complained, he left us. Soon after this she became very pale, said she thought she was going to die, and requested her mother to make her a pallet on the floor, such as was often made for children to sleep on in warm weather. This was done, and she was laid upon it. The paleness increasing, we became alarmed and all gathered round her, some chafing her hands, some her feet, and some fanning her. She breathed only a few times after this, and then her gentle spirit passed away. At first we could not realize that she was gone. It seemed incredible. But it was even so. Her soft, blue eyes were closed forever. Thus died, in her early bloom, one of the little twins, the first born of the family. She had been baptized just one month before her death.

The other twin, your aunt Nancy Morrison, lived on amid the usual vicissitudes of human life, until February 23d, 1862. The circumstances attending her death were likewise such as not to be soon forgotten. Her health had not been good for many years in consequence of a fall from a buggy, which greatly impaired her nervous system and confined her much of her time to her bed. Soon after the first great battle of Manassas, your brother Reuben, while walking over the battle-ground, picked up a bomb-shell, which he brought home as a curiosity. This had been carried about from place to place, until finally it reached your uncle Morrison's, as you no doubt remember. There it remained until a few days before the battle of Fort Donelson, when, while your cousin Eugene, her only son, and some others, were endeavoring to extract the powder it contained, it exploded, a fragment of the shell striking him and inflicting a dangerous wound, from the effects of which his recovery was long doubtful.

This, in her weak state of health, produced a shock from which she had not recovered when the news of the fall of Fort Donelson was received, in which the fate of so many dear to her was involved. In her feeble condition she was unable to bear up under it, and soon afterwards breathed her last. Thus, in darkness and in sorrow, the days of her pilgrimage ended, which, in Heaven's mysterious providence, has been the lot of so many whose hearts like hers were full of Christian charity and devotion to the happiness of others. She sleeps by her father and mother at the Old Place, where many others whom she loved also repose, and nothing could be more appropriate than the portion of the inscription on her tomb, " Blessed are the pure in heart, for they shall see God." The sisters were baptized at the same time, July, 1816, and were members of the Little West Fork Church. They were born Sept. 12th, 1799, and were two years and a few days older than myself.

When little children, it was difficult to distinguish one from the other. I think, though, that a close observer could perceive that your aunt Nannie's face was a little less oval than her sisters. She had also a mark on her shoulder, the exact resemblance of a strawberry, which always betrayed her, if we could catch and hold her long enough to find it. They would often try to pass themselves off one for the other, were mightily pleased when they succeeded in doing so, and were so inseparable that when you saw one you involuntarily looked for the other. We were playmates and confidants, and they were so gentle and loving in their disposition as to permit me to domineer over them a good deal; and, when I got into disgrace for misconduct—which they seldom did—I received a world of sympathy from them. It is pleasant, even now, to think of the happy years we passed together, and how completely our lives were identified in every respect.

13

CHAPTER XXVIII.

ELDER ROSS EXPLAINS HIS VIEWS.

WE will now pass on to the year 1817, which may be regarded as an epoch in the life of your grandfather, since during this year he gave utterance to those views which culminated in his separation from his hyper-calvinistic brethren, and in the organization of the Bethel Baptist Association.

At the commencement of his ministerial labors, as was to have been expected, he adopted the rigid views of his family and of the church to which they belonged,—in which faith so many great and good men have lived and died. It would, perhaps, not be extravagant to say that many of the brightest intellects from the earliest ages of the church down to his own time had contended for these views as for " the faith once delivered to the saints."

They believed in particular and unconditional election and reprobation, that Christ died for the elect only, and that not one of the elect would ever be lost, or one of the non-elect ever be saved. That the Almighty, who knows the end from the beginning, looking down, as it were, upon the generations of men yet unborn, without the least regard to character or conduct had elected or selected one here and another there to be saved and had passed all others by as vessels of wrath fitted to destruction.

These views, as he thought, represent the heavenly

Father as a parent who had lavished all his care and tenderness on a part of his children only. These he had provided with food, raiment, instruction, and all things necessary to their comfort and happiness. The rest he had left to struggle on as best they might for a time against hunger, cold, and neglect, and finally to perish, not because they were less deserving than their brethren, but simply because it was his *will* and pleasure to pass them by.

Early in his ministry his mind became perplexed and troubled on this subject. He could not understand how this could be when the sacred writings declare that his tender mercies are over all his works; that " he is no respecter of persons, but in every nation he that fears him and works righteousness is accepted of him." But such was his reverence for the wisdom, knowledge, and piety of those who had gone before him and held these views, that he would not permit his thoughts to dwell upon them when he could avoid doing so.

When he came to the West he found his brethren here of the same belief, and tenacious of it to the last degree. They watched over it with the utmost solicitude, and over every member of their communion in regard to it, and especially over their preachers. If one of them was suspected of being unsound in the faith or Arminian in his tendencies, they turned away from him, and his usefulness among them was at an end.

Could this doctrine be true? he often thought. Does the Bible teach that our happiness after death depends on unconditional election? That if elected, we shall be saved simply because we are elected, and if lost, it will be because we are not elected.* He doubts this and is determined to

* The advocates of election would be slow to admit that this is a cor-

bring all the faculties of his mind to the investigation of this subject, one of the most important in his estimation in the whole range of Christian theology.

On one side of this great argument stands John Calvin, of Geneva, with his hard, cold, merciless, but powerful logic. On the other, James Arminius, of Holland, no less able, with his warm, generous, and merciful interpretation of the sacred writings.

Mighty men, so to speak, have fought under these leaders respectively, and for a long time victory seemed to be perched on the banners of the former; but, in these latter days, the signs are, that the views of Arminius will triumph in the end.*

In calling to mind the disadvantages under which your grandfather labored, one can but regret the strait he was in; and nothing shows more clearly what manner of man he was than the patience and courage manifested by him. He was almost literally without books. He did not own a Concordance even—a work so indispensable to the Bible student. With the Bible alone he went to the work, and, beginning at the beginning, he passed through it again and again, comparing chapter with chapter and verse with verse, often carrying it to the field with him when at work there, and opening its pages when occasionally resting from

rect view of the doctrine, They certainly do not believe that election saves independently of a compliance with the requirements of the gospel, but that election leads to such compliance, and that God in choosing ends chooses means to accomplish them. On the other hand, it is not scriptural to represent sinners as lost and punished, because they are not elected; but they are lost and punished for their sins, and for no other reason.   J. M. P.

* The biographer here expresses his opinion, which he had a perfect right to do; but from this opinion many, no doubt, will dissent.
                    J. M. P.

his labors. It is not strange, therefore, that his knowledge in after years was so extensive and accurate.

Gill's " Body of Divinity" was a book held in high estimation by Baptists at that time. He greatly desired to get it, hoping it might throw much light on the subject of his studies, and he knew where it could be had for six dollars. But six dollars were something to him in those days. I remember to have heard him and your grandmother often speak of purchasing this book. Sometimes they almost made up their minds to buy it, and then again declined doing so. He was always afraid of debt, and used to say, that, next to a bad conscience, debt ought to be avoided.

The book, though, was at last bought, and for days we saw but little of him, so much was he absorbed in its perusal. Some time after this he procured another book, " The Gospel Worthy of All Acceptation," by Andrew Fuller, of England,—a work which greatly interested him.*

After a while he bought Butterworth's " Concordance." It was a thin folio volume, and lies by me at the present writing. When afterwards he procured another, more convenient for use on account of its shape, he made me a

* Andrew Fuller, in his day, found the state of things among the Baptists in England quite similar to that referred to on the theater of Elder Ross's labors. It was to them a troublesome question whether the gospel should be preached to sinners at all. Dr. Gill hesitated about the matter, as we learn from Dr. Cramp's " History of Baptists." Fuller differed from Gill, and believed in an " objective fulness " in the provisions of the atonement of Christ, sufficient for the salvation of all men. He therefore insisted that the gospel is worthy of all acceptation, and is to be preached to men, not as elect or non-elect, but as sinners under the wrath of God and in perishing need of salvation, Eternity alone will reveal all the good accomplished, by God's blessing, on Fuller's " Gospel Worthy of All Acceptation."   J. M. P.

present of this.   On one of the blank leaves is written :
" James Ross' Book, a present from his father, Reuben
Ross, Sept. 22, 1818.   Price $4."   The above is in his
own handwriting, and the most perfect specimen of it I
have.   I need hardly say I value it much.   This book he
found to be a treasure indeed, saving him much time and
labor in finding and comparing various texts and portions
of the sacred writings.

He would often speak of the delicacy of his position
during these years.   He was all the time engaged in
preaching, and it was of the utmost importance to express
himself so that it might not transpire prematurely to what
his investigations were tending.   For ecclesiastical history
shows that as much wisdom and sound discretion is necessary in religious movements as in those of governments
and armies, and that, for want of these, many great and
good men have failed in effecting much needed reforma-
tions.

Fortunately for him, the Baptists in this country at that
time were divided in sentiment in regard to preaching to
sinners or calling them to repentance ; one class knew
that if they were reprobates, it would all be of no avail.
Others thought it would do no harm to scatter the seed
broadcast, since none but the elect germs would, after all,
vegetate and bear fruit.   He availed himself of this state
of things to the full extent, and urged all alike to repent
and believe the gospel.

As he proceeded in his investigations, he saw that the
Bible, from beginning to end, was instinct with the doctrine that all our blessings, both spiritual and temporal,
are more or less conditional.   To our first parents it was
said : " For the day thou eatest thereof thou shalt surely

die." They, however, disregarded the condition, and thus

"Brought death into the world and all our woe."

To fallen Cain it was said : "If thou doest well, shalt not thou be accepted ? and if thou doest not well, sin lieth at the door." He did not choose to do well, murdered his brother, and was driven forth a fugitive and vagabond, with the mark of Heaven's displeasure branded upon him.

Here, then, in the early dawn of twilight, as it were, of the revelation made to man, he is informed that good and evil, blessing and cursing, life and death, are set before his eyes, and that his fate depends upon his own voluntary choice. If he is obedient — chooses the good and shuns the evil—all will be well with him. If not, calamity and sorrow await him.

Moses in his dying address, Solomon at the dedication of the temple, and all the ancient seers and prophets reiterated the same great principle of the divine government, that happiness and misery, joy and sorrow, life and death, were conditional, more or less, on our own conduct, and not on *foreknowledge, election,* or *predestination.*

Though his memory was stored with numberless passages from the Old Testament bearing directly on this subject, none I ever heard him repeat were more conclusive, at least to my mind, than those remarkable texts to be found in the Prophecy of Ezekiel, 18 : 21–24, 27, 28, 31, 32.

"But if the wicked *will return* from the sins he hath committed, and keep all my statutes, and do all that which is lawful and right, he shall surely live, he shall not die. All his transgressions that he hath committed they shall not be mentioned unto him. In his righteousness that he hath done shall he live.

"Have I any pleasure at all that the wicked should die? saith the Lord God, and not that he should return from his ways and live? But when the righteous turneth away from his righteousness and committeth iniquity and doeth according to all the abominations that the wicked man doeth, shall he live? All his righteousness that he hath done shall not be mentioned. In his trespass that he hath trespassed and in his sin that he hath sinned, in them shall he die.

"When the wicked man turneth away from his wickedness that he hath committed and doeth that which is lawful and right, he shall save his soul alive. Because he considereth and turneth away from all his transgressions that he hath committed, he shall surely live, he shall not die.

"Cast away from ye all your transgressions whereby ye have transgressed and make you a new heart and a new spirit, for why will you die, O house of Israel? For I have no pleasure in the death of him that dieth, saith the Lord God; wherefore turn yourselves and live."

"Who," he would say, after reading these texts, "can doubt that man's salvation is conditional?" And not only are the blessings of life and salvation conditional, but those of a temporal character also. This underlying principle he taught was everywhere visible. Industry, economy; and prudence are the conditions of wealth; temperance and exercise, of health; good order and system, of success in business; uprightness and integrity, of esteem and confidence. This has been the judgment and belief of all mankind.

To the husbandman his Creator had given the fertile soil, the early and the latter rain, the sunshine and the dew; with strength and intelligence to cultivate his crops and bring them to maturity, on condition that he will do his part. But the Creator will not plow his fields or gather in his harvest. This he must do for himself, or, like the sluggard, who will not plow by reason of the cold, in harvest he must beg and have nothing.

In the New Testament, likewise, this doctrine is everywhere taught. The merciful are to obtain mercy. The pure in heart are to see God. The peace-makers are to be called the children of God. Those who ask are to receive. To those who knock it is to be opened. Those who believe on the Son are to have everlasting life. Those who believe not on the Son are not to see life.

When asked if there were not texts which seemed to teach differently? he would reply that many good men thought there were such; but that conditional and unconditional salvation could not both be true, since this would involve a contradiction in terms; and hence the conclusion that they were misunderstood, and that, were this not the case, all parts of the sacred writings would be found to harmonize on this subject.

By supplying a word or phrase, now and then, which is done in every language, to bring out the meaning (and nowhere oftener than in the Bible, as may be seen by the number of italicised words on almost every page), there would be found, as he thought, but few texts not in accord with the drift and scope of the Bible in its teaching in regard to salvation as being conditional or unconditional.

In the text that reads: " For whom he did foreknow he also did predestinate to be conformed to the image of his Son," were the reading thus: " For whom he did foreknow" *would love and serve him,* " he did predestinate to be conformed to the image of his Son,"* what an important

---

* Would not this turn the text from its true meaning? The question is whether the love of God's people is the cause of his foreknowledge, or whether his foreknowledge has a *causal* influence on their love? The mysteries of foreknowledge and predestination are proverbially deep.

                                                J. M. P.

turn it would give to this text? And so of others like it.

The same method of reasoning should hold in the interpretation of Scripture that does in all other writings.

When the great law of nature is established, that all ponderable bodies are attracted towards the earth, it must not be set aside because smoke and vapor are often seen to *ascend* from it. The exceptions must yield to the rule, not the rule to the exceptions. So when the Bible clearly teaches that all our blessings, political and temporal, are conditional in a greater or less degree, if a few texts *seem* to teach differently, we must conclude that, for some reason, they are not well understood, rather than that the Bible contradicts itself, which we are compelled to do when we make it say that salvation is both conditional and unconditional, this being a contradiction in terms and consequently absurd, as already observed.

He now bade adieu forever to the Calvinistic dogma, "That God hath chosen a certain number of the fallen race of Adam in Christ before the foundation of the world, unto eternal glory, according to his immutable purpose and of his free grace and love, without the least foresight of faith, good works, or any conditions performed by the creature ; and that the rest of mankind he was pleased to pass by and ordain to dishonor and wrath for their sins, to the *praise of his vindictive justice.*" (Buck's *Theological Dictionary*. Art. *Calvinist*.)

What next claimed useful investigation was the nature and extent of the Atonement made for sin. That is to say, whether it was made for all or limited to a part of the human race only. He concluded the shortest and best way to ascertain the teaching of the Bible on this subject, was to ascertain the nature and extent of the *invitations*—since, if the Scriptures teach that all are *invited*, the natural inference would be that the Atonement was made for *all*. And here, with deep emotion, he would repeat those glorious texts which forever set this question at rest. To him this was a delightful theme; one on which he loved to dwell; one every way congenial to his nature. Some of these I remember as distinctly as if I had heard him repeat them yesterday. Among them were such as these :

" Look unto me and be ye saved all the ends of the earth, for I am God, and beside me there is none else."

" Ho, every one that thirsteth, come ye to the waters, and he that hath no money : come ye, buy and eat ; yea, come, buy wine and milk without money and without price."

" And the Spirit and the bride say come, and let him that heareth say come, and whosoever will, let him take of the water of life freely."

" Let the wicked forsake his way and the unrighteous man his thoughts, and let him return unto the Lord and he will have mercy upon him, and to our God, who will abundantly pardon."

" He is the propitiation for our sins, and not for ours only, but also for the sins of the whole world."

" God is no respecter of persons, but in every nation he that feareth him and worketh righteousness is accepted of him."

These texts, and many others like them, left no doubt on his mind that the Atonement was general and unlimited, and that " Christ had, by the grace of God, tasted death for *every* man " (Heb. 2 : 9) who would become his follower and learn to love and serve him.

Having thus satisfied himself that man's salvation is conditional and depends on his character and conduct * and

* More scripturally accurate to say, according to his faith in the Lord Jesus Christ or his continuance in unbelief and in " neglect of so great salvation."   J. M. P.

not on election or predestination, and that the atonement is general, he determined henceforth to preach in accordance with these views, and a fitting opportunity soon after presented itself to address the people in regard to them.

In the month of July 1817, he was requested to preach the funeral sermon of Miss Eliza Norfleet, who had died some time previously near Port Royal, Tenn. From what I have heard of this young lady she was greatly esteemed and beloved in the community in which she had lived, on account of her gentle and amiable character,—one of those bright flowers so often seen to bud, bloom, and fade away in the morning of life. The place where the funeral sermon was preached was a short distance only from Port Royal, on the road leading thence to Nashville, distant only a few miles from the spot where ten years before he had first been heard as a preacher in Tennessee; and now as then in a grove of shady trees and in a community where he was highly esteemed both as a man and as a preacher. The wish was general to pay marked respect to the memory of the departed, and to hear a favorite preacher on the occasion. I have seen lately several old gentlemen of the highest respectability who were then present and from whom I learned many interesting particulars.

Your grandfather, on that occasion, preached a sermon remarkable, both on account of the deep impression it left on the minds of the people who heard it and on account of the important consequences that followed. In the conclusion of his discourse he gave utterance to those views which characterized his preaching until the close of his ministerial labors; they were as follows:

That the human race in consequence of disobedience, are in a state of alienation and rebellion against their Creator and they must become reconciled to him before they can obtain his favor and forgiveness,—that Christ by his suffering and death has made an atonement sufficient for the sins of the whole world,—that salvation to all who will accept the terms, is as free as the light of heaven or as the air we breathe,—that he has given his word to teach them the way and plan of salvation and the terms on which they will be forgiven and received into favor,—that these terms are repentance, faith, love, and obedience—in a word to become followers of Christ;—that in addition to the word the Holy Spirit is given to influence men directly to believe in Christ, to love and serve God, and lead pious and godly lives; yet that he never operates with such power on the human soul as to destroy its free agency, but leaves to man the fearful responsibility of deciding for himself whether he will serve God or not.

That is, if we yield to the influences of the Holy Spirit and become followers of Christ, we shall be pardoned and saved. If not, we shall be lost. If we are lost, it will be our *own* fault. If saved, it will be on account of the goodness and mercy of God and not for any merit in us. That the election spoken of in the Bible is not unconditional, but always has reference to conduct or character. That the Almighty before the foundation of the world elected those to be saved, that he knew from the beginning would love and serve him.

These views, it is said, were received with great favor by the people, and a suppressed expression of approbation was heard to pass through the multitude.

When his discourse was ended he descended from the stand, passed silently through the crowd, mounted his horse and rode home, about twenty miles distant. He does not wish just now to meet face to face his kind old brethren; those who ten years before had received him with open arms when he first came a stranger among them; who had given him so many proofs of sincere friendship, and came to hear him as one of the ornaments of the church. He prefers at present to persue his solitary ride and indulge his feelings of regret that so often in this life duty and friendship cannot go hand in hand together.

But while he is wending his way homeward let us return to the grave he had just left. Here a little apart from the dispersing crowd might have been seen a group of men, many of whose heads were gray with age, in earnest conversation trying to decide what was best to be done under the circumstances. It was finally settled that Elder Fort should go down to see your grandfather; expostulate with him in regard to his strange course; and try, if possible, to induce him to reconsider what he had said in his sermon, and save his church from the great reproach he had brought upon it by falling into the grievous heresy of Arminianism.

Elder Fort had a kind heart, was greatly attached to your grandfather, and dearly loved the church to which they both belonged. On going, he found him in his field plowing his corn. Riding up to the fence, after the usual greeting he at once made known his business, told him he had caused great trouble among his brethren by the wild Arminian doctrine he had preached at the funeral, and he had come down at their request to try to convince him of his error and to persuade him, if possible, to alter his course.

He answered that he would take his horse from the plow, go to the house, get the Book and examine the subject with him. To this Elder Fort replied, that he would prefer taking a seat with him under the trees and discussing it where they then were. This was done. A long and careful examination ensued, at the close of which Elder Fort rose up and said, "Brother Ross, I believe you are right; I am with you;" and henceforth they stood side by side in proclaiming a free salvation to all who would repent, believe, forsake their sins, and turn to God.

When Elder Fort returned and reported that Brother Ross still adhered to the views he had already expressed, and that he himself had come to adopt them, his brethren turned from him as from one no longer of their faith, and thus commenced that estrangement which continued to increase and widen until a separation took place and a new Association was formed, as will in due time be related.

It is proper here to add that although a difference of opinion in regard to election and predestination, or rather to the grounds of election and predestination, was the chief cause of the wide spread dissatisfaction among the churches at this time, yet this was not the only cause of alienation and estrangement. There was a wide difference also among them on the subjects of an educated ministry and Foreign and Domestic Missions. The Old School Baptists, as we may now term them, were violently opposed to everything of this sort, and in favor, so to speak, of letting all these things take care of themselves. The others felt a deep interest in sending the gospel into foreign lands, to those sitting in darkness and the shadow of death, to the heathen nearer home, and also to giving the ministry the advantages of learning and general culture.

CHAPTER XXIX.

AFTER DECIDING UPON HIS CHOICE.

HAVING thus, after long and careful study of the Bible, satisfied himself in regard to what it was his duty to preach, he never afterwards hesitated to proclaim that ample provision had been made for the salvation of all men; that a great and generous feast, as it were, had been provided, and all were affectionately invited to partake of the bountiful provision freely, without money and without price; that the Atonement was general and unlimited; that the Holy Spirit had been poured out on all flesh according to the ancient prophecy; and that all who yield to his divine influence, repent, believe, forsake their sins and turn to God, have the promise of the life that now is and of that which is to come.

These views which sounded strange, coming from a Baptist minister, drew together crowds of attentive hearers. Many of his old brethren adopted them heart and soul, and rejoiced to believe that the gates of heaven were open to receive not only their children and friends, but all nations, kindreds, and tongues who were willing to enter in. And being no longer held in check by the chilling dogmas of unconditional election and reprobation, their zeal became more lively and active. Each one felt more like trying to aid the good cause, instead of waiting with folded hands until the Holy Spirit should come with irresistible power and convert the sinner notwithstanding all

292

his efforts to the contrary.   And thus most of the churches and communities where he preached seemed to awake, as it were, from a deep sleep and manifest greater interest in the subject of religion.

It may be remarked here that the Baptist communities, extending over the region of country in which he preached, were even then a very respectable body of Christians, though a little antiquated and primitive in some respects, as already stated, when compared with those of the present times.

Their democratical form of church government was their pride.   They would not permit king or Cæsar to interfere with their spiritual rights.   They were, indeed, in this so straight, that, like the Indian's gum-tree, they leaned a little over to one side.   Their beloved and time-honored act of baptism, hallowed by Christ and the harbinger in the sacred Jordan, was and is a great bond of union among them in every land.   This love of order and decorum was so great that in their worship they often seemed cold and formal.   If a good sister, giving way to her emotions, kindled by the warm and glowing descriptions of heaven and eternal rest, clapped her hands and shouted for joy, the preacher even then generally came to a dead pause, waited till she " got through," and then went on again, and the good soul often felt rebuked for what she had done.

Aware of the damaging effects of the love of money, they contributed but little to the support of the preacher; and, other things being equal, esteemed him more highly if he managed to support himself.   They would have gazed with astonishment at a man, " hat in hand," passing through their congregations, begging money for their preachers; yet they often showed by their kindness and liberality to their brethren, friends, and neighbors, that this was more from principle than from the love of money, of which, indeed, they had but little to give in those days. Without the assistance they rendered your grandfather and his family in various ways, it would have been impossible for him to have given his time and thoughts, as he did, to ministerial work. In planting his crops and gathering them in, his brethren and friends often came and assisted him with their own hands, or sent their servants when they had them. The kind sisters would often come themselves or send their daughters to help your grandmother in times of sickness, and they sometimes remained for weeks together, not to be waited on, but to render most needful assistance. Many of these gentle nurses I remember well.

As time rolled on and their circumstances improved some of the churches for whom he preached gave him small sums of money. This was first done by the Spring Creek Church in 1824. The amount made up for him there was, I think, sixty dollars. He likewise married a great many young people. Sometimes as many as three couples a day, often living at some distance from each other. For this he sometimes received small sums. Frequently at the request of friends at a distance he spent two or three weeks preaching funeral discourses, and some of these were considerate enough to make him some compensation. If they were not, nothing was ever said. His little income from these different sources, together with the excellent management and economy of your grandmother, enabled him to live in a plain, inexpensive way, and to give his time and thoughts to the work in which he felt so deep an interest. Much, though, as his heart was set on this work he always considered his duty to his family paramount, remembering that the sacred volume placed those who did not provide for their families lower than the infidel himself.

As they became more prosperous the Baptists of this country exhibited a commendable spirit of liberality in supporting the ministry, contributing to aid in spreading religious knowledge, building up churches, schools, and colleges, and promoting the general interests of society.

I have already told you that your grandfather's preaching, after he began to proclaim a free salvation, became more and more impressive. The terrible thought that perhaps a large portion of each congregation he addressed was predestinated to eternal death no longer haunted his imagination, nor like an incubus, weighed upon his spirits and paralyzed his strength. He now no longer felt it incumbent on him to investigate the endless mazes of liberty and necessity, free-will, fatality, and predestination. But to call upon men everywhere to repent and to publish the glad tidings that "God is indeed no respecter of persons, but that in every nation he that fears him and works righteousness is accepted of him."

It was his earnestness, based upon his deep conviction of the truth of what he proclaimed and his compassion for his fellow men, that gave such emphasis to his preaching during these years. He no more doubted that eternal happiness or endless woe depended on the conduct of men in this life, than he doubted his own personal existence. With him this was no myth or fable,

"No idly feigned poetic dream,"

but a tremendous reality. Hence, when he contemplated

the thoughtless and giddy multitudes passing swiftly over the narrow space allotted them in this world, like shadows over the ground, and then plunging, as it were, without preparation into the shoreless ocean before them, his pity knew no bounds; and he often spoke in accents little less moving than those of the old prophet when he exclaimed : '' Oh that my head were waters and mine eyes a fountain of tears, that I might weep day and night for the slain of the daughter of my people!'' And very few, indeed, could remain unmoved by his affectionate appeals when he would earnestly pray them as in '' Christ's stead '' to be reconciled to God.

During these and the following years, his thoughts dwelt much on the nature of the soul and its capacity for happiness before and after its separation from the body. There is in it, he would say, a certain class of feelings or sensations that produce a high degree of enjoyment or happiness, such as those caused by the contemplation of excellence, beauty, and goodness. Also, a consciousness of rectitude and of having done or tried to do our duty in all our relations to our Creator and our fellow man. On the other hand, there is another class which produce intense unhappiness in the soul, such as the feelings of sorrow, regret, remorse, and guilt.

When preaching from the text : '' What shall it profit a man if he gain the whole world and lose his own soul ? or what shall a man give in exchange for his soul ? '' as he often did, he would call attention to this interesting subject. The lost soul, he would say, is the soul that has lost its happiness by continuing in sin until the time for repentance has been closed by death. On the contrary, the soul that is saved is the one that has gained endless happiness, by laying hold on the hope set before it in the gospel and " by patient continuance in well-doing," until called away to its reward.

Although both our happiness and unhappiness in this life may be great, there is, he would say, reason to believe that it bears no comparison to what it would be capable of when, released from the clay tenement, it became a pure, disembodied spirit. With all its powers and capacities enlarged either to bear an exceeding and eternal weight of glory and happiness in the presence of the King of kings, surrounded by all that is beautiful and good; or to bewail forever its blindness and folly, with remorse and anguish for having lost an inheritance so bright and a destiny so glorious. What profit now, had it gained the whole world, with all its power and riches and glory? How willingly would it barter them for the happiness forever lost!

Two other distinguished preachers, about this time, adopted your grandfather's views, and joined heartily with him in preaching a free salvation ; the first of these was his beloved brother and friend, Elder William Tandy.

Elder Tandy was born in Virginia on the 27th of February, 1778, and was consequently about two years your grandfather's junior. On removing to Kentucky in 1815,* he settled in Christian County, near Bethel Church, which immediately licensed him to preach. The next year (1816), in the month of July, he was ordained by Elders Jesse Brooks, Leonard Page, and your grandfather. And

* This date should probably be changed to 1811. My father removed to the same county in 1812, and one of the strong reasons that induced him to buy the tract of land on which he settled, was, that it was in what was called the " Tandy Settlement."   J. M. P.

in July, 1817, one year after his ordination, he was called to take charge of Bethel Church as its pastor.

I was often at his house when a boy, and remember it well. It was a pleasant place to visit, so orderly and quiet. He was both a polished gentleman and a pious Christian minister. One hardly knew which most to admire—himself or his amiable, gentle wife.

He completely won me over. For, seeing me greatly pleased with a beautiful copy of Goldsmith's "Animated Nature," filled with pictures of birds, beasts, fishes, and reptiles, he permitted me to carry it home with me. I considered this a great favor, and found it little less interesting than the Arabian Tales, written, as it was, in the beautiful style of the author whom, as I think, Dr. Johnson used to call the "inspired idiot." Especially was I charmed with the description of that monster of monsters, the Kraken, which it was said, when basking on the surface of the sea, the mariners mistook for an island, according to Milton, and cast their anchors in its scaly rind.

Elder Tandy was a man of fine abilities, and greatly beloved and admired as a preacher. Very soon after beginning to speak, his eyes would fill with tears, and this would continue until the close of his address. Although his appearance was stout and manly his voice was low and weak ; and, in order to hear what he said, all endeavored to make as little noise as possible while he was speaking. One needed to listen to him but a few moments to become deeply interested in what he said. For about twelve months at one time his voice failed him entirely. It was then touching to see him with his tablet and pencil trying to converse with his friends. He partially regained his speech, however, but never so as afterwards to be able to speak in public.

After his voice failed him, your grandfather was chosen to take his place as pastor of his church, and continued to act as such about seventeen years. In this church he made his last public address, as we shall have occasion to mention in its proper place. Here, too, in July, 1860, his beloved brother, Rev. J. M. Pendleton, preached his funeral sermon.

During the years he was pastor of this church, I think your grandfather's success as a preacher was more splendid than at any other period of his ministry; not only within the bounds of the church, but in all the surrounding country. Here, too, on one bright summer morning in 1838, he baptized at one time sixty-six converts. Though often before and afterwards he baptized many at the same time, I think this was the greatest number he ever baptized on one occasion.

He was greatly attached to this people and to Elder Tandy, who rejoiced to see his church grow and prosper under his ministry. Among them he chose to spend the last years of his life, and some of them were around him when he breathed his last.

Of Elder William Tandy it has been said :

" He was an every-day Christian, who exemplified the precepts of the gospel he preached. He was a man of vigorous intellect, sound judgment and affectionate heart, and remarkable for his knowledge of church discipline. There were, owing to his judicious management, but few difficulties in the churches that enjoyed his ministry. His sermons were plain, full of truth ; and often were the emotions of his heart such as to impede his utterance and fill his eyes with tears. There was eloquence in those tears, for they were the exponents of feeling, to which language refused to give expression. After many years of faithful labor, having been at one time entirely deprived of his voice, he fell asleep in Jesus, and, as Peter said of David: ' his sepulchre is with us unto this day.'"

Elder William Tandy was born in Virginia, February 27th, 1778, and died in Christian County, Kentucky, Oct. 12th, 1838, in the sixty-first year of his age, and was buried on the place where he lived when I first knew him in my boyhood. After his death his name was never mentioned but in terms of the highest esteem and regard by your grandfather. The love between them much resembled that of David and Jonathan.

Elder Ambrose Bourne was the other of the two brethren alluded to. He removed, I think, from Bourbon County, Kentucky, and settled near Allensville, Logan County, then and now considered one of the most fertile and beautiful regions of the southern portion of the State. I cannot say at what date he came among us. I notice, however, in some of the minutes of the Red River Association, that he and a Mr. Stephen Trabue were sent by the Mount Gilead Church as Messengers to an Association held at Cave Spring Meeting-house, in Robertson County, Tennessee, in 1816.

Elder Bourne was below medium height, well-formed and active, lively and cheerful in company, and possessed of a good deal of pleasant humor when among his friends ; the more striking because, when he chose to do so, he could assume an expression of countenance that indicated anything rather than wit and humor. Your grandfather had many amusing anecdotes to relate of him.

I heard him say that once he and Brother Bourne set off together to a big meeting at a distance, when the roads were nearly impassable. He on his grey mare Juno, with his saddle-bags on his saddle under a piece of buffalo-robe, to protect them from the rains; his umbrella tied to the pommel of his saddle with a thong of buckskin; his great coat rolled up and strapped behind his saddle on a small pad, to prevent being soiled by the sweating of his horse; and in a suit somewhat travel-stained and worn. I may here remark that something like this was his usual outfit when out on active service.

Brother Bourne, on the other hand, being a widower, had a new buggy with silver mounting, drawn by a handsome Kentucky horse, and was dressed in a suit of fine broad-cloth—a marvel of an outfit for those times. On stepping into his buggy, before giving his horse the reins, with a serio-comic expression that he could so well assume when he chose, he said : " Brother Ross, I know how you must feel. I was a poor man once myself, and had to ride on horseback just as you do now. But don't be discouraged; see how I have risen in the world. Your time may come some day. And, as I shall not see you again before we reach the meeting-house, I bid you good morning," dashed off and was soon out of sight. But the fates were against Brother Bourne that day. The roads grew worse and worse and the buggy moved more and more slowly. Juno seemed to be in a lively mood that morning, and fell into a long, swinging trot, as if she thought she and her master were behind time. In about an hour he began to see the glinting of the bright mounting of the buggy. At length he came in full view of it and could see Brother Bourne whipping up his weary horse and occasionally putting out his head and looking back. It was clear he did not wish to be overtaken at that time by his pursuer; but there was no help for it, and soon they were side by side. It so happened that just then something on the other side of the

14

road seemed to attract Brother Bourne's attention, at which he continued looking long enough for your grand. father to have passed on. But he did not.

At length he said, turning his face to him : " Brother Ross, what disgusting things these buggies are ? If it were not for the grandeur of the thing, I would much rather be on horseback like you." Here they both broke down and had a hearty laugh. "The grandeur of the thing," became a saying with your grandfather afterwards, and he would repeat it when he observed any one sacrificing comfort and convenience to show.

Subsequently, Elder Bourne and several other preachers were entertained by one of their hospitable brethren, where were several handsome young ladies, one of whom was named Charity. After they retired to their rooms, a discussion rose about the comparative beauty and accomplishments of the young ladies.

An appeal was finally made to Elder Bourne for his opinion, when he said : " In my judgment, my brethren, the greatest of these is Charity." I know you will be interested in learning that he and the fair Charity, in whose favor he decided, were afterwards married.

Elder Bourne heartily concurred in your grandfather's views, and said, as Elder Fort had done before, they were right, and he never intended to preach the hard old doctrine again, but proclaim the great truth which he thought the Bible clearly taught, that salvation is free to all who will avail themselves of the offered pardon.

He was a very fluent speaker, and, when animated, had a peculiar tone of voice which many thought very pleasing. His discourses were adorned with many beautiful quotations from the Bible, selected and applied with taste and judgment.

I remember to have heard him when speaking of those who come to see and feel their own sinful nature, repeat with great effect some of the sublime verses in the sixth chapter of Isaiah:

" In the year that King Uzziah died I saw also the Lord sitting upon a throne high and lifted up, and his train filled the temple. Above it stood the seraphim; each one had six wings; with twain he covered his face, and with twain he covered his feet, and with twain he did fly. And one cried to another and said: Holy, Holy, Holy is the Lord of Hosts; the whole earth is full of his glory. And the posts of the door moved at the voice of him that cried, and the house was filled with smoke.

" Then said I: Woe is me for I am undone, because I am a man of unclean lips, and I dwell in the midst of a people of unclean lips, for mine eyes have seen the king, the Lord of hosts."

He often made quotations from the older British poets, such as Milton and Young, with whom he seemed familiar, and the lines he repeated were always appropriate, giving force and weight to his thoughts. I first heard him preach near the residence of a worthy brother named Ransom Tinsly, near what is now called the " Big Pond," formerly, " Renfroe's Pond" in the southern part of Todd County, Kentucky.

Elder Bourne was born in Virginia, September 12, 1778, and died October 13, 1823, in the fifty-first year of his age. It pleased the Master in whose vineyard he had labored long and faithfully to remove him to his reward, though in the midst of his usefulness and in the maturity of his faculties. The news of his death brought sorrow to the hearts of many, but to none more than to the brother by whose side he stood when friends such as he were few.

I may in passing here state that about this time in the year 1818, the Little West Fort Church was organized.

Until then it was an arm or branch of Spring Creek
Church. When constituted your grandfather became its
pastor, and acted as such about forty-two years. Of this
church you and your grandfather were members when they
died. Elder S. S. Mallory became its pastor after his death
in 1860. Seldom perhaps has been witnessed a greater
degree of esteem and brotherly love than subsisted between your grandfather and Elder S. S. and John Mallory who were members of this church. They were raised
up under his ministry; and on the one side there was
something resembling filial love and reverence; and on
the other, parental affection and regard, which knew no
abatement to the last. In his old age their names seemed
to sound pleasant in his ears, and a visit from them appeared to afford him the sincerest pleasure. It was one
of those pure unselfish friendships, so pleasant to witness
and so creditable to the human heart. Only one of these,
S. S. Mallory, is still living—an honored member of the
old church.

In its palmy days the Little West Fork Church was a
large and flourishing body of Christians imbued with as
much of the true religious element as could any where be
found. When a boy I was a regular attendant at these
meetings, and well remember many of the old brethren
and sisters, who, on account of their piety and Christian
spirit, still remain with me the ideals of the Christian
character. Many of these are dead; many moved away
to find homes elsewhere; but I learn it still numbers
about eighty members. May it again revive and flourish
as in the days of its former prosperity.

CHAPTER XXX.

FORMATION OF BETHEL ASSOCIATION.

ALL the churches of the Red River Association became at length more or less agitated by the preaching of the new doctrine. They had the same creed, but all the ministers were not preaching in accordance with it. A direct collision, however, seldom or never occurred. A coolness was at first observable. To this succeeded something like aversion, until finally the brethren could no longer be seen sitting together in the same pulpit.

The advocates of the milder doctrine boldly proclaimed their views, but avoided the mistake, too common among reformers, of discussing them incessantly. When these subjects came up naturally in their preaching they noticed them, and then passed on to that which lay nearer their hearts, trying to persuade men in Christ's stead to be reconciled to God, and leaving the impression on the minds of the hearers that they wished them to become Christians rather than proselytes. This is a great element of success in all public speaking. He that leaves on the minds of his audience the impression that it is their good he has at heart, and not their votes or support, will always be listened to with greater interest, all else being equal.

In some of the churches a majority was in favor of the old, in others of the new, and in others again they were nearly equal. In none of these cases, however, did they bring to trial and excommunicate each other, but granted letters of dismission, which each one could take, and unite with any other church that held views similar to his own. In these letters the old formula of " the same faith and order"—was not often inserted, I think, but an acknowledgment simply of their being in good standing and fellowship in the churches they had left. In this way, by the simple operation of the forces of attraction and repulsion, the kindred elements, so to speak, were brought together and united. In a few cases, however, an effort was made to do something more.

In the year 1823, his brother, Christopher Owens, a worthy member of Spring Creek Church, preferred a charge of preaching unscriptural doctrine against Brother Ross. The church immediately took action in the case, and decided by a unanimous vote that in its judgment, Brother Owens was mistaken, and he withdrew the charge. But it is probable he was not satisfied on the subject, as he and his wife soon after applied for letters, and left the church. He has been mentioned in this narrative before —was a good man and one of your grandfather's earliest friends. I believe it was thought he had been put forward by some other person who did not wish to be known in the affair. Had the charge been that your grandfather had preached contrary to the creed, it could have been easily sustained, for it was clear he had been doing this. No doubt, the old brother thought the Bible and the creed were pretty much the same thing, and that preaching against one was the same as opposing the other.

About the same time one of the sisters, a prominent member of the same church, who always expressed herself freely, demanded a letter from the church as she said " on principle," declaring it to be her belief that "if she was a child of God, at all, it was long before she was regenerated." In this, as one might say, "*rem tetigit acu*," "She touched the subject with the point of her needle," for all orthodox Calvinists believe they were the children of God while yet in their sins.* She requested, moreover, that this declaration should be committed to record, and accordingly it was put on the journal and her letter given her.

Elder John S. Wilson about this time preached a sermon at Drake's Pond Church from Rom. 1 : 16, " For I am not ashamed of the gospel of Christ : for it is the power of God to salvation unto every one that believeth." In his remarks he said, " The Atonement is general, and all who will may avail themselves of its benefits." Soon after a number of the brethren and sisters met—drew up a protest against such a declaration, and set their names to it. Some of these you have seen and remember well—honest and upright men, as well as high toned Calvinists.

I mention these incidents to show you what was going

---

*This does " Orthodox Calvinists" great injustice. They do not believe that any who are "in their sins" are *really* the children of God, whatever they may be in the divine purpose. There are certain statements of the Scriptures which they fully believe, and which clearly settle the whole question :—1st. The Apostle says to the Galatians, " Ye are all the children of God by faith in Christ Jesus ;" of course then, not before faith is exercised. 2. He says to the Ephesians, " After that ye believed, ye were sealed with the Holy Spirit of promise," not before they believed. 3. He says again to the Ephesians, that when in their unrenewed state, they "were without [outside of] Christ, being aliens from the commonwealth of Israel and strangers from the covenants of promise, having no hope and without God in the world ; but now in Christ Jesus [that is, after that ye believed], ye who sometimes were afar off are made nigh by the blood of Christ." It is often difficult to do exact justice to those whose views do not accord with our own.   J. M. P.

on during these years among the churches. Coming events were beginning to cast their shadows before. Many lamented the breaking up of the old brotherhood which now seemed inevitable, and days of fasting and prayer for the peace of Zion were often appointed by the churches, as may be seen by referring to the church records of the time.

"At length, in 1823, a convention of delegates from the churches of the Red River Association was appointed to meet at Union Meeting-house, in Logan County, Kentucky, with the view professedly of establishing peace within its bounds." To this convention your grandfather, your granduncle, Edward G. Walton, and Mr. Bryan Whitfield were sent as delegates by the Spring Creek Church. "The proposed object was a good one, and it is not strange that a majority voted for the measure."

But when the Convention met it soon became apparent that it was the object of many leading members who were opposed to your grandfather's doctrinal views to put *him* on his trial, condemn and suppress *them*. The charge, though, was that he had disturbed the peace of the Association by preaching doctrines contrary to the creed, or "*Abstract of Principles.*" This took him rather by surprise, as he expected to be called to account for preaching doctrines not in accordance with the Scriptures.

His promptness, sagacity and coolness on this occasion, I remember to have heard spoken of with admiration long afterwards. He at once refused to be tried by the Creed as of any binding authority, and said :

"Inasmuch as that instrument itself declares that the word of God *is the only rule*, then there is no other, and I will be tried by no other The creed itself confesses its want of authority when it declares, in its very first article, that the word of God·is the *only* rule. The creed i the work of man ; the Bible, of God ; and as the heavens are higher than the earth, so is the authority of the Bible higher than that of the creed. I object not to a creed as such. It simply expresses one's belief as to what the Bible teaches, and so far is not objectionable. All men who believe anything have a creed, either written or unwritten. The word creed means a belief. Prove that my preaching is not in accordance with the Bible, and I submit. Quote the Bible, and I listen with reverence ; but not the creed, for the sake of our holy religion and a decent respect for the common sense of mankind. I stand here able to prove, as I think, that the doctrinal views I advocate are in accordance with the sacred oracles. That the Atonement is general and unlimited, sufficient for all. That salvation is offered to all who will accept it, without money and without price. That all men are the proper subjects of gospel address, and that the gospel is indeed the power of God unto salvation to every one that believeth."

The victory, so to speak, was now won. When the scene shifted from the creed to the Bible it was decisive. There was no one willing to meet him there, for few had studied it as he had done.

One of his friends, whom I mainly follow on this subject, says :

" Never did he display a loftier moral courage than on this occasion. His opponents were taken by surprise. They expected to make it appear that his preaching conflicted with the ' Abstract of Principles ;' but when he took his stand on the capital truth announced in the first article, it threw them into an embarrassment from which they could not recover. They were afraid to meet him in argument if the Bible alone was to be appealed to. He presented his views, and sustained them by the word of God.

" His opponents now proposed that the whole subject be dropped, and that they should live in peace. This was agreed to. But when the Association met next year, there was no peace, but the same collision in doctrinal sentiments. Elder Ross now proposed in ' Committee of Arrangements,' a peaceable division of the Association. * * * The recommendation of the Committee was adopted by the Association, and the body was divided.

" The division was nearly equal in *numbers*, though a majority of the churches remained in the Red River Association. Those who withdrew

14*

from the body, recommended to the churches of which they were members to send messengers to meet at Mount Gilead (now Allensville), with a view to the formation of a new Association. The recommendation being carried out, the Convention met October 28th, 1825, and organized a new Association which was styled, and is yet styled, Bethel.

"The churches entering into the organization were the following: Red River, Spring Creek, Drake's Pond, Mt. Gilead, Bethel, Little West Fork, Hopkinsville [then called New Providence], and Pleasant Grove. The three following churches were received by petition afterwards—Elkton, Lebanon, and Mount Zion.

"As soon as it was resolved to form a new Association, the messengers from Union and Russellville withdrew. They were in favor of a different policy. They wished the Red River Association to remain undivided and still hoped that peace might be restored. It is proper to say that these two churches, not many years after, united with the Bethel Association, Russellville, in 1828, and Union in 1830."

After the division was agreed upon, it was carried out in a way highly creditable to both parties, as the following, extracted from the minutes of the nineteenth session of Red River Association, will show:

"The Association agrees to divide, as recommended in the report of the committee, as follows: We recommend that the Association be divided into two Associations. The upper district to be called the Red River Association; the lower one to be called ————, giving each and every church in each district choice as to which Association it will join and live in. And further, if this plan should be adopted, we recommend to the Association to advise the churches, if any member or members should be dissatisfied on conscientious sentiments of religion, to give them letters of dismission to join any church in either Association.

"*Resolved*, That we recommend the above advice to the Churches.

"*Resolved*, That all the delegates from the churches who feel themselves now authorized to unite with the lower Association [Bethel], enter into the house and appoint the time and place when and where they will meet to organize and name such Association; and that those who wish to unite with said lower Association are requested to meet at Mount-Gilead by their messengers on Friday before the fifth Lord's Day in October next, agreeable to this resolution. Of those who feel themselves authorized to form said lower Association, it is requested that each send three messengers. Elder William Tandy is requested to preach the Introductory Sermon.

"*Resolved*, That our Treasurer, after paying the expenses of this Association, divide the balance of the money between the two Associations, having respect to the number of churches in each."

Thus, nineteen years after its organization, the old Red River Association, which so long represented all of Baptist sentiment in this portion of the country, was, for satisfactory reasons, divided.

At the formation of Bethel Association it consisted of eight churches, as already stated, and about seven hundred members. Before your grandfather's death, there were sixty-two churches and *more than seven thousand members !* This, too, notwithstanding the numbers that left it and joined what is now called the " Christian Church." This high success cheered him in his declining years — a proof, he thought, that his labors and those of his brethren had not been in vain. It was now a power in the beautiful country over which its churches were spread, destined, as he fondly hoped, to be a blessing to generations in the far distant future.

Of all the ministers who met in the Convention at Mount Gilead, not one is now living; and of the delegates, since the recent death of the venerable D. J. Burks, only one is left, A. G. Slaughter, of Hopkinsville, Kentucky, an intimate and long-cherished friend of your grandfather, who, as you may remember, stood near his grave at his burial in 1860.* Thus the stream of time, on its mighty but silent current, bears away the generations of men.

You will see by my quotations how much I am indebted to the *Funeral Discourse* by Rev. J. M. Pendleton, in the " Southern Baptist Review," September, 1860.

* Since dead.

CHAPTER XXXI.

AFTER the formation of Bethel Association in 1825, it continued to grow and flourish for a number of years under the labors of its pious and influential ministry. And as I remember to have seen them all and to have heard them preach frequently, I propose giving you briefly the impression left on my mind in regard to them as respects their character and style of preaching.

But before doing this, in order to keep you advised of our family history, I must inform you that in 1824 your grandfather sold the tract of land on which we had lived the ten or twelve years preceding, and removed to the place he called Cedar Hill, some ten or twelve miles farther east, but still in Montgomery County.

He had become convinced by sad experience that the place was unhealthy, or this, together with the belief that he would never be able to procure water on it by digging wells, was his chief inducement to leave it. You will remember that cisterns had not then come into use.

This new home lay on the north side of Spring Creek, which you, when a little child, used to call Grandma's Creek, in which you loved to wade and dabble so well. From a mass of rocks on the north side of the creek, where also was the house, issues the small spring of pure cold

312

water, so highly prized by him after having lived so long without this great luxury.

The old house, as you remember, stands on an elevation overlooking the creek, which is here bordered by cedar trees.   Its name was suggested by the hill and the cedars growing on it.   Here he lived about thirty-two years; and to it was more attached than to any place he had ever owned.   I need not describe to you the fine old oaks, interspersed with the sugar-maple, mulberry, and other trees, that surrounded it, or the deep verdure of grass growing under them.   It was a pretty place when you last saw it, is so still, and there is reason to believe it will long so continue, since it has great natural beauty and has come into the possession of a family of taste and refinement who can appreciate it.

The house was built by your grandfather, assisted by the neighbors, who were little less interested in the work than himself, so much were they pleased to have him among them.   Here he lived till age and infirmity made it necessary for him to leave it, and live with some one of his children.   His intention at first, you may remember, was to live with me, but he finally decided to make his home in the family of your aunt Nancy Morrison, near Pembroke, Christian County, Kentucky.   His desire to be among his brethren of the Bethel Church and the people of that community, for whom he always retained a particular attachment, decided him to make his home there.

After this digression, I continue my reminiscences of the preachers of the Bethel Association as proposed.

As Elders Fort, Tandy, and Bourne, have already been mentioned I will next speak of Elder Robert Rutherford.

He was born near Jedburgh, Scotland, in 1785. This place, famous for its ancient monastery, and for the school in which Thomson, the poet, was educated, is situated about thirty-six miles southeast of Edinburgh; near the Cheviot Hills.

He left England in 1816 for the United States, and in 1818 or 1819, came to Russellville, Kentucky, where, being a tailor by trade, he worked some time at that business. I regret not being able to give you some account of his history, as it would no doubt be very interesting.

As a man and a Baptist preacher he was so prepossessing that he soon won the esteem and confidence of the whole brotherhood, and of none more than of your grandfather, who soon came to love him as a brother, and, like Paul and Barnabas, they traveled and preached together for many years among the churches of Bethel Association.

In 1833, when your grandfather visited his native State, Elder Rutherford accompanied him, and became greatly endeared to him by his kindness during the journey. They left home, in the month of November, intending to spend the winter in North Carolina, preaching to the people and visiting old friends and localities interesting to him on account of early associations, and returning home the next spring. His brother James, then an old man, and his youngest sister Elizabeth were still living; the former in Bertie, the latter, in Martin County. These he greatly desired to see once more, and to visit again and for the last time the graves of his father and mother which he had left behind twenty-six years before.

The weather soon after they left became very inclement, and in crossing the mountains your grandfather took a deep cold, so that when he reached the end of his journey he was quite ill. This deranged all their plans and brought on a depression of spirits from which he could not rally. This was increased when he noticed the changes that had taken place. Nearly all whom he wished to see were either dead or had removed to distant States as he had done, some to Kentucky, some to Tennessee, and others again to Alabama or Mississippi.

A singular illusion, too, which he attributed to the state of his health, took possession of his mind. The very face of the country seemed to have undergone a great change. Where he thought there had been little hills or elevations there were none. The ground on which his father's house had stood, and which he remembered as being somewhat elevated was now a dead level. One thing and one only seemed unchanged, the beautiful Roanoke, on whose surface he had sported in his boyhood and youth, still swept along its sandy shores.

Finding he had contracted a slow fever, and believing if he remained there, he would not recover, he stayed a short time with his brother and sister, and preached a few discourses only, and then bade them adieu, and turned his face homeward. To our amazement, in the middle of January, when we thought they were in Carolina safe among their friends, they rode into the yard and dismounted.

He was so changed by fatigue and sickness that we hardly knew him, and he always afterwards seemed to think of his journey with a sort of horror. No one could have been more grateful for the kindness and sympathy of his friend during this long and weary journey than he was.

I remember to have heard him, after his return, mention a few incidents that occurred. One was the beautiful meteoric display of what was called the "falling stars" on the 13th of November while they were among the mountains of Tennessee. This he described as one of the most beautiful sights he had ever seen. They fell thick all around from the upper regions of the atmosphere in large flecks of snowy whiteness, and from a cloudless sky.

He spoke also of the deep emotion manifested by Elder Rutherford, when gazing upon the sublime mountain scenery often presented to view; he would stop in the road at certain points, and, sitting on his horse, survey in the distance mountains piled on mountains, lost in admiration of the beauty and grandeur of the scene. Did they bring to his mind the gray, historic mountains of his native land?

I heard him more than once speak of a little incident that occurred near Chapel Hill, where is the famous University of North Carolina, of which he always seemed to think with interest and pleasure. Here they stayed all night, and were put into a room to sleep where were several beds. Soon after they, weary with their day's travel, had lain down to rest, two little boys who were there at school came into the room, and, after they had undressed, knelt down by their bedside, placed their hands together, palm to palm, and repeated their prayers; then lay down and fell asleep. He could but invoke a blessing on them as they lay in their peaceful slumber.

Elder Rutherford, being skillful with the needle, made up all his own clothing, even his shirts. The sisters complained of him for this, and would most cheerfully have done all his sewing for him had he permitted them. Sometimes, when he had clothes to make or repair, he came to your grandfather's and remained several weeks, sewing, reading, and conversing alternately. In his intercourse with the family he was very pleasant and cheerful, and when I happened to be at home from school, during his visits, I enjoyed his society very much. Seeing him at work one day on a pair of trowsers, he appeared to get on with them so easily, I thought I could make a pair, too, and went to your grandmother for the cloth. She gave it to me, and he cut them out and showed me how to put them together. I took a seat by him, and we talked and sewed away like two tailors for some time. The next day I finished them except the button-holes, and commenced on them. On finishing one, I thought it had rather a queer look. It was perfectly round, and such edges! I thought I had better show it to him before beginning another, and carried it to him for that purpose. On seeing it he dropped his work, put both hands to his face and laughed until the tears ran down his cheeks. I was rather disconcerted, for though I did not think myself it had the right look, I had no idea it was so bad as that. It was some time before he became composed. When he did he made me pick out all the stitches and work it over again. When finished, he pressed them for me, made me put them on, and said : " they did very well, considering."

On asking him one day when we were talking of Scotland and Burns, which of his songs he thought most beautiful, he answered without hesitation : " Of a' the Airts the wind can blaw." On turning to the book and reading it, I thought he could not be far wrong. It ran thus:

> " Of a' the airts the wind can blaw,
>   I dearly like the west,
> For there the bonnie lassie lives,
>   The lassie I lo'e best.

> There wild woods grow and rivers row,
>   And mony a hill between ;
> But day and night my fancy's flight,
>   Is ever wi' my Jean.
>
> I see her in the dewy flowers,
>   I see her sweet and fair ;
> I hear her in the tunefu' birds.
>   I hear her charm the air.
>
> There's not a bonnie flower that springs
>   By fountain, shaw, or green,
> There's not a bonnie bird that sings,
>   But minds me o' my Jean."

This set my fancy at work, and I soon made out a sad, romantic story. He had been in love that was certain. And this beautiful song, in his mind was associated with some fair Scottish maid, who had either died or married another, I could not tell which. After this there was no place left for another love. Then bidding adieu to his native land where all his young hopes lay buried, he crossed the stormy seas. It was distressing to think of it.

He made his home with Mr. William Dickinson, who lived in Christian County, Kentucky. Here he lived about twenty years, I think. Mr. Dickinson and his wife were kind-hearted, friendly people who had no children, and were members of the " Christian Church," while Elder Rutherford was a thorough Baptist in principle ; yet such was the Christian charity of these excellent men, that no abatement of friendship and esteem was ever felt.

Elder Rutherford was a zealous, earnest, and impressive preacher. He studied the Bible much, and his knowledge of its teachings was thought to be both extensive and accurate. His memory was stored with numberless beautiful passages which he used as gems to adorn his sermons. He spoke with ease, and his rich native brogue was very pleasant to the ear. His countenance while speaking beamed with love and good'will to all mankind, and all were delighted to see him rise in the pulpit to address them. I doubt if a purer man ever lived among us; or if there was in all his acquaintance an individual who did not love and esteem him. For many years he was the beloved pastor of Mount Zion and Salem churches. He and your grandfather preached much together, not among the neighboring churches only, but in distant localities which were destitute of religious instruction.

But at length the work assigned him by his Master was finished. Being on his way to the Concord Association, he was prostrated by an attack of congestive fever at Springfield, Robertson County, Tennessee. There, after a few days' illness, he died. Those who stood near him in his last moments remember to have heard him more than once repeat, in a low tone, the word: " Victory." Yes; the battle had been fought, the victory won.

He died on September 12, 1841, in the fifty-sixth year of his age. His grave may be seen where he died, far from his early home and the land of his fathers, but among a people and a brotherhood in whose memory his name and his virtues remain embalmed.

He was about the medium height and well formed. His complexion was generally fresh and healthy, but sometimes a little pale. His general appearance was serious and thoughtful, though in the social circle he was quite talkative, very polite and affectionate, and extremely fond of an innocent joke. His manners were dignified and easy.

Since writing the above, I have seen an obituary of Elder Rutherford, written by Elder Robert Williams. It is so appropriate and interesting, I know you will read with pleasure the following extract:

" Elder Rutherford was born in Scotland, but I know nothing of his history before his coming to this country, eighteen or twenty years ago. From that time he has been a useful and able minister of the New Testament, as well as a pious and devoted Christian. Our lamented brother was universally esteemed by all who knew him for his purity and amiable disposition, and was very remarkable for his prudence. I have known him for the last fifteen years, but never heard any one say he had acted imprudently in anything. Indeed, all who saw him might have said: ' Behold an Israelite, indeed, in whom there is no guile.' He was one of the most evangelical preachers in the land, and all were much edified and delighted with his sermons, which were but a tissue of Bible thought. When preaching he manifested great earnestness and great affection for his congregations. The goodness of God and his love manifested for a lost world, together with the practical duties of religion, were the themes on which he delighted to dwell."

But I need not attempt to describe him. His character is too well known. His praise is in all the churches, and he yet lives in the memory of his brethren, and will long continue to do so. His death was such as might have been expected. " Mark the perfect man and behold the upright, for the end of that man is peace."

From the commencement of his illness he expressed entire resignation to the will of God concerning life or death. He said to a brother: "I shall not rise from here; but I have a desire to depart and be with Christ.'

CHAPTER XXXII.

ELDER WILLIAM WARDER, if I remember correctly, was a little above medium height, of a frame rather spare and delicate, with a mild and prepossessing countenance. When he rose in the pulpit to speak all soon became fully impressed with the belief that he felt a deep interest in their spiritual welfare. Notwithstanding his emotional nature, he was a close and logical reasoner, and very soon fixed the attention of his audience by the strength and force of his arguments.

He often traveled and preached in company with Elders Isaac Hodgen and Jeremiah Vardeman, two distinguished Baptist preachers from upper Kentucky. They held the same doctrinal views as did the Baptists of Bethel Association, and sometimes visited their brethren in the Green River country and preached among them. No church in those days was large enough to hold the immense crowds that would assemble to hear them. In summer they collected under the trees and covered, as it seemed to me, whole acres of ground.

Elder Vardeman, I thought then and still think, was among the most eloquent speakers I ever heard. His face was large and handsome, his head massive, sitting finely on his shoulders, his height six feet, and his weight over three hundred pounds. A noble specimen of the Kentuckian of those days.

321

The earliest glimpse we have of him may be seen in the life of Elder John Smith, that famous old hardshell Baptist, who afterwards joined the "Christian Church," and according to President William, his biographes, *whipped out* nearly everything in upper Kentucky that encountered him during the religious wars of that period.

It is stated that in the early setlement of Kentucky, having been sent by his father to a mill about one hundred miles distant, to procure a little seed corn, on arriving there he heard the lively strains of a violin, and the nimble feet of dancers on a puncheon floor in a house near by. He approached it and saw the fiddler himself, the most conspicuous figure in the merry group, "a young man of fine face and form, dressed in a gay coat and yellow velvet trousers." This was young Jeremiah Vardeman, afterwards one of the most distinguished pulpit orators of his day in Kentucky.

This was perhaps about the time your grandfather, on the other side of the mountains, was leaving home at night and attending similar frolics to the great unhappiness of his parents. Verily it is difficult to tell where the youth of eighteen or twenty, full of life and gayety, will be found twenty or thirty years hence. Other thoughts after this took possession of young Vardeman's mind which led him to high distinction among the people as a preacher.

When he arose to speak in the midst of a vast assemblage the hum of voices soon died away. At the first he would speak in a low, but very distinct tone, and to my fancy had the appearance, for some moments, of one contemplating some distant object. Gradually his voice, which was rich and powerful, became more and more elevated in its tones, his attitude more and more commanding, and his words and sentences fell with greater emphasis and power, until finally his oratory, like an inundation, would sweep over his audience. and seem to amaze, astonish, and bewilder it. For me, after hearing Elder Vardeman preach, I never doubted the effect Paul's discourse is said to have had on Felix the imperial governor of Judaea; or Cicero's on the great Roman Dictator, or Sheridan's on the British House of Commons in the trial of Warren Hastings.

These were the palmy days of eloquence in Kentucky. Not only the pulpit, but the bar, the forum, and the national councils were illustrated by it—the days of Clay, Barry, Crittenden, Pope, Rowan, and others. Strange, is it not, that poetry and eloquence will rise and flourish at certain periods in such perfection, and then fall into neglect and comparative decay?

Thinking that perhaps, being young, I might have formed exaggerated notions of the effects of Elder Vardeman's preaching, I have inquired of others since, and particularly of one who was born and brought up near where he lived in Kentucky, attended his church, knew him well, and often witnessed the effects of his preaching. He fully confirmed the truth of my early impressions. From his description of what he had seen and heard, one would be forcibly reminded of the days of Whitefield and the Wesleys.

Elder Vardeman, however, lived to see his usefulness and influence greatly impaired. When the doctrines of the " Current Reformation " were first presented to the people by Elder Campbell, he adopted them to some extent; but when he saw their tendency more fully, he retraced his steps. Thus he lost favor with the new party, and, at the same time, with the old brotherhood. This involved him in trouble and perplexity and he determined to leave the theatre of his brilliant success in former years and remove to Missouri. He accordingly sold his Kentucky home, settled in that State, and soon after died, affording a melancholy example of the vicissitudes of human life. It is probable the troubled condition of the churches he so much loved during the upheaval caused by the Reformation under Alexander Campbell, contributed to his untimely death.

Elder Warder, accompanied by Elder Isaac Hodgen, visited Virginia on a preaching tour in 1817, and I have heard that their success was great beyond their expectations. The Virginia Baptists were delighted with this visit from their western brethren; religion was revived among them, and great numbers added to the churches where they preached.*

He was for many years pastor of the Baptist Church at Russellville, Kentucky, near which place he lived. To this church, and to the sister churches in the surrounding country he delighted to preach, and of no one could it be said with more truth that, like Paul, he " warned every one night and day with tears," until removed to a higher and nobler sphere.

On account of the purity of his life and his beautiful Christian character he will be held in affectionate and lasting remembrance by the churches of Bethel Association.

---

* These two able ministers attended the Old Triennial Convention for Foreign Missions, which met in Philadelphia in 1817. On their way home, they preached for some time in Virginia, and there was a remarkable revival of religion under their labors. No doubt there are now a few living in Virginia who remember that year as one of " the years of the right hand of the Most High."   J. M. P.

Elder Warder was born June 8, 1786, and died August 9, 1836, in the fiftieth year of his age. His grave may be seen in the Baptist cemetery at Russellville. On the stone that marks his last resting place these words are written:

" In the days of his youth he became pious, and devoted himself to the ministry of the gospel. In the thirty-sixth year of his age he was united in marriage to Miss Margaret Morehead. He was a kind husband and fond father. Before his God, he walked humbly; before man, uprightly."

Elder JOHN S. WILSON was born in Franklin County, Kentucky, July 3, 1795. Much care is said to have been taken with his early religious education by his pious and excellent mother, and he remained under its influence until about fifteen years of age, when religious restraint became irksome to him, and he finally threw it off altogether, and became thoughtless and wicked.

At length in the eighteenth year of his age, under the preaching of Elder Isaac Hodgen, he was converted, and baptized at Mount Gilead Church, Adair County, Kentucky, of which he became a member. In the twenty-third year of his age, he was married to Miss Martha Waggener, whom I have often heard spoken of as being a most estimable lady. She was a first cousin of your uncle, S. T. Waggener of Russellville, Kentucky. In the year 1822, in the twenty-seventh year of his age, he was led to believe that it was his duty to preach the gospel, and would often engage in exhortation and prayer. The church, being pleased with his promise of usefulness, granted him license and requested him to preach for them. Soon after he was ordained to the ministry and received a

15

call to the pastoral care of the Lebanon Church, Todd
County, Kentucky.

I may here remark that opinions differ among the various denominations of Christians in regard to whence the
call to preach the gospel is derived. Some think it comes
directly from the church, and that the individual should
be prepared for ministerial duties by a course of regular
study, as for the practice of law, medicine, or any other
profession. Others, and among these the Baptists, believe
the call comes directly from the Holy Spirit, who im-
presses the minds of some men in a special manner with a
belief that it is their duty to preach the gospel ; and that
the individual so impressed feels a desire above others,
for the salvation of men and the spread of the gospel.

They do not, however, undervalue learning, study, and
general information. On the contrary, these are held in
high estimation. But the ability to edify the church ; to
expound the Sacred Writings by a close personal study of
the Bible ; to awaken their fellow-men to a sense of the
value and importance of religion, and to adorn the doctrines they preach by a pious life and godly conversation,—these they value in their preachers more than all
besides.

It is customary with them when an individual of the
church professes to have the above-mentioned impressions
of duty, to grant him a license to preach, and then, if he
gives promise of becoming a useful laborer in the vineyard, though an humble one, to call a presbytery and have
him solemnly set apart for the work by the laying on of
hands and prayer.

This your grandfather considered one of the most re-
sponsible and important duties of the churches, as the

cause of religion depended much on the evangelical character and zeal of those sent out to publish the glad tidings.
And he often took for his text, when preaching ordination
sermons, 1 Tim. 5 : 22 : " Lay hands suddenly on no man,
neither be partaker of other men's sins." That is to say,
by putting them in a position to injure the cause of religion, and by inattention to the lives and characters of the
candidates

It was while he was pastor of the Lebanon Church that
I first saw Elder Wilson and heard him preach in the old
brick church that had been built by Elder Finis Ewing
and his Cumberland Presbyterian brethren. He was a
man of diminutive stature, and apparently unable, physically, to perform the arduous duties assigned to him in
his field of labor. In argument he was thought to be less
able than others of his brethren in the ministry. But, in
persuasive eloquence and exhortation he had few equals, if
any. In his efforts of this kind, he seemed to be able to
touch in rapid succession every topic that could influence
men to turn their thoughts to religion. The forbearance
and long-suffering, goodness and mercy, of God ; Christ's
humiliation and death, in the great work of redemption ;
eternal happiness and endless woe ; the grave, the resurrection, and the final judgment,—were the themes of his
impassioned appeals.

He was, I think, one of the first of the class of preachers among the Baptists called Revivalists. It was something new among them to see men singing, praying, shaking hands, and exhorting all at the same time. Anxious
seats and mourning benches were hardly known. These
things seemed at first to be out of place and indigenous to
other soils and climates. Nor do they seem to be at all

needed, judging the future by the past, which wise men tell us is all we can do.

Elder Wilson preached with success in Southern and Central Kentucky until 1833, when he was chosen as its pastor by the First Baptist Church in Louisville. He was one of the leading spirits in the great revival in and near Shelbyville, Kentucky, in 1835, the most considerable ever known, perhaps, in that part of the State, and thus described by Elder George Waller:

" On the Friday before the fourth Lord's Day in May, 1835, a meeting was convened at Shelbyville by John S. Wilson and other brethren in the ministry, most of whom participated freely in the glorious work which then and there commenced, This meeting continued fifteen days, in which time one hundred and one were added to the church in that place by baptism.

"The brethren on their way home stopped at Bethel, five miles east of Shelbyville. Crowds who had been at Shelbyville flocked to Bethel, and in three or four days seventy or eighty were received for baptism. This church continued to receive members till in three months, one hundred and nineteen were received for baptism. Buck's Branch shared lightly, Dover, Buck Creek, Elk Creek, Plum Creek, Taylorsville, and Little Mount, have shared freely in this glorious revival,

" Others of us have borne our humble part in this good work. Among the rest of my brethren it has fallen to my lot to· baptize one hundred and twenty up to this time. Upwards of eight hundred have been added to the Long Run Association in the last three months, and by accounts received it is believed that not less than twelve hundred are the fruits of this glorious revival, commencing at Shelbyville. "

These were brilliant successes; but they were Wilson's last. Like the gallant warrior he won them, but fell in the achievement. He was taken severely ill at the close of these labors, and being conveyed home found that his aged mother, whom he tenderly loved, had just breathed her last. This in his weak and suffering state, hastened his end; and he soon expired. His last words were, "Mother, I am coming after thee." He was about forty years of age when he died. He sleeps in the beautiful cemetery of Louisville; a simple marble slab marking the place where he lies.

You have no doubt been told that when your beloved mother and I were united in marriage he performed the marriage ceremony; and, as is usual in such cases, we ever afterwards thought of him with peculiar interest and regard.

CHAPTER XXXIII.

SKETCHES OF ELDERS CONTINUED.

ELDER ROBERT T. ANDERSON was born in the State of Virginia, April 9, 1792. He emigrated to Green County, Kentucky, 1818, was baptized by Elder William Warder in 1812, and became a member of Mount Gilead Church in Adair County, where in 1828 he commenced preaching the gospel.

He was above medium height, well formed, with dark hair and eyes, a pleasing and cheerful expression of countenance; and more social and lively in company than his brother, Henry T. Anderson, who was an able advocate of the Reformation, and used to preach for us at the Oikadelphia Church.

Of him, Rev. J. M. Pendleton thus speaks :

He was a man of kind heart and excellent qualities. He was between thirty and forty years of age when he began to preach ; his time having been devoted to teaching. Nor did he abandon the school when he became a preacher. He loved to preach, and though willing to devote himself exclusively to the ministry, he found, after making the experiment, that he and his family, could not live entirely of the gospel. Hence, for the greater part of his ministerial life, he taught school five days in the week, preaching every Saturday and Lord's Day, and frequently at night during the week. He was a laborious man, with a large heart, and in proportion to his means, he gave much to objects of benevolence. His sermons were chiefly of the expository class, and many of his pulpit efforts were quite happy. He was a useful man,

330

and baptized many converts, who were the fruits of his labors, and will doubtless be gems in the crown of his rejoicing. He was, for a number of years, Clerk of Bethel Association.

He was fully persuaded for several years, that he had discovered a method by which deaf and dumb children could be taught to speak intelligibly. His benevolent heart was much engrossed with this subject for a time, and he had a number of little boys under his instruction and treatment. The public generally became greatly interested in his scheme, and many thought it would be successful. But it proved otherwise, greatly to his disappointment and regret, since, had it succeeded, he would have been placed high on the roll of public benefactors.

For several years before his death, he was much engaged in what, perhaps, has proved to be the most unprofitable of all the intellectual labors of many good men —the interpretation of the dark prophetic portions of the Bible. It was thought by some that his mind became so much engrossed by these subjects, that its vigor was somewhat impaired.

When the prophet Daniel besought the angel that stood upon the waters, to reveal to him the meaning of his vision, it was said to him : " Go thy way, Daniel; for the words are closed up and sealed till the time of the end." Are we not admonished by this, not to push our inquiries too far, as many have done, from the earliest times, and involved themselves and their readers, in the mazes of endless conjecture and doubt, only to learn when too late, that it all amounted to nothing, or worse than nothing? At the proper time the veil will be lifted, and all that is now obscure will appear distinct and clear. "The secret things belong unto the Lord our God; but the things which

are revealed belong unto us and our children for ever."
Deuteronomy 29 : 29.

As the poet Cowper, has well said :

> "God is his own interpreter,
> And he will make it plain."

Is it not probable that the chief advantages of the
prophecies are derived after their fulfilment? Then they
strike the mind with great force, and yield the most con-
vincing proof of their divine origin.

When the Jew before their accomplishment, read the
prophecies contained in the fifty-third chapter of Isaiah,
what could he understand of them? The most learned
Rabbi, on undertaking to explain them, would have found
them utterly incomprehensible. He never could have
made them point to the life, sufferings, and death of the
promised Messiah. But since their accomplishment, all
see with amazement that the inspired prophet, seven hundred years before, pointed out each particular, as though
he had been an eye-witness, and in the small space of one
chapter, of only twelve verses, has epitomized the gospel.

In 1830, Elder Anderson, preached for the church in
Russellville. In 1831, he settled near Pleasant Grove
Church, eight miles south of Russellville, of which church
he became pastor. He was then called successively to the
pastorate of Hopewell Church, Robertson County, Tennessee, in 1832; of Keysburg Church, in 1834 ; of Hopkinsville Church, in 1839; of Olivet and West Union Churches,
in 1840. He next became pastor of Salem Church, in
Christian County. Then he built up Locust Grove and
Pleasant Grove Churches, the former in Christian, the
latter in Caldwell County, Kentucky. Of this last, and

Olivet, he was pastor when he died. The above will show how much his ministerial labors were sought for, and how active and busy must have been his life.

Elder A. D. Sears, now of Clarksville, Tennessee, in an interesting biographical sketch of Elder Anderson, to be found in the March number of the "Christian Repository" for 1859, observes:

> "Some time last winter, the church at Pleasant Grove, Caldwell County, enjoyed a most interesting revival. The meeting continued several weeks. The cause seemed to demand of him more than usual exertion. He preached continuously through several days. The weather being inclement, he took a severe cold, which continued several weeks after the meeting closed, and finally terminated in neuralgia. This disease first affected his right arm, gradually moved to his head, and ultimately settled over his right eye and terminated in apoplexy, of which he died on the 8th of June. We are thus particular in describing the disease of which he died, because a rumor went abroad that Elder Anderson's mind was affected. This is untrue. Although at times a great sufferer for upwards of three months, the native strength of his intel ect remained unimpaired until the last; and he was always aware of his condition."

Thus, in the sixty-third year of his life, and in the twenty-fourth of his ministry, after long suffering, which he is said to have borne with submissive resignation, this excellent man closed his laborious and useful life, and entered into his final rest. Having turned many to righteousness, he will shine as the stars forever.

I heard Elder W. C. WARFIELD preach, and have seen him occasionally at your grandfather's. "His sermons were by no means of uniform merit. Some of them were well prepared, logical, eloquent, and delivered with great energy. Others betrayed some want of thorough preparation, and were defective in methodical arrangement. This

15*

was more noticed in him than in his co-laborers, on account of his superior educational advantages," and because he had been a student of Princeton Theological Seminary. When his feelings became excited, as was often the case in the close of his sermons, his appeals to the impenitent, in referring to " the terror of the Lord," were striking spec. mens of denunciatory eloquence. Sometimes, with apparent harshness, he admonished sinners of their danger, and warned them " to flee from the wrath to come." In the prime of life he fell beneath the stroke of death. He was born in Lexington in 1796, and died at the residence of Elder William Tandy in Christian County, Kentucky, November, 1835.

ELDER R. W. NIXON was born in Hanover County, North Carolina, May 3, 1799, where he lived till about twelve years of age. His father, Col. Richard Nixon, then emigrated to Bertie County, in the same State, and while living there, had his son placed in the Military Academy at West Point. In 1821, his father came to Tennessee.

Here the son married, in 1822, Miss S. C. Whitfield, daughter of Needham Whitfield, Esq., of Montgomery County, an early friend of your grandfather, mentioned in a former chapter. After his marriage he changed his place of residence to Brownsville, Tennessee, and sold goods for some time in that place. In 1827, he returned to Montgomery County and settled near his wife's father. He made a profession of religion in 1828, and was baptized by your grandfather, as a member of Spring Creek Church. In 1830, he commenced preaching, and in 1831 was ordained to the ministry by your grandfather, and Elder Robert Rutherford.

Some years after, when your grandfather resigned the

pastorate of this church, Elder Nixon was chosen his successor, and continued his pastoral care, until 1857, when he removed to Lauderdale County, Tennessee. "Besides his pastoral care," says a friend and brother, "he rode and preached extensively, as a missionary for the Bethel Association some three years. He spoke of his labors in that department with great satisfaction." After his settlement in Tennessee, he was pastor of several churches and also a missionary, under the patronage of the West Tennessee Baptist Convention.

He died of pneumonia, March 4th, 1881, in the seventy-second year of his age, after an illness of twelve days, during which he suffered exceedingly, often trying in vain to sing some familiar hymn.

"Elder Nixon loved to preach; it was his constant thought. He frequently said: 'A preacher ought to love his work.' His talent for preaching was above mediocrity. The order and systematic arrangement of his sermons were superior. His thoughts were well arranged, and presented to his hearers with a force and energy that arrested attention."

In the language of Elder Joseph Borum, from whose notice of the death of Elder Nixon, the above has been condensed, and for whom he had an unusual attachment, "His work on earth is done. He has gone to receive his reward. Christians will no more hear his words of encouragement. Sinners will no more hear his faithful warnings. Let all remember that the Lord has said : 'They that be wise shall shine as the brightness of the firmament, and they that turn many to righteousness, as the stars forever.' A beautiful and glorious promise to the faithful ambassador of Christ."

Elder Thomas Watts was born in Albemarle County, Virginia, in 1787. He emigrated to Sumner County, Tennessee, about the year 1810. In 1812, he settled in Christian County, Kentucky. After this he resided alternately in various border counties of Kentucky and Tennessee. In 1827, when about forty years of age, he professed religion. In 1830, he began to preach. As a minister of the gospel he was zealous and earnest. As a man and Christian he had the esteem and confidence, not of his brethren only, but of all who knew him. He died in Logan County, Kentucky, May, 1860, a few months only after your grandfather passed away; fortunately escaping the horrors of the impending civil war.

Elder John Mallory completes the number of the brethren in the ministry most intimately associated with your grandfather in giving stability and character to Bethel Association, who have passed away from "this mundane sphere." From a friend I have obtained a copy of the Record made by order of the church to which he belonged, immediately after his death; it is as follows:

"Elder John Mallory was born in Caldwell County, North Carolina, January 5, 1798. While a youth, his father emigrated to Tennessee. In 1828, he professed faith in Christ, and was baptized into the fellowship of the Little West Fork Church by Elder Reuben Ross. Not long after his connection with the church, he was chosen to the office of deacon, which office he held with acceptance and profit to the church until he was licensed to preach in November, 1839.

"In February, 1841, he was ordained to the work of the ministry. The elders who officiated at his ordination were—Reuben Ross, R. Rutherford, R. W. Nixon, and Thomas Watts. Shortly after his ordination he became Pastor of Blooming Grove Church. His work was greatly blessed, and many were added to the church.

"After resigning the pastorate of this church, he was employed several years by the Association as one of her missionaries to preach to the destitute within her bounds.

" On the fourth Sabbath in September, 1862, he was arrested by the Federal authorities at Bay Rock meeting-house, Stewart County, Tennessee, and carried to Fort Donelson, where he was kept a prisoner several days, but finally released on taking the oath of allegiance to the Government. He was soon after taken ill, his disease being contracted while a prisoner from exposure, and died in a few days after at his residence in Stewart County, on the 14th of October, 1862, in the 65th year of his age, leaving a wife and several children and many loving friends to mourn the melancholy close of his life. But their loss is his great gain, for a voice from the volume of inspiration says: ' Blessed are the dead who die in the Lord.'"

He was a good man. I remember him well. At the time of his death the clouds of war hung black and heavy over his unhappy country; but he soon reached the "sun-bright clime," where, " the wicked cease from troubling and the weary are at rest."

To my mind, the memory of such men as Fort, Tandy, Bourne, Rutherford, Wilson, Warder, Warfield, Anderson, Nixon, Watts, and Mallory,—names that have been mentioned in these sketches, is worthy of lasting preservation; for, in many respects, they challenge our admiration. They were all fully persuaded that it was their duty to preach the gospel to their fellow-men; and with this belief, under many discouraging circumstances, they gave themselves to the work. Not one of them, in the full import of the word, could be called a man of learning. Being in most instances poor, they neither had access to books nor leisure to read them. What time they could spare, after providing for their families, they devoted to preaching. Consequently, the Bible was the book they chiefly studied. It thus became the source and fountain of their religious knowledge. This they were compelled to study diligently and to form opinions for themselves in regard to its great and solemn truths, instead of learning the opinions of others from books and lectures.

Although in criticism and dialects they were by no means masters, their knowledge of the sacred writings was, in many instances, both accurate and extensive; and this, aided by no inconsiderable degree of native eloquence and talent, enabled them to present the teaching of the Scriptures with no small degree of power and effect.

The thing that lends a peculiar interest to the memory of these men, is their unblemished characters. It would, perhaps, be difficult to point to the same number of men anywhere, associated together for any purpose, whose lives and characters were more faultless and pure. On this account the churches of the Bethel Association have good reason to felicitate themselves. They stand as bright examples for imitation in the coming years. With men like these to give them dignity and character, they may anticipate a long career of usefulness and honor.

Your grandfather remained till almost the last of those had passed away. This produced a feeling of loneliness and desertion, like that of the traveller who has been left behind by his companions to finish his journey alone.

Remembering that these excellent men have finished their course and will never again appear in the fields of their former labors, their brethren that are left behind might well feel that their loss was irreparable. But, though Elder Williams is no longer in the bounds of Bethel Association, and the familiar face of Elder Holland will no more be seen among them, they still have a corps of able and efficient ministers to carry on the good work. Among them may be mentioned the names of Morrow, Baker, Keen, Sears, Gardner, Lamb, Plaster, Forgy, Crutcher, S. S. Mallory, and Dicken.

CHAPTER XXXIV.*

THE TRUANT.

In order to call your attention to some particulars which could not have been introduced so conveniently at an earlier period, I will go back to the year 1818, and give you some account of them.

There was, at this time, in our vicinity a youth with whom I was well acquainted (it is unnecessary to mention names), who had a great desire to be well educated, and especially to acquire a knowledge of the Greek and Latin languages. He had somewhere picked up a work on Mythology, and read with much interest of the gods, god-desses, demi-gods, and heroes of antiquity. He had also read in Plutarch's Lives, of Cæsar, Hannibal, Pompey, Alexander, and other illustrious characters, and had a great desire to read of all these in the language in which they were originally written. Moreover, he had heard that a course of classical studies would be of great benefit to one who might study a profession, which he hoped he might at some time be able to do. He could not see how he could accomplish these ends, as his father was unable to incur the expense, and, being a preacher, he was a good

* The critical reader may doubt whether this chapter, strictly speak-ing, should have a place in this volume, especially as it does not appear in chronological order. The matters related, however, are not only in-teresting but exciting ; and it is not too much to say that those who read the chapter will be glad of its insertion.

J. M. P.

deal away from his family, which made it necessary that this youth should stay at home to protect and assist his mother, and also to aid in the work of the farm.

Not being able to solve the problem himself, after much reflection he concluded to get the advice of a young man who attended the school, whom he considered a true friend and very wise withal, being several years older than himself. The student listened to the youth's statement of the case very attentively; then inquired if he knew enough to teach a school. He was told that he could read and spell very well, knew a little of Arithmetic and Grammar, and was pretty well up in Geography. " But what about your writing?" His copy-book was produced, and, after examination, he was told it would do.

" Now," said he, "if you will go over into Muhlenburg County, Kentucky, where I am acquainted, you can get a school of fifty scholars, if you want them. The people there, in some places, are thickly settled, and would be the gladdest in the world to have their children taught to read and write a little. But, as you can teach Arithmetic and Grammar, especially if you are willing to *board round*, you can make from one hundred and fifty to two hundred dollars a year with all ease. In this way, in the course of two or three years, you may have four or five hundred dollars in your pockets, and go to school and learn Greek and Latin to your heart's content, study law if you choose, and become famous, perhaps, like Clay, Rowan, and the rest of them."

This scheme appeared so grand and beautiful, and also so *practical*, that he was completely fascinated. It is probable that most boys, at his age, have felt a similar temptation. A few days after this consultation, just as the October sun was rising above the hills east of Hopkinsville, might have been seen a youth about seventeen years of age, with a small bundle in his hand, walking briskly through that part of the town where the old brick semi- nary used to stand. He desires much to pass through this place unknown, so as to escape observation and trou- blesome inquiries. In order to accomplish this, on the night previous, immediately after his supper, he went to his room, made up his bundle, wrote a short note to his mother, as cheerfully as possible, in which he informed her he had started out into the world, to make his fortune, and expected wonderful success; that she was to feel no anxiety on his account; that all his plans had been well considered, and could not possibly fail of success; that, in due time he would write and tell her how he succeeded. He concluded by requesting her to persuade his father to give himself no trouble on his account, or to try to hunt him up, as it would be altogether useless. This note he folded and laid on the table, took his bundle, stepped out into the darkness, and started for Muhlenburg County, via Hopkinsville.

After passing the town as above stated, it being no lon- ger necessary to hasten, he slackened his pace, and pro- ceeded quite leisurely. The day was delightful. No tropic plant in full bloom could outvie in gorgeous color the trees of the forest; every leaf was brighter than the gayest flower, and clothed the forest in variegated and romantic beauty. The traveller, somewhat fatigued by the long walk of the morning, occasionally stopped by the way, and reclined at the roots of some giant tree or on the margin of a stream; thus at the same time he rested himself, and enjoyed the beauty of the surrounding scenery. It was at the season when the woods were filled with wild pigeons, and the squirrels busy, gathering nuts and acorns to store for the coming winter. Whether he reached Muhlenburg County a little earlier or later was to this traveller of little moment.

The feeling that, henceforth, he could act in every respect, just to suit himself, untrammeled, independent, was new and strange, and very agreeable.

At noon, or perhaps a little earlier, he stopped at a wayside cabin and procured refreshment. For this he paid a mere trifle which was received rather reluctantly. After this he pursued his journey till near the close of the day, when he called at a house and obtained lodging for the night. The family consisted of an old man, his wife, and daughter. They were in a good deal of trouble at the time. The husband of the daughter, who had been lately married, had gotten into a difficulty of some kind, which rendered it necessary for him to leave home. After supper, the traveller learned, rather to his embarrassment, that they were all to sleep in the same room. After taking off his coat and hanging it on the back of the chair, as a sort of screen while undressing he turned down the cover, and rolled into bed. He never forgot the luxury it was to relax his weary limbs in that comfortable bed.

He now for the first time, began to feel some misgivings in regard to what he had done. That is, to doubt if he had acted right in leaving home in the manner described. The more he reflected the more uncomfortable he became. He finally determined that if he could not throw off these unpleasant thoughts, rather than be thus annoyed, he would straightway return home. He then fell into a deep sleep from which he did not awake till broad day.

After breakfast he took leave of the kind old people who had entertained him so hospitably. They refused to receive any pay for their trouble and with kind wishes he departed.

With a light heart and buoyant step, he now began the second day's journey, but he had not proceeded far when the unpleasant impressions of the night returned, and continued till noon, when he entered a house on the roadside to rest and procure dinner. The man of the house proved to be a very inquisitive and excitable fellow, and a number of questions and answers ensued as follows :

"If it is a fair question," said the host, "may I ask where you are from ? "

"From Tennessee," was the reply.

"And where may you be going ? "

"To Muhlenburg County, Kentucky."

"From what part of Tennessee did you come ? "

"From Montgomery County."

"And what may be taking you to Muhlenburg County, pray ? "

"I am going there to teach school."

"Indeed ! To teach school did you say ? "

"Yes; to teach school."

"And what can you teach, pray ? "

·"Spelling, reading, writing, arithmetic, grammar, and geography," pronounced very promptly.

"Well, I declare ! you boys, over in Tennessee, must be *peart* lads. What is the name of that last thing you teach ? "

"Geography."

"And what is *that ?* "

"Geography means a description of the Earth its—

lakes, rivers, mountains, oceans, islands, continents, king-doms, and empires."

He begins to show off.

"The Lord save us! And can *you* teach all them things?"

"They are nothing. I can explain to you the torrid, frigid, and temperate zones; the Arctic and Antarctic circles; the eclipses of the sun and moon; the planets primary and secondary, and the tides of the ocean."

"Holy Angels! Stranger, if it's a school you want, you need not go a step from this place. I will get on my horse directly after dinner, go round among the neighbors, and have them all here after breakfast in the morning, and we will make you up a school before you know it. And I want you to board here too. I like to hear you talk."

"Many thanks, but I will first go on to Muhlenburg, and if things do not look favorable there, I can return as you seem to think I can do well here."

"*Think*, did you say? I *think* nothing about it. I *know* it. But, bless me! I don't even know your name yet."

Here the stranger tells his name.

"There it is again," said he. "The very name of the preacher that was down here at the big meeting lately. Any kin?"

"I believe," said the stranger, "nearly all of that name think they are related. But tell me, did the preacher of my name talk pretty well?"

"You may say *that*," said he. "He told us what *a* awful fix we would all be in when we die, if we didn't re-pent and believe the gospel, and begged us so hard to be good, and seemed so sorry for us, that we all fell to crying like our hearts would break, and some of the meanest old sinners in the whole settlement cried like young gals when they are in trouble. Some of them *jined* the church, and they *aint* been so wicked as they *was* before. Some of us were *kinder* shamed of ourselves, for taking on so, but we couldn't help it, for I tell *you* he preached powerful."

The youth never forgot this interview, and it was ever after a pleasant recollection.

After dinner he bade adieu to his lively and kind-hearted host, and started, not for Muhlenburg, but straight for home, which he reached late in the evening of the third day after leaving it. Had he encountered real hardships and dangers on his wild adventure, his reception, on returning, would have more than compensated him. His mother and the children were greatly delighted, and praised him extravagantly for returning, and on his telling her that when he came to think about it, he was satisfied he had acted wrong, and turned back on that account, his mother said, that was just what she thought he would do from the first. This pleased him not a little. He related to her all he had experienced on his travels, and it is probable so poor a tale had never been listened to with deeper interest. It was often mentioned, years after, by the family, as a remarkable event in its history.

When, in turn, he was told all that had occurred during his absence; how business was suspended; the wheel and loom forgotten; how they all sat up till late at night, listening for him to knock at the door; how they watched the gate and looked down the road all the long days; how the neighbors would come in and inquire about him, shake their heads and go away. But it is time we were looking after the youth's father. When he returned home, only the day before his son, from a tour of preaching, and learned what had taken place, he, to use a phrase now in vogue, " was very much demoralized." It was not uncommon at that time, and still less so some years earlier, for wild young " scamps," to leave home for the purpose of "*running the river*," as they called it, which was to get on a keel-boat, barge, or flat-boat, and become regular boatmen. This often made ruffians of them, especially if they ran the lower Ohio River, which was long infested by desperadoes of the worst type. Many no doubt, still remember the bad reputation of " Ford's Ferry" and its vicinity in former times, when traders were murdered for their money, and owners of trading boats with their families were said to have been killed, the goods taken *out*, and the boats burned, and where Ford himself, who it was thought belonged to the gang, was shot dead in his own house, by whom, it was never discovered, though the house at the time was full of men drinking and carousing together. I remember to have seen somewhere a description of the cave, called " The Hole in the Rock," in which these men lived. It was said to be near the river and not far below the Ferry. I once heard a gentlemen speak of an amusing incident in reference to this old Ferry, years after the death of Ford.

He stated that, being on his way to look at some of the fine lands in Illinois, he reached the ferry late in the evening, where he had expected to stay and cross the river next morning. But every thing about the premises appeared weird and uninviting, and brought to his mind the ugly tales he had heard about the place. These took such hold of his imagination, that, notwithstanding respectable people were then owners of the premises, he offered an extra price to be set over the river at once. When he reached the Illinois shore he felt much relieved, but his rejoicing did not last long; for, while riding across the gloomy bottom, he saw a man sneaking along the undergrowth, evidently intending to get into the road just before him. He concluded at once that the man was a robber. Holding his bridle in his left hand, and putting his right into the pocket of his overcoat, where was his pistol, he cocked it, intending, so soon as the suspicious-looking fellow put his hand on the bridle, to shoot him down. Instead of doing this, he stopped short, took off his hat, and bowing politely, said: " Stranger, if you have any to spare, please give me a little piece of terbacker." The " terbacker" being given, there were two happy fellows— one because he had a plug of fine tobacco, the other that he had escaped a rencounter with a supposed robber.

The youth's father had more than once expressed to his mother much anxiety on his account, having observed that his mind seemed to be too much occupied with tales of romantic adventure. Being an ardent admirer of Daniel Boone, who was then hunting and trapping in Missouri, he sometimes, in a rather peculiar way, would say to his mother: " You needn't be surprised if some day I leave home to join Daniel Boone." Having his fears now fully aroused, the father of this truant now determined to set out early next morning in search of him, before he wandered off too far, and I doubt not would have rivaled Ceres in his fabled search for Proserpine, had he not found him; for he was not easily deterred from anything he undertook. Knowing this, the young adventurer made all haste to depart. Late in the day he was happy to discover he was, in Indian parlance, on "the right trail;" and a little before nightfall met a man who said he had seen his father dismount at Elder Horne's gate and go into the house.

Elder Josiah Horne was a Baptist preacher, an excellent man,—one whose "praise was in all the churches" on account of his gentle Christian character. He resided in what was called the Blooming Grove Settlement, some ten or twelve miles below Clarksville. His father had been vainly trying to ascertain what direction the truant had taken, and, when night came, found himself near his friend's residence, and concluded to remain there for the night.

It was dark when the lad reached the place where his father was, and, getting off his horse, went to the door of the room where he and Elder Horne and other members of the family, with several neighbors, were sitting round the fire, rather a melancholy group, having heard the sad news. After knocking, and being invited to "enter," he stepped in. In a moment all were on their feet. Going to his father, he shook hands with him—told him he had reached home safely, and, on learning he was in search of him, had started almost immediately to find him, and had succeeded in tracing him to this house. His father was greatly delighted, and the boy never remembered having seen his expressive countenance more radiant with pleasure than on that happy occasion.

It was evident that a load of anxiety had been lifted off his mind. All gathered round, and a general shaking of hands ensued. "Old Brother Horne" was the happiest person present, your grandfather excepted—for I suppose it is not necessary to use our thin veil any longer.

We had an excellent supper, spent the evening very happily and on the morrow returned home.

CHAPTER XXXV.

DR. CHARLES MERIWETHER AND HON. JOHN W. TYLER.

THE spring after the adventure narrated in our last chapter, your grandfather informed me that there was a school near Dr. Charles Meriwether's, taught by a Mr. Boyer of Todd County, Kentucky, and that he had been invited to take me there to board in the family and attend the school. This proved to be a most fortunate arrangement for me, for there I was received as one of the family, and treated with the utmost kindness. The Doctor had three sons, one near my own age, two younger, and if there was ever any difference made between us, I never perceived it. This kindness made a deep and lasting impression on me; remaining green and fresh in my memory though the changing vicissitudes of many long years. Dr. Charles Meriwether was a native of Albemarle, Virginia. He was a large and handsome man. Let no one suppose he sees his real likeness in the portrait still to be seen in the parlor at Meriville. His form was noble and commanding. His features were cast in nature's finest mold. His smile was of the utmost suavity and kindness, and his expression striking and engaging. However, you need not to be told this, who remember him well, though later in life. I have no doubt that he was the most educated and highly cultivated gentleman in the West at that time. His grandfather, generally known in his day as " Parson Douglas " belonging to the Church of England, came from

Scotland, and settled in Virginia in early times. He was descended from the ancient and powerful house of Douglas, so famous in Scottish history. His mother, Margaret Douglas, married a Welsh gentleman named Meriwether.

Parson Douglas was considered a man of extensive learning and ability. Many books may be still seen at Meriville, the name of the family seat, in which is written : " *Ex libris Gulielmi Douglass.*" One of the books of William Douglas.

After having passed through a liberal course of study in Virginia, Dr. C. Meriwether was sent to the far famed University of Edinburgh, in Scotland, then in its palmy days, where he remained a number of years, and graduated in the school of medicine. I used to get his Diploma—the first one I had seen, and which was a showy affair—and try to decipher the Latin, but with indifferent success. During his sojourn at Edinburgh, he formed the acquaintance of many of the great men who shed luster on the University at that time. I have heard him speak of interviews with Robertson, the historian, then principal of the University ; Blair, the famous rhetorician, and others distinguished for science and literature, who attracted students from all parts of Europe.

After graduating he returned to his native state and practiced medicine. Having an ample fortune, he paid but little attention to collecting his fees. He once showed me a large, well bound book in which all his accounts were made out with care and neatness, which had never been collected. The total amounted to a large sum of money.

About the year 1817 he emigrated from Virginia to Southern Kentucky, and purchased a large body of fertile land in what is now Todd County, lying along the State line. Here he was living when I entered his family as a boarder. I, of course, was amazed at the extent of his knowledge. From the humble, the fascinating science of botany, to the profound subjects of physical and metaphysical learning, he was familiar, having explored them all. And when, after supper, he would remain in the dining-room an hour with me, as he sometimes did, conversing on these and kindred subjects, so interesting was he, the time glided swiftly away. Chemistry seemed to interest him more at that time than any other subject, as wonderful discoveries were then being made in that department. He also took much delight in Mathematics. He said to me on one occasion : " If you will remain with me during the holidays, I will give you any assistance in Geometry you may need." Accordingly I procured Euclid's Elements, the work then in common use, and went to work. When the demonstration of a proposition did not appear clear to .my mind, he would explain, and show me wherein the demonstration lay, in so few words and with such perspicuity, as to excite my admiration and surprise. He concerned himself in all natural phenomena, and when in 1825 those singular and beautiful circles appeared around the sun, which some may still remember, he became greatly interested, and he and Mr. Jefferson, President of the United States, were in correspondence on the subject. They were very wonderful as well as beautiful. Your uncle, Charles A. Meriwether, has in his possession a diagram which his father left, showing the manner in which these circles intersected each other. But in the diagram the lovely rainbow tints were wanting. I think Mr. Jefferson and Dr. Meriwether together discovered what they considered a satisfactory solution ; but, I regret to say, I do not now remember what it was.

During the years I remained in the family, the doctor enjoyed life very much. It was at the time when Sir Walter Scott held the literary world spell-bound. First, by his poetical works, and then by his novels, nothing comparable to which, in the realms of fiction, had appeared previously. The Scottish character was well understood by the doctor, having lived so long in Edinburgh; and when it was so well delineated by the magic pen of the " Wizard of the North," it afforded him unmixed delight.

It was with the comic or lower characters, such as Mompliss, Dandie Dinmont, Captain Dalgetty, that he was most delighted. Old Mause, who appeared to such advantage at the battle of Loudon Hill and on other occasions, was a great favorite with him. Her sneer at " the old woman in scarlet, who used to sit upon seven hills," " as if *one* was not enough for her," amused him particularly. I have heard him say that he had no doubt of having seen the original of the Black Dwarf, the famous " Canny Elshie."

Quite a friendship at this time existed between him and ex-Governor Blount of Tennessee. The latter would come occasionally and spend several days with the doctor. It was a great entertainment to me, at such times, to hear their conversation. Doctor Meriwether was familiar with the progress of literature, arts, and sciences in the old world, and could relate anecdotes of the distinguished men, many of whom he had seen. The Governor, on the other hand, was well versed in the history of our own country, the thrilling events of its early settlements, Gen. Jackson, and the Indian Wars. The Governor was remarkable for being very spare. I doubt your having seen any one more so, who was in health. He often made this

matter of amusement. Being on one occasion at a fashionable watering-place among the mountains of Tennessee,
he was seen by some of the mountaineers, who had
brought venison and other game to sell. They looked at
him inquisitively. At length, one, a little more forward
than the others, said: " Mister, please tell me what
might be your ailment?" "I am afflicted," said the Governor, " with a swelling of the legs," pulling up one leg of
his trowsers to show them. " Well, I never," said the
mountaineer, " the water of these springs is *powerful.*"
The Governor was a most agreeable gentleman, and one
whom Tennessee delighted to honor.

Dr. Meriwether's ideas of economy differed from those
of most men, both then and now. He lived strictly on
his income. If his crops brought him large sums of
money, it was well; if not, it was likewise well. Much or
little, he never went beyond it. This kept him free from
all annoyances of indebtedness. He never bought any
thing because it was cheap. I have heard him say that he
never had during his life, purchased any thing to sell
again, or to make profit on it, but to keep for his own use.
He disapproved of all kinds of gaming and betting. When
any one he esteemed bet money and lost it, he always rejoiced, and would say, " that was the best that could happen to cure him, as no advice and warning is likely to do
any good while one is successful." He was, at the same
time, kind-hearted and liberal, and assisted your grandfather and his family more than any other individual
among his friends. His wife, was also, a very excellent
character. As the mistress of a family she had no superior. Order and system every where prevailed. " She was
not afraid of the snow for her household." It was pleasant

to see her servants in their clean, warm, and comfortable
clothing. All their wants were well supplied, both in
sickness and in health. The most striking trait in her character was her extensive, but unostentatious charity. All
the needy in her vicinity were her beneficiaries. Like the
glorious woman mentioned in the Bible, "She stretcheth
out her hand to the poor, yea, she reacheth forth her hand
to the needy." In the day when " secret things shall be
revealed," but not till then, will all her good deeds be
known. It is pleasant to write and think of characters
such as these. Your maternal grandmother, Mrs. Barbara
Barker, was her sister, and resembled her in all her excellent qualities, and benevolent impulses. The two sisters,
your beloved mother, and Dr. Meriwether were baptized
by your grandfather, and now, after the journey of life,
sleep tranquilly together, in the cemetery at Meriville.

The Shakers, a strange new set, first made their appearance in our country, while I was at Meriville, and
were very active for some time in making proselytes. We
attended one of their meetings, at a place then called the
Cross Roads; since, Graysville. Several elders were present. Their costumes were plain and neat, though singular; their appearance, rather striking.

We had several discourses on that occasion. They said
that all the world eventually would become Shakers.
One of them spelled atonement thus, " at-one-ment" and
said it indicated that all people would, eventually, become
one; and that, *then* Shakerism would appear in all its
beauty and excellence. In conclusion, they sang one of
their songs to a lively air called, " Fire in the Mountains." The chorus of which was

" Babylon is fallen, is fallen, is fallen,
 Babylon is fallen to rise no more."

Some years after this, being on my way to Louisville I
visited their village, South Union, then rather a new
place. At that time dancing was one of their public religious exercises. I saw them perform on Sunday. Two
lines were formed facing each other and extending quite
across their handsome church. A man with a fine voice
sang a quick air, and all fell to dancing, keeping time to
the music, and dancing forward and back. This they continued with spirit until, on a signal, all would stop a few
minutes, during which a short exhortation was given, and
then dancing was resumed. After they had been well
exercised in this way, they were dismissed. There was
no appearance of gayety whatever; yet still, I imagined,
it was rather a pleasant excitement. I have learned
that dancing in public has been discontinued by the
brotherhood. The Shaker religion seems to have been the
most absurd of all " *humbugs*," if I may use a slang term.
The credulity of a large portion of mankind may be re-
lied on to an almost unlimited extent, but it was asking
too much to require belief that the old Lady, Anne Lee,
was a second " manifestation of Christ." This, was bad
enough, but when they forbade " marrying and giving in
marriage," many considering this as being mostly what
they were made for, there was no longer a hope of success. Mahomet and Brigham Young understood human
nature better, and were " wiser in their generation" than
the Shakers. Shakerism must in the nature of the case
die out.

The school at Meriville closed some six or eight months
after I entered. In the mean time Hon. John W. Tyler, a

Virginian by birth, had opened a school in the vicinity.
To this I was sent. I soon came to admire and esteem our
teacher very much. He reached my ideal of a gentleman
in every respect. His knowledge of the Latin was accurate. He translated with great ease and elegance, in
strict accordance with its idiom and grammatical construc-
tion. It was delightful to hear him translate a fine passage
from the classic authors.

After reading Latin with him for several months, I was
one day expressing regret, at not being able to read the
Greek also; he then remarked that he once commenced
learning that language, but for some reason discontinued
it, and added that if I was willing, he would resume it,
and we would study it together. I went into the arrangement with pleasure, hunted up the old Greek Grammar
given me by Judge Brown, and committed it to memory;
then with some difficulty, procured the "Lexicon Schrev-
elii," the meaning of every word in which was given in Latin, and also a very valuable Greek Testament, with a Latin
version, and took my first lesson in John's gospel, which
we read through. We declined all the nouns, pronouns,
adjectives; conjugated all the verbs, pointed out the principal parts of the tenses formed from them, and also the manner of formation, even to the " *Paulo post futurum*," that
terror of the school-boy of those days, and in search of
which an old Greek student is said to have lost his wits.
Westenhall's Grammar gave us a specimen of the Greek
Tree, which consisted of the root of the verb, and all the
tenses or branches formed from it. We took great pleasure in seeing this tree grow up under our pencils, and
spread out its branches, one after another, until it attained
perfection. You must understand that Mr. Tyler was

then a young man, only five or six years older than myself, so that there was a good deal of sympathy between master and pupil. I dwell the longer on these small matters, first, because they go to show the truth of the old adage—" Where there is a will there is a way," and also, because it is pleasant to think of those old school-boy days, in the morning of life.

After John's Gospel we read other books, *Graeca Minora* and *Majora*, Lucian's *Dialogues*, the *Anabasis* and *Cyropœdia* of Xenophon etc., and finally plunged into *The Iliad*, that grand old epic whose sublimity and beauty, notwithstanding its gray antiquity, remain and will remain, a marvel and a mystery; and which, like the deity it describes,

> " Its glory shrouds,
> In gloomy tempest and night of clouds."

Mr. Tyler, from this time continued at the head of a large and flourishing school, till his death in 1866, except the years he was in the Tennessee Legislature, both as senator and member of the lower house. His death filled the whole community with lasting sorrow.

Between him and his family and your grandfather, there were for many years relations of a pleasant kind, the result of mutual esteem and friendship. I always considered him a superior, and in many respects a remarkable, man. While all proceeded smoothly in his school, he was singularly mild and gentle. But when insubordination or defiance made its appearance—which he was quick to observe—and the crisis came, he met it with a nerve that never failed fully to impress all with the knowledge that he was "master of the situation." On account of the fine

16*

qualities of both his head and heart he was greatly beloved by his pupils, and "Old Luke," as he was familiarly called among the boys, will long be remembered with affection and tenderness by many, who have not forgotten the happy school boy days spent under his instruction.

CHAPTER XXXVI.

ALEXANDER CAMPBELL.

For several years after the organization of Bethel Association, all looked bright and cheering. Peace reigned in all her borders. New churches were constituted, and her membership was constantly on the increase. Not a cloud was visible on the distant horizon. The most experienced mariner would have predicted a long and prosperous voyage over a tranquil sea. But even then, far away among the distant Alleghanies, a storm was gathering, destined to try the timbers of the goodly ship.

The storm king, on the present occasion, was the celebrated Alexander Campbell. He was a native of Ireland, born in 1788 in the county of Antrim. He was finely educated, and possessed talents of the highest order.

He landed in New York city in 1809, having in charge his mother and sisters, all on their way to join the husband and father, who had come out two years previously to prepare a home for them on their arrival. The history of their voyage is of uncommon interest, especially that relating to their shipwreck during a storm on the coast of Scotland, which caused a long separation between the father and his family. From New York they proceeded to Philadelphia—thence, across the Alleghany Mountains, to Western Pennsylvania, where Elder Thomas Campbell, the father, attracted by the romantic beauty and fertility of the country, had selected his home.

He was a minister of the gospel belonging to the denomination of Christians known as the Seceders, who seceded from the Presbyterian Church of Scotland in 1733, on account of their opposition to what was called the "law of Patronage." All accounts describe him as an excellent character. He was distinguished alike for learning, talents, philanthropy, and piety.

In emigrating to this country he seems to have had two objects in view—providing a home for his now large family, where land was both cheap and fertile, and hoping, or rather dreaming, that he might here be instrumental in bringing the various religious denominations together in one great brotherhood, where all would see "eye to eye, and speak the same thing," preparatory to the introduction of the Millennial glory. There is reason also to believe that he had largely imbued the mind of his son Alexander with this idea, which in after years suggested the name of his periodical, the *Millennial Harbinger*.

When Thomas Campbell, in 1807, reached Washington County, Pennsylvania, he was happy to find among the pioneer settlers a number of his Seceder brethren, who had already organized presbyteries and a synod. They received him with open arms, and considered themselves highly favored in having among them so good a man and a preacher so able; and, as was natural, they anticipated much happiness in the future. But these hopes were not to be realized, for Elder Campbell soon began his reformatory measures, by permitting persons to partake of the Lord's Supper, who, by the rules of his church, were not authorized to do so. This produced trouble, and he was finally summoned for trial before the Presbytery, which decided against him, when he took an appeal to the Synod.

Finding this also unfavorable, he seceded from his brother Seceders, and, as is usual in such cases, carried off a number of his brethren with him.

The turn things had taken seems to have perplexed the old man greatly, finding almost at the commencement that he was about to add another denomination to the number which, according to his views, was already far too great, and which he had fondly hoped to reduce. Finally, however, as there seemed no alternative, he formed his followers into a body, not to be called a church, but "A Christian Association," to meet at stated periods for worship. He recommended to this body the adoption of the formula, that "When the Bible speaks they would speak, and when the Bible is silent they would be silent." This formula Dr. Richardson, Alexander Campbell's biographer, considers as containing the germ of the "current Reformation." Here he began to foresee the difficulties that lay in the way of his progress. For no sooner had he announced this principle in the meeting than Andrew Munro, a shrewd Scotchman, rose and said : "Mr. Campbell, if we adopt that as a basis, there is an end of infant baptism." Mr. Campbell replied, in substance : "If infant baptism is not found in the Bible, according to our rule, we must give it up." Here another brother arose, and, with tears in his eyes, said : "I hope I may never see the day when my heart will renounce that blessed saying of the Bible : 'Suffer little children to come unto me, and forbid them not, for of such is the kingdom of heaven.'" The Seceders were thorough Pedobaptists. However, by common consent, they agreed to waive the subject of infant baptism for the present, and to publish a "Declaration or Address" to the people.

Elder Thomas Campbell, still feeling uncomfortable in the position he and his little flock occupied, next concluded to make an overture to the Presbyterians to unite with them, they differing but little from the Seceders in faith and practice. This movement was disapproved by his son, Alexander, who had by this time joined his father and took a deep interest in what was going on. The Presbyterian Synod, fearing probably that, on account of their latitudinarian and reformatory proclivities, they would occasion trouble, declined to admit them into their communion. This called forth a severe philippic from Alexander Campbell against the Presbyterian Synod, whence may be dated his war with that influential denomination, which was waged with much vigor on both sides for many years.

The Christian Association now determined to form themselves into a regular church organization, chose Elder Thomas Campbell as their pastor, elected deacons, and ordained Alexander Campbell as a minister of the gospel, who immediately began to preach in the surrounding country with marked ability.

The members of the " Brush Run Church," as this was called, were at first Pedobaptists ; but what Andrew Munro had said, seems to have set them to examining the subject, and they found, as they thought, that there was no authority in the Bible for infant sprinkling, and they were all finally immersed, Father Campbell and Alexander included.* Some of them at first, however, did not come

---

* This comprehensive statement does not enter into details. The historical fact is that Thomas and Alexander Campbell and others received immersion June 12, 1812, at the hands of Elder Mathias Luce, a regular Baptist minister, a pastor in the Redstone Association.

to believe in immersion so readily as afterward. On one occasion, when several were to be baptized, Father Campbell took them down to Buffalo Creek, to a place where the water was quite deep, coming up to the shoulders. He himself did not enter the water, but stood up on a root that projected a little over the surface, and bent their heads down until they were buried in the liquid grave, repeating in each case the baptismal formula. This was now, essentially, a Baptist Church, Calvinistic in doctrine,—as the Baptists generally were of that day,—opposed to sprinkling, believing immersion alone the proper act, and believers only the proper subjects of baptism. But for some cause it did not seem to take root and flourish, notwithstanding it had two of the ablest preachers in all the country. Its membership being at this time only about twenty-eight, Father Campbell felt quite distressed at their slow progress, and still greatly desired a union with some religious body. This was eventually effected.

There was at that time, 1813, in the rich valleys among the western slopes of the Alleghanies, a number of Baptist churches organized into the Redstone Association, so called from an old Indian fort of that name, on the Monongahela River, sixty miles above Pittsburgh, where the town of Brownsville now stands. This Association numbered over thirty churches and about eleven hundred members.

From what we can learn of the " laity " of this Association they seem to have been a quiet and orderly body of Christians, fond of reading the Bible, the *Pilgrim's Progress*, the *Holy War*, Booth's writings, and other standard works of Baptist literature, and guarding with special care the baptism instituted by the Great Head of the Church

himself.   But, although this honorable testimony was
borne to the character of the members of these churches
by Elder A. Campbell, he gives an invidious picture of the
" clergy " of the Redstone Association when he says :

" The people were much more highly appreciated by me, than their
ministry.   Indeed, the ministry of most sects, is, generally, in the
aggregate, much the worst part of them.   It was certainly so, in the
Redstone Association· thirty years ago.   They were little men in big
office.   The office did not suit them.   They had a wrong idea, too, of
what was wanting.   They seemed to think that a broad rim on their
hat instead of a narrow one, a prolongation of the face, and a fictitious
gravity, a longer and more emphatic pronunciation of certain words,
rather than spiritual knowledge, etc., * * were the grand desiderata."

In the above we have an illustration of that bitterness of
feeling towards " clergymen " that so much marred the
beauty of his Christian character.

Still feeling isolated and lonely, Father Campbell and
his little flock next turned their eyes to the Redstone
Association, and petitioned for union with them.   Admitting the Baptists to be harmless as doves, they certainly
were not wise as serpents.   For unlike the Presbyterians
and Seceders, they received them with open arms, and
rejoiced, no doubt, at having in their number, those two
able preachers.   But this proved to be a fatal step to
them, and was the " beginning of their end."   " The fatal
machine had entered their city."

Elder A. Campbell soon preached doctrines that sounded
strange in their old Baptist ears.   By some these new
doctrines were approved, by others condemned, and war
was inaugurated. Those opposed to Elder Campbell's views,
at one time thought they had matured a plan to excommunicate him, or throw him overboard, as the frightened

mariners did Jonah of old, during the storm that threat-
ened them with destruction. But they little knew their
man. When they were about to take the vote for this
purpose, to their amazement, they found that Jonah had
already gone on board another ship that was near by,—
that is, had transferred himself to the Mahoning Association ; and thereby having checkmated his adversaries, as
Dr. Richards says, was out of their jurisdiction and still
in the Baptist denomination. Still the fight went bravely
on among the Redstone people, long after the cause had
left them, and it continued till scarce a vestige of the Redstone Association was left. One can but feel sorrowful at
their fate, when he remembers how cozy and comfortable
they were before the evil days came upon them. We may
say, in passing, that Father Campbell, when he saw his
little bark, that had so long been drifting about at sea,
safely anchored, gave the helm into the hands of his son,
and was no more seen actively engaged in its management.

For several years after Elder A. Campbell united with
the Baptists, he preached a good deal, and his reputation
for learning and talents was on the increase. In 1820, he
and a Presbyterian minister named Walker had a debate
on the subject of Baptism, in which he gained additional
laurels and proved himself to be an able debater.

The year 1823 was an important era in the life of A.
Campbell. In this year he held his celebrated debate with
Rev. Wm. C. McCalla, also a Presbyterian minister ; the
subject again was Baptism, and again he obtained fresh
laurels. It was in this debate he turned the laugh upon
his adversary (who had been saying a good deal about the
unhealthiness of the practice of going down into the water

and being immersed), by requesting the audience to look first at Elder Jeremiah Vardeman, one of the moderators, a man of magnificent proportions, over six feet high, and weighing about three hundred pounds, who had perhaps immersed a greater number of converts than any other man in America,—and then, at a little, dry Presbyterian minister (another moderator), sitting near him, who during all his ministerial career had been sprinkling babies, and *then* decide on the unwholesomeness of immersion.

In this year also, the publication of the "Christian Baptist" was begun by Elder Campbell, which had a wide circulation, and added to his reputation, by proving him to be a ready writer as well as an able debater. This work created considerable interest among all religious parties, especially among the Baptists, many of whom considered some of its teachings not so much reformatory as unsound and revolutionary.

Although the Baptists in Southern Kentucky felt a little uneasy at the boldness and novelty of some of his views, yet, as they thought, he had defended them so gallantly against the Pedobaptists, their old hereditary opponents, they could not conscientiously turn against him, by saying anything to his disadvantage. He was the pride of their hearts, especially of those who were present at the McCalla debate, which was held in Washington, Mason County, Ky.; after which he occasionally came down and preached among us.

In one of these visits, he came as far south as Elkton, Todd County, and preached in the old court house. The house was closely packed. His reputation bringing many from distant points, I rode fifteen miles to hear him on that occasion.

He was then somewhat out of health, and remained seated most of the time while speaking. The people generally, were disappointed, as they had come with the expectation of hearing a great display of oratory, and his discourse happened to be rather didactic on that occasion. He told us of the Temple and the utensils used in it, and what they symbolized. I remember becoming greatly interested in what he said of those things. Toward the close of his discourse, he rose to his feet and treated us to some very fine oratory, in which Kentuckians delighted especially in those days, On leaving the court house, after the discourse ended, while standing near the door, some one called my name, and on turning around, I found it was our old family friend, Mr. William Dickinson, whom you remember no doubt, and a great admirer of your grandfather. He asked me my opinion of the discourse? I told him I thought it very fine. "Yes," he said, " I suppose it was, but your grandfather can beat him any day in the year, give him an even start." I replied, I had my doubts about that. He said, " I have none whatever," but I suppose he thought differently afterwards, as he finally went over to the Reformers. This was the gentleman with whom Elder Robert Rutherford resided till his death. I saw Mr. Campbell twice after this, once at Doctor Meriwether's and again at Oikadelphia Church, where I heard him preach a second time. Your mother and I, with a number of others, spent the evening with him at Doctor Meriwether's at the time alluded to, and heard him converse with much interest and pleasure. A gentleman present, inclined to infidelity, got into an argument, and Elder Campbell soon disposed of his case in a very pleasant way, leaving no disagreeable feeling. He was a superb

talker, and passed gracefully from one interesting subject
to another, till a late hour of the night.

Some years after this, when on his way to Nashville,
he again visited Doctor Meriwether, spending several days,
and a messenger was sent, requesting your grandfather to go
and be with him while there. He did so, and they spent
two nights and a day together, during which interview,
they talked over all the new issues that had been raised
by Mr. Campbell concerning faith, baptism, and spiritual
influence.

After your grandfather returned home, desiring to hear
his report, I rode over to see him. He said, he had been
very favorably impressed by Elder Campbell, both as a
gentleman and a Christian, and added that " when he un-
folded his views in conversation, they seemed less objectionable, than when seen in print." Being asked if he thought
union and harmony could be preserved among the Baptists,
he shook his head and said, he " feared not," and that
much trouble was in store for the Baptist churches, and
that many friendships of long standing were destined to
be broken up. This he felt very acutely. After this Mr.
Campbell at one time would seem to moderate a little, and
then again to go to greater extremes. In his discussions
with Elders Semple, Meredith, Broadus, and others, at
times, he would so express himself as to encourage hope
of their coming to an understanding. He, and old Bishop
Semple, as he was sometimes called, went so far as to get
in the same bed and sleep together.* This was really,
very encourageing, and it would seem that some good
ought to have come of it, but unfortunately, none ever did.

* See *Memoirs of Mr. Campbell* by Dr. Richardson.

CHAPTER XXXVII.

DISSENT FROM ELDER CAMPBELL.

I PROPOSE now to notice some of the points wherein your grandfather differed from Elder Alexander Campbell. These were often the subjects of conversation during the rise and progress of what was called the " Current Reformation."

He had read with care all that Elder Campbell had written and published both in *The Christian Baptist* and in *The Millennial Harbinger.* And when, in 1835, he published a small volume entitled : " *Christianity Restored,*" he perused that also with special care, as it was supposed to contain his more mature views. He was now fully satisfied that they were unsound on several subjects, especially so in regard to faith, baptism, and spiritual influence.

As to faith, he differed from Elder Campbell in this : That the Bible clearly teaches that the forgiveness of sins. is predicated on faith in its true, scriptural import, in which is always ˙ implied a disposition to love and obey God : whereas, Elder Campbell taught that no one's sins are forgiven unless he is baptized, immersed in water. It was your grandfather's custom, in order to determine what the Bible taught on any subject, to group together a sufficient number of passages bearing on it, like so many independent witnesses to a particular fact. This method

369

would leave on the mind a conviction little less strong than demonstration. Some of the texts he cited to prove that forgiveness of sin was predicated on faith, were as follows :

" And, as Moses lifted up the serpent in the wilderness, even so must the Son of man be lifted up . That whosoever believeth on him should not perish, but have eternal life."

"He that believeth on him is not condemned ; but he that *believeth not*, is condemned already, because he hath not believed in the name of the only begotten Son of God."

" He that *believeth* on the Son hath everlasting life ; and he that *believeth not* the Son shall not see life ; but the wrath of God abideth on him."

" Jesus said unto her : I am the resurrection and the life. He that *believeth* on me, though he were dead yet shall he live."

" By grace are ye saved, *through faith*." " And whosoever believeth on me shall never die." " Whosoever *believeth* that Jesus is the Christ, is born of God." " For I am not ashamed of the gospel of Christ ; for it is the power of God unto salvation to every one that believeth, to the Jew first, and also to the Greek."

Now it seems, as your grandfather would say, little less than incredible that any one should come to the conclusion that salvation is not predicated on faith, after reading these texts and many others like them. And if language like this could be explained away, who can say that anything certain can be learned from the Sacred Oracles ? He would remark that, not only the voice of Revelation teaches this great truth, but Reason also. The faith of the Bible that brings salvation is a faith in Christ, " that works by love," disposing men to love, reverence, and obedience. This brings them into the relation of children, whereby they can say, " Abba, Father," for the apostle says, " Ye are all the children of God by faith in Christ Jesus," and hence, " heirs of God, and joint heirs with

Christ." Just as Noah's faith moved him to build the ark, as God commanded, and saved him and his family from being swept away by the deluge; so does faith in Christ,—it works by love and brings the sinner into fellowship with God and with his Son Jesus Christ. They are then "in Christ;" and thus by grace are they saved, through faith. Hence, he would say, both reason and revelation predicate pardon and eternal life on the faith of the gospel. But, since the Bible speaks of a living faith, or "faith that works by love," and a dead faith which is of no value, every one should *take heed to the kind of faith he possesses.* The former he compared to a tree planted by a fountain, bending under its load of fruits; the latter, to a blighted trunk, with decayed branches and withered leaves. The man who has living faith—the faith that looks to Christ, and rests in him, and longs to be with him—he likened to one who, having confidence that there is a better country, with more fertile soil, a milder climate and more salubrious air, begins without delay his journey to this "better land;" while he whose faith is dead, never moves away from the bleak and sterile soil on which he first drew breath. Many, he feared, who simply admitted or assented to the truths of the gospel, mistook this for true faith. No one, though, need be deceived on this momentous subject. If his faith leads him to love and reverence God, and to walk in all the ordinances and commandments of the Lord, blameless, he need have no fears on the subject. And of this no one need have doubt, as it is a matter of consciousness. "He has the witness within himself." One can as certainly know that he loves the Heavenly Father, as that he loves an earthly friend and benefactor.

According to your grandfather's views, the faith which saves the soul involves not only the assent of the understanding to the truths of the gospel, but the consent of the will, and the approval of the heart. He thought Mr. Campbell's view defective, because it makes faith almost exclusively an intellectual exercise. If "faith works by love," it has to do with the heart, for it is the heart that loves. It is not necessary for me to enlarge, as you can see wherein your grandfather and Mr. Campbell differed.*

Elder Campbell's views on baptism, also, were objected to. On page 213 of "Christianity Restored," he says :

" If, then, the present forgiveness of sins be a privilege and a right of those under the new constitution in the kingdom of Jesus, and if being ' born again,' and being ' born of the water and the Spirit' is necessary to admission ; and if being born of water means immersion, as is clearly proved by all witnesses, then *remission of sins in this life cannot be received or enjoyed* previous to baptism.   The remission of sins, or coming into a state of acceptance, being one of the present immunities of the kingdom, cannot *be received or enjoyed by any one previous to baptism.*"

* It is well to emphasize the fact that Christ is the object of gospel faith. He who exercises this faith not only believes what the gospel says *about* Christ, but believes *in* him. Faith is a personal matter, not merely because it is the act of a person, but because Christ, its object, is a person. No belief of any propositions concerning Christ has any saving element in it, apart from faith in him as a personal Saviour. Faith is a trustful reception of Christ as the only Saviour. This faith *follows* repentance. There is, of course, a faith that precedes repentance. That is to say, a man must believe there is a God against whom he has sinned, before he can repent; but this differs from faith in Christ. It is only a preparation for the exercise of faith in Christ. He who is convinced that he is a ruined sinner, in perishing need of a Saviour, is ready to give to the Lord Jesus that reception which the gospel claims for him. Receiving Christ is inseparable from love to him, and therefore " faith works by love." J. M. P.

Here, then, Elder Campbell unequivocally teaches, that without immersion there is no remission of sins.

No Baptist, perhaps, living or dead, had ever believed or even dreamed of a dogma like this before; and, consequently, it fell like a bombshell in their ranks. Its very novelty, though, seems to have had a kind of fascination for some.

Notwithstanding the great importance your grandfather always attached to baptism, in its proper place and import, he never believed that the forgiveness of sins was predicated on it. Faith, in its Bible import, as already stated, and *no bodily act* whatever that men can perform, is the condition of salvation. Men ought to be baptized, as an emblem or symbol of death to sin, and resurrection to a new life, and not to obtain the forgiveness of their sins. But are not the "Reformers" beginning to reconsider this doctrine? An article has recently appeared from the pen of Henry T. Anderson, whom we used to hear preach so often at our old Oikadelphia Church, in the stormy days of the beginning of the Reformation, and who was then considered one of the most uncompromising advocates of Elder Campbell's views, in which he says:

"Baptism in water for the remission of sin can never be sustained, for water affects only the body. But the blood of Christ affects the heart, as seen in the words above quoted, and can affect the heart only through faith." * * * "In Rom 6: 4, 6, we have language that teaches the meaning of baptism. It is the *likeness* of Christ's death and resurrection. Is it not then a symbol, or if any one prefer, an emblem? These two places are sufficient for our purpose. Christ died, was buried, and rose again. We are buried in water and raised again as a likeness of what he did. But the likeness of his death can never affect our sins. We must apprehend him, lay hold on him by *faith*, and be baptized in water as a symbol of our being baptized into him in Spirit."

17

Thus we see that Elder Anderson, a veteran in the army of the Reformation, and a laborious student of the Bible, having given what is thought to be an excellent translation of the New Testament from the original Greek, after the lapse of forty years, holds the identical views your grandfather did from the beginning, namely, that baptism is a symbol or emblem of the forgiveness of sins, and not *that* by, or through which, the pardon of sin is obtained.

Elder Campbell's views in regard to Spiritual Influence were not in accord with your grandfather's views. On page 350 of the volume referred to, Elder Campbell says:

" As the spirit of man puts forth all its moral power in the words which it fills with its ideas, so the Spirit of God puts forth all its convert-ing and sanctifying power in the words which it fills with its ideas." * * * "If the Spirit of God has spoken all its arguments, &c., then all the power of the Holy Spirit that can operate upon the human mind is spent."

From these and kindred passages, your grandfather said it was clear that Mr. Campbell believed and taught that all the converting power of God was in the word alone. Now, he believed equally with Elder Campbell that the Holy Spirit operates on the human mind, by and through the word, but not by and through the word *alone*.* He

* It is safe to say that the Holy Spirit operates through the word. It is not, however, necessary to say that he always confines himself to this method of operation. We disparage the Spirit if we say that he cannot gain access to the human heart without words; for we vir-tually represent him as unable to do what Satan does every day. Some of Mr. Campbell's opponents, forty years ago, did him injustice in insist-ting that he identified the Spirit and the word. He never did this, but the view which he urged was that the Spirit is in the word—so that if we have the word we have the Spirit in all his converting and sanctify-

believed and thought that the Holy Spirit often influences the souls of men, entirely independent of the word, but always in accordance or in harmony with it; that he influences the human mind, even in the dark corners of the earth, where the word has never been; and that to this divine influence is to be attributed all that is good and virtuous in heathen lands. "Why," he would ask, "may not the Good Spirit, without words oral or written, influence the minds of men, since Satan, the Evil Spirit, and according to the Scriptures the enemy of God and man, is now, and ever has been doing this without any word oral or written?"

Elder Campbell's reason for not believing this was that no one could understand how it was possible that Spirit could act directly on spirit, except through the medium of words. Your grandfather thought this objection not only unscriptural but unphilosophical. All know that matter attracts or influences matter. Of this they have no doubt. But the greatest philosopher, living or dead, could not tell how it was done. He could say, that matter is attracted by attraction or influenced by influence, and that would be the end. He would say that men know *something* about many things, but understand very few things fully, either in the natural or the spiritual world. And that he was a wise man who said, he that believed only what he understood, had the shortest creed known. And he concluded that Mr. Campbell was mistaken when he denied that Spirit could operate on spirit, unless through the medium of words

ing power. This, however, may not have been his uniform view, for he often changed his opinions, and, indeed, came as near as any man of modern times, to passing through all the signs of the theological zodiac.

J. M. P.

"filled with ideas;" since, according to the Bible, the Old Enemy and his emissaries are "going about seeking whom they may devour," or lead to destruction by their wicked influence, independent of words. When he wishes to make one murder his neighbor, or do any other wickedness, great or small, he does not hold a talk with him, but by temptation, suggestion, or impulse induces him to commit the deed. Or he enters into the wretch, as he is said to have done into Judas Iscariot, to tempt him, without the use of language, to betray his master. We believe that there are many other passages of Scripture, which led to the belief that Spirit operated on spirit, directly, without the intervention of words, such as " My Spirit shall not always strive with men." " The Spirit of God came upon him." (Balaam.)

The personal experience of each individual also, he thought, proved the *voiceless* influence of the evil spirit on the mind. He would say that probably most persons remember times when suddenly, by some evil influence, their whole nature, for the moment, seemed to be changed for the worse, and then slowly "to right up again," as if by some beneficent influence or spirit. And, also, times when his nature seemed to be mysteriously exalted to a higher degree of purity and excellence. So far then, from believing with Elder Campbell that, all the power of the Spirit of God upon man is in the word alone, and that when the word was given *all* was given, he thought that even dead inanimate matter was often governed by the Spirit as when in the early days of creation he *moved* upon the waters, bringing order and beauty out of chaos. When Christ spoke to the storm-tossed waves of the Sea of Galilee, the power that stilled them, was not in the *words*, for these the waves could neither hear nor understand. When he laid his malediction on the barren fig tree, and it withered and died, when he called the lifeless form of Lazarus from the grave, it was not the words alone that produced the effect, but an awful and invisible *power* beyond them.

Indeed, there was no subject on which I ever heard your grandfather converse more interestingly than that of the Holy Spirit, whose power, he thought, pervaded all the realms of creation, ever bringing good from evil, and counteracting the baleful influence of the Prince of Darkness and his emissaries.

CHAPTER XXXVIII.

END OF THE REFORMATION.

WE learn, from his Memoirs by Dr. Richardson, that Elder Campbell made a profession of religion in his youth. And his *experience*, as then given, seems to resemble all those of the times.

"As his convictions deepened he underwent much conflict of mind, and experienced great concern in regard to his own salvation ; so that he lost, for a time, his usual vivacity, and sought in lonely walk and by prayer in secluded spots, to obtain such evidence of divine acceptance as his pious acquaintances considered requisite.   'Finally, after many strugglings,' he adds, ' I was enabled to trust in the Saviour of sinners, and feel my reliance on him as the only Saviour. From the moment I was enabled to feel this reliance on the Lord Jesus Christ, I obtained and enjoyed peace of mind.' "

I doubt not that during the interview at Dr. Meri-wether's, Elder Campbell gave your grandfather this account of his conversion, and of his subsequent Christian life, as we are informed he did to Elder John Smith. After his conversion he became a member of his father's church, and before leaving the old country, it is probable they conversed often concerning the possibility of doing something in the new world to aid the cause of religion and Christian union (which seems to have occupied much of their thoughts), as here civil and religious liberty were fully enjoyed. On arriving in this country, taking it for granted that religion was in its depressed state on account of the number of sects, creeds, and errors in doctrine that everywhere prevail; and concluding that if these could be all thrown overboard, and what he called "Primitive Christianity, or the ancient order of things, restored," the church would spring into new life and beauty; and supposing also that he could make others see this as plainly as he himself saw it,—he commenced war upon them all, being naturally of a sanguine and determined character. This brought down upon him, in turn, the ministers of all the various denominations almost in solid phalanx. He accepted battle and fought like a Titan. And, if what some witty fellow has said be true, namely: "that an Englishman is never so happy as when miserable, a Scotchman never so much at home as when abroad, and an *Irishman* never so much at peace as when at war," Elder Campbell, for many years, must have enjoyed a peaceful and happy time.

But Elder Campbell, your grandfather thought, made a capital mistake at the beginning. He was in the predicament of a physician who had failed in the diagnosis, and was treating his patient for one disease while he was dying of another. It was, he used to say, not the number of sects, creeds, and false doctrines, that was doing the mischief; these were the *effects* of the malady, not the cause, and would disappear when the real cause should be removed. What the Christian world needed was *religion*. What Christianity needed was *Christians* to exhibit its power and beauty in their lives and conduct,—men and women who would "let their light so shine before men, that they, seeing their *good works*, would glorify their Father who is in heaven."

There is nothing in any form of church government, he thought, to prevent any member thereof from leading a truly Christian life and serving God "in the beauty of holiness." "What is a Christian," he would ask, "but one who loves the Christ and delights in his service?" He is a good citizen, obedient to the laws made for the benefit of society. He is a kind husband, a kind father, a kind master, a kind neighbor, just and honorable in all his dealings, a friend and benefactor of the poor and destitute, and according to his means, "abounding in every good word and work."

Now, supposing all "who name the name of Christ" to come up to this standard, what would be the result? The power of Christianity would subdue the world, and truth and righteousness extend from the rivers to the ends of the earth, and "fair as the moon, clear as the sun, and terrible as an army with banners" (to all evil doers); and it would soon "cover the earth, as the waters cover the face of the great deep." Of course, there would be a breaking down of all the dividing walls between the followers of Christ. He taught that the downfall of creeds, false doctrines, and sects, depended on the *rise* of Christianity, in its power and beauty, and that the Reformer should devote his talents and zeal to *this* object with unremitting ardor.

When the doctrines of the Reformation reached our part of Kentucky, they produced quite a sensation among all classes of people, both religious and irreligious. The turmoil was greatest, I think, between 1830 and 1840. The din of politics was, for a time, not so loud. Clay and Jackson, Whig and Democrat, Tariff and anti-Tariff, were no longer the only subjects of debate and controversy; but Campbellism and anti-Campbellism were endlessly discussed.

The Baptists in our section of Kentucky were much

agitated, though not as much so as in the northern counties. The questions of hyper-Calvinism had been pretty
much settled among us; and Campbellism, as it was called,
was the only cause of discussion. But in the northern
counties they had both hyper-Calvinism and Campbellism
to fight. To add to their distress, they lost several of their
distinguished preachers, who deserted their ranks and
joined the Reformation; among whom were the Creaths,
and Elder Philip S. Fall. With the latter your grandfather became acquainted, and loved and esteemed him as
a highly cultivated Christian and an ornament to the Baptists. He is the father of Elder James S. Fall, an acquaintance of yours, late of Russellville, highly esteemed
as a preacher.

The Reformers had quite an advantage over their opponents in one respect. They had an able leader, who used
a press of his own, and by this means, through his periodi-
cals, could furnish his disciples with his views, and the
arguments to be employed in their support, all prepared
for use, which, when well learned, all were equipped for
fighting in column and to act in concert; whereas, their
adversaries had each to choose his own ground and make
his own fight as best he could.

A number of preachers, some of whom possessed good
talents and popular manners, came into our country from
a distance, among whom were Elders Jesse B. and John
D. Ferguson; and, some years later, their venerable father
from Baltimore, Elder Charles M. Day, and Henry T. Anderson from Virginia, to whom Elder Isaiah Boone, a good
local speaker, rendered efficient aid. He had been raised
up under your grandfather's ministry, but went over to
the Reformers. These men, well suited to giveres pecta-
17*

bility to the cause, were very active and influential, and
some of them good debaters; they canvassed very thoroughly the region of country in which your grandfather
lived, and made many proselytes and converts.

The feature of the new doctrine, that seemed to be most
fascinating, was "*baptism for the remission of sins.*" They,
everywhere, and on all preaching occasions, promised the
forgiveness of sins, and the gift of the Holy Spirit, to all
who would make what they called "the good confession,"
viz: that Jesus Christ is the Son of God, promise to obey
the gospel, or submit to immersion. Elder H. T. Anderson told them one might obtain the forgiveness of his sins
in three minutes, as well as in a thousand years; and at
another time said to me, standing on the bank of the stream
while he was baptizing: "If you will go with me down
into the water, I will bring you up from it free from sin
as an angel."

These terms seemed so easy and favorable, that many
availed themselves of them, and were baptized; others,
again, fearing there might be some mistake in this, held
aloof, thinking they ought first to show some "fruits meet
for repentance," or be conscious of a change in themselves
for the better, before they professed to the world that they
were followers of Christ. Those who accepted this doctrine
to the letter, earnestly entreated all they loved, without
delay, to obey the gospel, viz: be immersed, and were
amazed that any one should hesitate for a moment in ob-
taining the pardon of sin, when it was made so easy;
others were alarmed, lest those they loved should be hurried on to take a step for which they were utterly unprepared. "Crimination and recrimination" followed, and
many of the oldest and purest friendships were broken up

forever. Husbands and wives, parents and children, were in many instances, unhappily, estranged. There are, indeed, few things more sad to contemplate than a disturbance of the religious peace and harmony of families and churches, when there is no good reason for it. There is always a greater amount of unhappiness produced than is at first apparent. Sorrows and regrets often remain through life, though they may never be mentioned. The common family altar has lost its interest and charm, and the old church, where those that once loved each other used to meet and worship, is deserted and falling into decay and ruin. My thoughts revert to our own Oikadelphia Church, where, in other days, so many loving friends and relatives met for worship.

While the Reformers were busy in dissseminating their views and making converts, your grandfather and his brethren in the ministry were not idle. They changed their manner of preaching but little. Seldom selected a text which indicated that they intended preaching a sermon of a controversial character. This was especially the case in regard to him. But he always expressed himself freely when any of these subjects came incidentally in his way.

The necessity of "repentance towards God, and faith in Christ;" the importance of making preparation during life for the solemn hour of death and the final judgment; and of walking blameless in all the ordinances and commandments of the Divine Master, formed the burden of his earnest appeals to the people, from which he seldom deviated. His warning voice was not heard in vain, and many were added to the churches, even in those troublous times.

Many of his brethren, some from a distance, visited him in their perplexity and trouble for advice and counsel. And many, who were not in any church, but were interested in their individual salvation, came to learn of him the way and plan of salvation. In this manner, and by his conversations in the family circle, when out on his tours of preaching, his influence was felt throughout the country. At last the din of battle began gradually to die away, and when the smoke had lifted, a new denomination was the result, in addition to the number, already too great. It was found that the Baptists had fully maintained their ground in the contest, and that their banner still waved over more than sixty churches, composing the Bethel Association, with prestige unimpaired.

It is sad to remember how many who fought in this fratricidal war have passed away, and now, after their work is done, sleep in their silent graves, where—

> " The storms that wreck the wintry sky
> No more disturb their last repose,
> Than summer evening's latest sigh
> Disturbs the rose."

CHAPTER XXXIX.

PHRENOLOGY,—MESMERISM,—SPIRITUALISM, ETC.

AFTER the quiet, which had been disturbed by the promulgation of the new doctrines advocated by A. Campbell and his adherents, was restored, another season of peace and prosperity prevailed among the Churches of Bethel Association, which continued until the commencement of our great civil war, in 1860, which paralyzed all the interests of the country, both civil and religious, in a great degree.

Several things followed in succession during this period, to interest and amuse the people in our parts of Kentucky and Tennessee, which, perhaps, should be noticed in giving an account of these times. These are Phrenology, Mesmerism, Spiritualism, etc.

Phrenology, I believe, aspires to the dignity of a science. It professes to be able to throw light upon the character, disposition, temper, and the moral and intellectual qualities of each individual, by the size, location, etc., of the bumps, or protuberances, to be found on his cranium. Each of these is supposed to have a significance of its own ; and he who could read it, could tell every one his character, and lay it bare to the inspection of spectators. The idea seems to be somewhat like this: In the substance of the brain the feelings, passions, desires, and intellectual powers have each a particular location, and operate there with such force as to cause an upheaval of the bone immediately above them, as the forces below the earth's surface sometimes raise hills, mountains, and other inequalities. So, if one can know the character of the force that produces these bumps or inequalities, he can know, also, the character of the individual on whose head they are found. This the adept professes to be able to ascertain, as each has its local habitation and its name.

Accordingly, the use and value of phrenology may be seen in this. If one desires to know his standing in morals and intellect, he has only to procure a chart of his head from an adept, and with pencil set down all his good qualities or bumps under one head and his bad ones under another, and compare the difference ; he can thus see at a glance his standing, whether he is an honest man or a knave, a wise man or a fool, or whether he is between the two extremes, where, perhaps, the majority will be found. He must be careful to take into account the size of the bumps, of each kind, as well as the number, for if the evil bumps are very large, though fewer in number, they may outweigh the good, and *vice versa*. Yet, notwithstanding all this, by the skillful use of Algebra and Arithmetic, something may be done. . Another benefit to be derived from a knowledge of Phrenology is, that it enables a parent the better to manage the education of his children. If the son has no capacity for grammar, let him omit it, and pursue something the bumps indicate as more congenial. Should the daughter manifest no aptitude for the solid branches of education, let her drop them, and turn her attention to those merely ornamental—music, painting, etc.

While Phrenology was attracting much attention, I was

conducting a school near Trenton, Kentucky, as you, no doubt, remember. The students would often obtain permission to go and hear a lecture, have their heads examined, and get a chart. This gave me a good opportunity for comparing, in many instances, the lecturer's chart with what I already knew of the abilities and tastes of the boy, and I was often struck with the wide mistakes made. One student, in particular, who was making unprecedented progress in Latin and Greek, was advised never to think of studying these languages, as he had no aptitude whatever for them.

In the times of which we are now speaking, young people seemed very much entertained in the towns and villages, attending these lectures and having their heads examined. Judging though from what I hear and see in the literature of the present times, I conclude phrenology has lost the interest formerly felt in it.

Mesmerism, or animal magnetism, also attracted much attention at this period. This is supposed to be a force or fluid, by means of which a peculiar influence may be exerted on the animal system. It was at first thought to be caused by a mineral magnet only, but afterward it came to be considered a force belonging to the human body, and also to some of the lower animals. When spoken of in reference to these, it is called fascination or " charming."

Those persons who possess influence in a high degree, are noted for strong wills and healthy constitutions, while those, on the other hand, most easily influenced are of a more feeble will and constitution. Writers speak of five or six phases or degrees of this mysterious influence. In order to produce it, the magnetizer seats himself immediately in front of his subject, and places the palms of his hands and balls of his thumbs, in contact with those of the subject. After sitting thus a short time the influence begins to be felt, when he makes what are technically called " passes " with open hands and outstretched fingers, over the subject, from head to foot. During this process, he keeps his attention fixed on the subject, and by a silent exercise of the will, commands him to become magnetized. In the first stage, the subject professes to feel a strange sensation pervading his body, and frequently a prickling somewhat like that felt in a limb when the circulation is retarded or, as is commonly said, it is asleep. The second state is that of drowsiness. The third is that of coma, or senseless sleep. The fourth state is somnambulism. He has now consciousness and sensation, but not his own ; they are those of the magnetizer. He tastes as the magnetizer tastes, hears as he hears, sees as he sees, feels as he feels, and smiles as he smiles. His own sensibility is obliterated, but he feels all the impressions made on the body of the magnetizer. The fifth state is that of clairvoyance. This is a heightened or intensified degree of the fourth stage. In this, the subject has means of perception unknown to man, in his normal state, and if judged from the common experience of mankind, seems to be an impostor. He can see with his eyes closed and bandaged. In that condition he sees what waking men cannot see with their eyes open. He can see what is going on in rooms above, below, and around him. He sees things not only outside of the body, but inside of it also. His own sense of smell, taste, or touch, is generally dull. A teaspoon full of the strongest cayenne pepper placed in his mouth, does not affect him. He inhales the strongest ammonia, through his nose, and it produces no effect. Pins may be thrust through his hands, or he may be pinched, or have an arm or leg cut off, without feeling pain. He will even laugh and talk while this is being done. Yet should his magnetizer be pinched, or have a pin thrust into him, or have his hair pulled, the magnetized feels it sensibly, and rubs the places on his own body, to relieve the pain. The sixth state is stated to be still more wonderful. This is that of perfect clairvoyance. He sees what is going on hundreds of miles away; reads the thoughts of persons about him ; reads the past and foretells the future. His soul dwells in light and delight, and he often regrets that he cannot remain in that state forever. (See "*New American Cyclopedia. Article, Animal magnetism.*")

Mesmerism, like Phrenology, for a time greatly interested and amused the people. They attended the places where the itinerant lecturers, with their trained attendants, showed off the wonders of their so called science. They were somewhat awed at some of its manifestations, but still would laugh to see how the person magnetized would jump and run, when a pin entered the skin of the magnetizer, or when his hair was pulled ; and the faces he would make, when ammonia or snuff was put into his mouth. But when it came to be known that a person frequently mesmerized by another, was more or less liable to be unduly influenced by him afterward, and that bad men had often taken advantage of this to effect their wicked puposes, it fell into general disrepute. I remember to have heard it said, that ladies complained that at church, even, they had felt their minds disturbed and confused, and on looking round would see the eyes of some one in the congregation gleaming upon them trying to exert a mesmeric influence.

After the interest manifested in the phenomena of mesmerism had subsided, "another wonder" of still greater interest came to light, which has since acquired gigantic proportions. I allude to what is known as modern spiritualism, which began to attract attention, as you may remember, in the year 1848, in the State of New York, under the "mediumship," as it is called, of two young girls, the Misses Fox. This teaches that the spirits of the dead are still in communication with the living, through the agency of what are called mediums, of which there are said to be three kinds, *speaking, writing, and rapping* mediums.

Such persons as have but little will of their own, or are of a yielding, passive disposition, and are easily brought under the mesmeric influence, are thought to make the best mediums, because they yield more readily to the influence of the spirits, and can deliver their revelations more accurately than persons of a more decided will and character. Many of these mediums profess, also, to have a power of vision unknown to common mortals. They claim to be able to see spirits daily, walking on the earth, standing still, or floating in the air above. You, no doubt, still remember several who professed to have this wonderful gift. This, though, is so contrary to the experience of mankind generally as to be considered one of the many freaks of an abnormal imagination, which so frequently makes dupes of people sound of mind in other respects. Such is the power of this wonderful faculty, that, you remember, it caused one lately to publish to the world that he saw a spirit step out from a closet into a well-lighted room, then fade away and become invisible, then gradually reappear, more and more distinct, until it stood clear and well defined as at first. And, had it not been proved afterwards, that this was really a young woman, the mother of a living child, he would have lived and died in the belief that he had seen a spirit.

The belief in spiritualism spread far and wide after its appearance in New York, not only over the United States, but in Europe also, till the number of those now professing to believe in it is said to amount to several millions. Many reasons may be assigned for the hold it has taken on the popular mind. It teaches that the living are still surrounded by the spirits of those lost by death, and that they still feel a deep interest in their welfare, and will continue to do so till they, too, enter the "Spirit Land." This, to many, is a source of real happiness, and they cherish the belief accordingly. Spiritualism also teaches—unlike the Bible—that men have still another chance, or probation, after death, which is very consoling to a poor mortal, who has been taught to believe that his fate hereafter depends on his conduct in this life. He, very naturally, hails with delight and embraces with cordiality the new gospel, which teaches that, however deep the stains of a sinful life—however polluted the soul may be with the blackest crimes—after death, it will enter upon a state of endless progression, and rise from sphere to sphere, until it finally reaches perfection and becomes a bright and glorious spirit, worthy to dwell in the presence of Deity. But, perhaps, much the larger number have become Spiritualists because they honestly think they have satisfactory evidence for the grounds of their faith.

To illustrate :

Let us suppose that A, an entire stranger, visits Louisville, where are a number of Spiritualists, and, as he has heard a good deal of the new *ism*, concludes to visit a seance, and judge for himself of its claims,—and that, on entering, he asks the following questions mentally :—" Where do I live ?"—" In the State of Arkansas." " Am I a married man ?"—" Yes." " How many children have I ?"— " Five." " How many sons ?"—" Three." " Is the eldest a son or a daughter?"—" A daughter." " What is her age ?"—" She is twelve years of age." " What is the age of the youngest ?"—" Three years." " What is the complexion of my wife ? "—" Very fair." " The color of her eyes ? "—" They are hazle." " The color of her hair ? "— " Dark brown."

A takes his hat and leaves rather hurriedly, with a feeling of awe, for every question has been answered accurately. He decides at once that Spiritualism must be true; since no living being could have known the correct answers under the circumstances, every question having been asked mentally. But, mark the sequel. A had a brother who had left home five years previously, of whose fate he was ignorant, not having heard from him from the time he left home. Thinking it an excellent opportunity to learn something concerning his brother, he returned to the seance the next night, told the circumstance of leaving home, and also that no information regarding him had been received to the present time. He inquired if his brother still lived, and was told that he was dead. " How long since his death ? "—" Two years." " Where did he die ? "—" Among the mountains of California, searching for gold." " Where was he buried ?"—" In the lonely spot where he died." " Was anything done to mark his grave ? "—" Nothing whatever." With a sad heart he leaves the circle and returns to his hotel. Not a doubt of his brother's death crossing his mind. Three days after, when he is about to leave the city, a knock is heard on his door. On opening it, who does he see standing before him but his long-absent brother, sound in body and in fine spirits, having met with gratifying success in business.

These illustrations show the condition in which Spiritualism stands at present. At one time the answers are all true in every particular; on another occasion they are false. The question now arises: Why were the answers in the first instance true? Answer: Because the answers to them were in the mind of A, and *reflected* from it to the medium. Why were the answers in the second case false? Because the true answers were not known to A, nor to any other person present, and, therefore, could not be reflected to the medium. Hence, a total failure.

"It is now believed that there is in nature a medium of communication between mind and mind, other than that by which communications are had through the ordinary channels of the senses, and that, through this force or channel, one mind may—when proper conditions are fulfilled—control the actions of the mental and physical powers of another mind." The conclusion, then, is that all the true information the inquirer receives comes to the medium from the mind of some other person or persons present, and that spirits have nothing to do with it; that, if no one present is cognizant of the true answer, not a " spirit from the vasty deep" can furnish it. All that a medium can do is to *guess.* Hence, the endless mistakes and contradictions.

At the beginning of spiritualism, we are informed by the celebrated Robert Dale Owen, that a peddler, known to have some money, suddenly disappeared from near

Rochester, New York. The spirits said, he had been murdered, and his body thrown into the canal. A crowd collected, and the canal was dragged, but no body found. The so called spirits then said the body would be found at another place. This was also dragged, with a like result. Two months after, the peddler returned and said he left suddenly, and went to Canada, because he learned that his creditors were on his track. According to the foregoing theory, no one present knew what had become of the peddler—the medium included. But numbers were impressed with the belief that he had been "made way with" in the manner stated, and this impression was conveyed from their minds to that of the medium, and she revealed it as coming from the spirits. It would seem that the mind of the medium is powerfully influenced by the belief or opinion of those about her. We are informed that the spirit of old Deacon Branch, in Madison, Ohio, when a crowd of Baptists were present, always said that immersion was the right mode of baptism; to the Pedobaptists, that sprinkling was; to those who believed in endless punishment, that *theirs* was the true belief; and to Universalists that all mankind would be saved. To a circle of friends who did not believe in Spiritualism he said, it was a miserable humbug.

That the thoughts, feelings, desires, and opinions of one person can be reflected to another, seems to be fully proved by experiments in mesmerism; and also all the ideas and sensations of the magnetizer passed directly to the person magnetized, so that he became, as it were, for the time, his "alter ego," seeing as he sees, feeling as he feels, tasting as he tastes, and thinking as he thinks. This will explain why it was that the ignorant young shoemaker—Andrew

Jackson Davis, when magnetized by Doctor Lyon, a man of learning and ability, could discourse by the hour on learned subjects, of which he was ignorant in his normal condition, receiving all his thoughts from Lyon himself. No one at all acquainted with the superstition of ancient Greece and Rome, can fail to see how nearly identical are modern Spiritualism and the ancient Oracle. So much are they alike, that, " nomine mutato," one might be taken for the other. Waiving all the arguments for and against the existence of spirits around us, and the influence they may exert on the human mind, your grandfather thought, admitting such to be the case, it was very sinful to court familiarity with them, since the Bible forbade this, even under the death penalty. He once made out a list of all the references in which this was condemned, which I regret is lost. He was fully persuaded, that they are things which we, in this life, ought not to know, as they would not contribute to our happiness. Our first parents, he said, wished to be like gods, " knowing good from evil." In an evil hour, this discovery was made, and with it the awful disclosure also, that they had brought down death and ruin upon themselves and their posterity. To keep each order of being in its proper bounds ;

" To hide from brutes what men, from men what spirits know,"

he thought was clearly the divine will, since from the beginning, all the attempts of men to look into the dark mysterious future, have been worse than useless. The few glimpses from the Bible are all the Creator has thought necessary for us to know until this great and mysterious drama is wound up. " Spiritualism," he said, " denies all the great truths of the Bible—the fall of man, the atonement of Christ, miracles, the divinity of Christ, his miraculous birth, a hell, a devil, a resurrection of the dead, and a day of judgment. Therefore, the teachings of spiritualism are utterly irreconcilable with the Bible, and he who adopts them will finally lay it aside." The desire to lift the veil that hides from mortals the secrets of the unseen world, he said was very improper, and for that reason, magic, necromancy, divination, oracles, demonology, witchcraft, the consulting of familiar spirits, and astrology, (which taught that the destiny of men and nations was controlled by stellar influences, and was believed in for ages by some of the most enlightened minds of Europe, as spiritualism now is,) should be abandoned at once and forever, since as the Apostle Peter tells us: "We have a more sure word of prophecy, whereunto ye do well to take heed, as unto a light that shineth in a dark place, until the day dawn and the day star arise in our hearts." His words, when speaking on this subject would bring to mind the following lines of the poet.

> "Heaven from all creatures hides the book of fate.
> All but the page prescribed, their present state;
> From brutes what men, from men, what spirits know;
> Or who could suffer being here below?
> The lamb thy riot dooms to bleed to-day,
> Had he thy reason, would he skip and play?
> Pleased to the last, he crops the flowery food,
> And licks the hand just raised to shed his blood.
> Oh! blindness to the future! kindly given
> That each may fill the circle marked by Heaven."
> * * * * ·* * * * * *
> "Hope humbly then; with trembling pinions soar;
> *Wait the great teacher*, death, and God adore."

Steam Doctors were among the things new and strange that sprang up in these times. It should not be forgotten or passed over in silence.

In the famous old State of Massachusetts, a man, calling himself Dr. Thomson, about the year 1822, published a little book which he called " *The New Guide to Health.*" He seems to have taken up the practice of medicine, without any education or previous preparation whatever. Hear what he says of himself:

" Possessing a body like other men, I was led to inquire into the component parts of which man is made. I found him composed of the four elements—earth, water, fire, and air. The earth and water I found were the solids, the air and fire, the fluids. The two first I found were the component parts, the two last kept him in motion. *Heat* I found was *life*, and *cold—death* And, again, it must be recollected that, if heat is life, and cold is death, fever is a friend and cold an enemy. It is therefore necessary to aid the friend and oppose the enemy, in order to secure health."

These extracts are given to show what stuff quacks are made of. You perceive, cold is considered not simply as the absence of heat, but as a real entity or substance. These two principles are considered as carrying on a ceaseless warfare. When cold gains the ascendancy, the man is sick, and it is the duty of the doctor to come to the aid of heat, and, if possible, to overpower and drive out cold. If this can be done, the patient recovers; if not, he dies. Heat and the doctor together can hold cold in check for a longer or shorter time. But cold in the end will prevail and triumph over all living creatures; consequently, to keep cold in check as long as possible is all that can be done by the doctor. In order to fight cold, the old doctor proposed certain heating medicines, numbering them from one to six. Lobelia, or what he called the *emetic weed*, was, I think, " No. 1." This was used to cleanse the stomach of "*kanker*" and enable it to digest food and supply heat to the system. Marvelous things were said to be

18

performed by lobelia. If an individual ate a variety of food at a meal, and any one article disagreed with him—cucumbers for instance—it was only necessary to give a dose of lobelia to the sufferer, and it would enable him to throw up the deleterious substance and retain the other food; and so, nothing that would be assimilated was lost. The strongest Cayenne pepper was the principal ingredient in " No. 2." That which grew in tropical climates was chosen, as having the greatest heating property. " No. 6," I think, was composed of capsicum and French brandy and other ingredients not remembered. When this was taken a writhing would follow, so great was its pungency.

These exciting preparations were given to drive cold from the interior to the surface of the body. When this was effected in some degree, the patient was stripped, placed on a chair and wrapped in blankets. Then the tea-kettle, filled with boiling water, to which a tin pipe or tube was fitted, through which the steam was conducted under the blankets around the body. If, during the time of taking this steam-bath, the patient seemed faint or dying, a little cold water was sprinkled on his face. This would revive him. By this arrangement the cold was between two fires,—the pepper within and the steam without,—and ignominiously routed. Occasionally, one was too weak to endure this, and died during the operation; but the wonder is, that no more succumbed to such malpractice.

Old Dr. Thomson himself was, once at least, indicted for murder in the first degree, and thrown into prison, where he remained " forty days and forty nights." This proved to be of great advantage to him. He cried, " Persecution," and his name and fame spread far and wide.

He obtained a patent for his "*invention.*" He employed agents, whom he sent all over the country, authorized to sell his little book and the right to practice medicine on this plan. The right was sold for twenty dollars. Farmers, blacksmiths, mechanics, and overseers bought the right, bought a stock of medicine, provided themselves with the complicated apparatus for steaming, mounted their horses, and scoured the country in search of patients, and reported wonderful and unheard-of cures. One of the most amusing parts of the farce was, to hear these ignorant fellows, who knew absolutely nothing about the human anatomy or the diagnosis of diseases, ridiculing the old, experienced, and scientific physicians of the country, whom they denominated "mineral doctors." This, too, like other popular delusions, has passed almost into oblivion, and made room for some other nine days' wonder, to die in its turn. The number of intelligent, practical people, who were carried away by this shallow quackery, can hardly be imagined by those who do not remember the excitement it created.

CHAPTER XL.

THE DEATH OF MRS. ROSS.

FOR a number of years after the troubles consequent upon the religious movement begun by Elder Campbell, the churches of Bethel Association enjoyed a high degree of prosperity, during which your grandfather devoted himself assiduously, cheered by the hope and belief that he was instrumental in turning many from the power and dominion of Satan to the light and liberty of the gospel.

The Baptist Denomination during these years, exhibited a good deal of activity, east, west, north, and south. Education; Home and Foreign Missions; Sunday Schools; and the great Temperance agitation, by which it was fondly hoped mankind would be redeemed from the curse of drunkenness, all claimed its attention. In all these "good works," he felt the liveliest interest, and to their advancement contributed cheerfully of his means, which he was now enabled to do, his circumstances having become less stringent than heretofore. The indications at this time were that a season of comparative ease and leisure lay before him, which would enable him to gratify his taste for reading and meditation. But these pleasing anticipations were not to be realized, as it is often the case in this checkered and uncertain life.

On the second day of June, 1847, your grandmother died, after which I perceived his interest in this life was lost, to a great extent. Though to the last he dearly loved his friends, and still felt a deep solicitude in the fortunes of the churches, and in the success of the gospel, his thoughts were now more of another world than this. Of all persons I have ever known, he spoke least of his own personal sorrows, though he spoke feelingly of those of his friends and neighbors. I have heard him say, that his bereavements were sometimes felt more keenly, long years after, than when they first occurred. Your grandmother had frequently been prostrated by severe indisposition, sometimes rheumatism, and sometimes a diseased condition of the stomach. The latter her physicians said was the cause of her death. For weeks previous she could retain neither food nor medicine. Her suffering was so great that it was evident to all that she ardently desired her release. She had nothing to fear after death. She had made her "calling and election sure," long years before, in the morning of life, and no expression of anxiety on that subject escaped her lips. For several days previous to her death she was unable to speak, and answered our questions by a slight movement of the head, signifying yes, or no.

It so happened that when she breathed her last, your grandfather and I, were the only persons standing by her bedside, the others having left the room a moment before. Her dissolution was calm and peaceful, preceded by a slight shudder and a moan just audible. I still remember how quickly my thoughts reverted to her, as she appeared to me when I was a child, and how distinctly I could trace her along the journey of life to its close. She had many noble traits of character, among which a strong and abiding sense of duty was the most striking. With her gentleness she possessed no small degree of firmness of character. Soon after her marriage, and long before your grandfather's thoughts were turned in that direction, and, even when he discouraged her, she made a profession of religion, and was baptized, became a member of the church, and all the remainder of her religious life was in harmony with this beginning.

In the discharge of her domestic duties, what she accomplished, considering her means and feeble health, seems almost incredible. In clothing her family, such material as linsey, jeans, and cotton cloth was spun, woven, and dyed at home. Sheets, quilts, blankets, counterpanes, and all kinds of bedding were provided abundantly in the same manner. And her house was always orderly and neat, however humble it might be. When unable from rheumatism to be on her feet, she found some work she could do sitting in her chair or lying on her bed. You, no doubt, remember how well cooked and savory was the food she set on her plain though neat table, and how, while the principal part of her meal was prepared in the kitchen by the cook, she would superintend something extra nice for us by the fire in her own room.

When your grandfather made a profession of religion, and came to believe it to be his duty to preach the gospel hoping he might do some good in that way, she determined to do all in her power to make his way smooth, and keep him in the field of his labor as much as possible, though well aware that it would entail upon her a life of self-denial.

She seldom enjoyed the pleasure of attending public worship, but spent most of her Sundays at home with her young children, in reading her Bible, and other religious

books.   The "Pilgrim's Progress," and the "Holy War,"
by Bunyan, were favorites when I was a child.   Her custom was to read aloud, and to pause occasionally, as if to
reflect on what she had read.   Her voice, when thus reading, was singularly soft and pleasant, and often attracted
me to her.   If she happened to be reading anything that
I could understand, and that interested me, I generally
lay down near her and listened.   The story of the old Pilgrim, after he fled from the "City of Destruction," and his
marvelous adventures, together with the terrible battles
fought around the beleagured city of "Mansoul," in the
"Holy War," I listened to with deepest interest.   I was
then at the happy age when we believe everything written
in a book—allegory, parable, etc.—to be true.   The stories of David and Goliath, Samson and Gideon; the death
of Saul and Jonathan, in the great battle fought upon the
mountain of Gilboa, and David's lamentation over the fallen
heroes, which are so wonderfully beautiful, she would often
read to me.   The infrequency of her attendance upon public
worship caused her to enjoy these rare occasions with peculiar zest.   She was universally beloved and admired by
her sisters and brethren ; for, although very gentle and
modest, she was sprightly and intelligent.   Later in life,
when she became more helpless from rheumatism, and
never left home, your grandfather would occasionally have
preaching in his own house, and invite his neighbors to
attend, that they might have an opportunity of seeing
them and uniting in worship at the same time.   On these
occasions, Elders Rutherford and Tandy were generally
the preachers.   They were his most esteemed friends,
and great favorites of hers.

Strange as it may seem, at one time she endeavored to

attain to a state of sinless perfection. In the neighborhood where we then lived before removing to Cedar Hill, there were several families of the Methodist Episcopal Church, as stated before, who were among our kindest and most esteemed neighbors. A daughter of one of these families, Miss Gilmer, a beautiful and interesting young lady of deep and fervent religious feelings, bordering on enthusiasm, became much interested in the possibility of becoming *perfect*,—a subject much discussed at that time by the denomination to which she belonged. Though so much younger, she and your grandmother, resembling each other in religious zeal, often met and conversed on this subject—examining the Bible in regard to it ; at the same time, to be able to live without sin was a pleasing thought, assimilating one to the angels.

They at length determined on the experiment. And while this was in progress they met at every opportunity to compare notes and report progress. Your grandmother was the first to decide that, for her at least, it was unattainable, as she could seldom pass a day, surrounded by so many busy cares, during which her conscience did not tell her that she had said or done something that was wrong. Her young friend, however, continued the attempt some time ; but she, too, finally reported failure. This grieved her much, as her heart had been set on becoming perfect. And some of her friends thought that this, with declining health, caused a state of settled melancholy, from which she never recovered.

After your grandmother's death, your grandfather was greatly interested in preparations for her funeral. It seemed to afford him a melancholy pleasure to be thus employed. He selected Elder Samuel Baker, then Pastor of the church in Hopkinsville, to preach the funeral sermon. Under a beautiful spreading oak tree, then and still forming a fine shade in the rear of the house, he had seats prepared, sufficient to accommodate a large audience. The beautiful day, the reputation of the preacher, and the respect felt by all for her memory, brought a numerous assemblage together, who heard a discourse so beautiful and appropriate to the occasion, that it would, perhaps, be safe to say, none who were present could have forgotten. The text was from the words: " And if Christ be in you, the body is dead, because of sin; but the spirit is life, because of righteousness. But if the Spirit of him that raised up Jesus from the dead dwell in you, he that raised up Christ from the dead shall also quicken your mortal bodies by his Spirit, that dwelleth in you." Romans, 8: 10, 11.

And here it may not be inappropriate to add, that while all honor is due to the memory of the pioneer preachers of the various religious denominations, for having endured so many hardships and dangers in spreading the light of the gospel in the wilderness,—no less praise is due to their pious, devoted, self-sacrificing wives. And it will perhaps be found in the end that their "crowns of rejoicing" are no less bright and enduring, though their names and their praises are less frequently heard among men.

Doctor Samuel Baker was born in Sussex County, England, in October, 1812. In 1833 he became a Christian, and was baptized. In January 1834, he left his native country, and from London embarked for the United States, and in March following landed in New York City. His first home in America was in Alton, Illinois, to which place he traveled on foot, from New York, carrying a small

18*

bundle in his hand, as I think I have heard your grand-father say.

On arriving at Alton, he entered Shurtleff College, which he was prepared to do, having received an English education in his native town. The college was a Baptist Institution, and from it he received his degree of A. M. In October, 1834, he was licensed to preach the gospel, by the Baptist Church of Upper Alton, and was publicly ordained, to the ministry, in December 1837.

The ordination sermon was preached by the Rev. Dwight Ives, pastor of the Lower Alton Church, from 2 Corinthians 2: 16. "And who is sufficient for these things?" The ordination prayer, was made by Elder Loomis, then President of the Shurtleff College. His first pastorate was at Cape Girardeau, Missouri. In 1839, he came to Kentucky, and was chosen as their pastor by the Shelbyville Baptist Church. In 1841, he became pastor of the Baptist Church at Russellville, Kentucky, for which he preached about five years, and then removed to Hopkins-ville, at which place he was living when he preached your grandmother's funeral sermon. After leaving Hopkins-ville, he became pastor of the First Baptist Church in Nashville. Finally, after serving as pastor of various other churches, in the beginning of the year 1870, he was chosen as their pastor, by the Herkimer Street Baptist Church, in the city of Brooklyn, New York. But when in the summer of 1872, he visited his brethren in Kentucky, who still retained affectionate recollections of him, they gathered around him, and entreated that he would again cast his lot among them. He consented, and in December following returned to Russellville, and was again called as pastor of the church at that place, where his many friends fondly hoped many useful and happy years await him.

I remember to have heard Doctor Baker preach on various occasions before he left Kentucky, and once in particular, at Spring Creek Church, from the passage "How long halt ye between two opinions? If the Lord be God follow him; but if Baal, then follow him." It was unquestionably a discourse of great power and effect.

Doctor Baker was the third Baptist preacher from England that came among us, according to my recollection. The first was a minister named Ebenezer Rogers. He was a young man highly esteemed and admired by his brethren, and indeed, by the people generally. He did not remain long, however, but went, I believe, to Alton, Illinois, and took charge of a Baptist church in that place. Your grandfather regretted his leaving, as he considered him to be both an earnest Christian and an able preacher. The second was Elder Robert Rutherford, of whom mention has been made. They all spoke with marked foreign accent, which, though novel, was rather pleasing to the ear.

CHAPTER XLI.

AFTER your grandmother's death, your grandfather
continued to live at Cedar Hill with his three old servants,
Jacob, Viney, and Fanny. Viney he had brought with
him from Carolina when a mere child. She kept his room
in order, washed, cooked, and attended to the poultry and
cows. Jacob and Fanny worked in the field and garden,
got up his fire-wood, and attended to his horse and other
stock. He always kept some good cattle, among which
were several fine milch cows.

These he highly prized. Next to his cows, his hogs
claimed his attention. He often called them together, and
fed them himself, enjoying the greediness of the little pigs
cracking corn at his feet. His horse was an object of
prime importance—his only means of transportation when
traveling from place to place among the churches. Three
qualities were indispensable. It was required that he
should walk well, four miles an hour, be strong and gentle,
and never under any circumstances to stumble. This
offence was unpardonable. If he did, he must be sold or
exchanged.

His field crops were corn, oats, and pumpkins, which he
usually grew in great perfection. His corn had to be worked
in a certain way, plowed a certain number of times, with a
certain number of furrows in each row—or he feared there
would be but a light yield. When sufficiently matured,

408

according to the old pioneer custom, the blades were stripped off the stalk as high as the ears, cured into sweet fodder, and stocked. Then the tops, above the ear, were cut off and tied around the stalks to dry. His field now would be quite showy –the large ears of corn in full view. The sweet-scented fodder, and the golden pumpkins scattered thickly over the ground, were to him objects pleasant to look upon. He had the finest apple orchard in the country—fruit of choice varieties, of his own selection. This was, to a considerable extent, public property. The boys and negroes would come with bags and baskets during his absence, and often when at home, and help themselves without asking leave. Yet, notwithstanding, he would put up quantities, more than he could use, and divide with his neighbors in winter, which afforded him gratification. When he went to his appointments, his saddle-bags were fragrant from the fine apples for the children where he visited. All his interest in fruit was for others, as he but seldom tasted any himself. He also took interest and pride in his bacon. As the time for killing hogs approached, he was watchful for suitable weather. He liked it to be quite cold, the wind from the north-west or north, and would sometimes get out of bed at night to ascertain from what point it was blowing. He did not believe that killing when the moon was on the increase or decrease affected the shrinking of the meat. His bacon was always very fine, and it delighted him to see his friends enjoy it, and to hear their praises, which gave him an opportunity to tell them his process of curing it.

Another thing he gave great credit to himself for, was his success in raising fine turnips. Perhaps he did not make a failure in raising them once in twenty years. Jaco ʲ

used to say: "Master has as great a gift for raising turnips as he has for preaching." He had a piece of ground
on which he penned his cows at night, which was plowed
frequently during spring and summer. When the time
for sowing came, it was neatly prepared, and on the Friday before the first Sunday in August, the seed were sown.
In this, you will see, he departed a little from the time-
honored day—

> " The twenty-fifth of July,
> Let the same be wet or dry."

If the first sowing did not succeed, on account of the fly
or dry weather, he continued sowing until he secured a
" good stand." The turnips were generally very fine, and
the tops, which he considered a great delicacy, supplied
himself and neighbors bountifully, while in season, which
continued through the spring months. Such were some
of his out-door amusements during these solitary years.

In his diet, when at home, he was very abstemious.
Coffee and cold biscuit constituted his breakfast and supper, for the most part; a piece of fried or broiled chicken
was sometimes added. His dinner consisted of something
boiled, with a few vegetables. Before each meal, when at
home, he always said a silent grace. At night, before
going to rest, he knelt down by his chair and engaged in
silent prayer. He read a great deal when at home, while
living alone. On my visiting him, he would tell me he
had been reading too much. The condition of the country
was now becoming alarming, and men of thought and reflection had many gloomy forebodings. The religious
denominations North and South were becoming violently
agitated, and none could tell what the end would be.

At the season of the year when there was a succession

of large and interesting meetings, he was from home most of the time, leaving everything in charge of his faithful servants. The days that intervened between meetings, when out on a tour of preaching, he spent with his brethren and their families. On visiting a family his presence seemed to be cheering and exhilarating to all—children and servants included. This was the result of esteem and affection. His ministrations at the family altar were solemn and impressive, leaving the conviction on the minds of all that he felt a deep interest in their spiritual and temporal welfare. No inconsiderable part of his influence was due to the character of his intercourse with the family circle.

In politics he was an old-fashioned Democrat. He believed ours to be the best form of government ever instituted, so long as the people remained virtuous and good; but, like Washington, Patrick Henry, and others of the revolutionary fathers, that it would soon fall into ruins, when the people became vicious and corrupt. He foreboded trouble to the country on account of slavery; not so much on account of the thing itself, as of the remorseless agitation and hate it would engender. Had it been "let alone" by impertinent meddlers, he believed it would have found a peaceful solution by the agency of gradual emancipation, and through the Colonization Society, which found advocates among the purest and ablest statesmen our country has ever known. This society was formed in 1817, and had for its first presidents, Judge Bushrod Washington of the Supreme Court, Charles Carroll of Carrollton, Ex-President Madison, and Henry Clay. It had for its first object the opening of a home for all colored persons who might obtain their freedom in the United States, where they might dwell, free from the overshadowing superiority of the white race. For its second object it had in view the civilization and Christianization of benighted Africa, where the people have so long sat "in darkness and the shadow of death."

In regard to gradual emancipation, it appeared clear to his mind that, if let alone, first one of the border states would have adopted it, then another, until finally it would have reached the Gulf, and accomplished, without havoc and bloodshed, all that has now been effected by civil war. Feeling the infirmities of age increasing upon him, in 1851, he thought it best to offer his resignation of the Moderatorship of the Bethel Association, which he had held from its organization.

The following is the report made by the Committee appointed by the Association on that occasion, written by Elder Pendleton:

" Elder Ross has been Moderator of this Association since its organization in 1825, a period of twenty-six years. He can with more propriety than any other man, living or dead, be designated the father of the Association. The influence resulting from the dignity of his Christian character, and from the salutary counsels he has through successive years imparted, cannot be fully known until the revelations of eternity supply all the elements necessary in making the calculation. This fact precludes the necessity of any attempt to make an elaborate report, and the committee request that the brevity they study may be considered more intensely impressive, than any thing they could say. They recommend the adoption of the following resolutions:

" Resolved,—That Elder Ross's resignation of the Moderatorship of this body constitutes an important epoch in its history; and that the thanks of this body are eminently due to him for the impartiality, dignity, and affectionate kindness, with which he has presided over its deliberations.

" Resolved,—That our ardent affection for him prompts us to comply with his request to be released from our service, and that in accepting his resignation we cannot suppress our emotions of sorrow.

" Resolved,—That we will cherish with affectionate veneration the name, the character, and the labors of our Father in Israel, and offer to God our fervent prayers that divine grace may sustain him amid the infirmities of age, and that the sun of his declining life may set in a cloudless sky."

The above resolutions have been extracted from a " discourse delivered at Bethel Church, Christian County, Kentucky, July 23rd, 1860, by Elder J. M. Pendleton," who goes on to add :

" This report was unanimously adopted, as expressive of the Association's high appreciation of the retiring Moderator. Such honor was due him, and was cordially rendered. It is appropriate to say in this connection, that for several years after the organization of Bethel Association, Elder Ross had, as co-laborers in the ministry Elders William Tandy, William Warder, Robert Rutherford, William C. Warfield, John S. Wilson, and at a later period Robert T. Anderson. Would that I were able to pay a worthy tribute to these men of God ! They were among the excellent of the earth." *

For the same reason that led him to resign the Moderatorship of Bethel Association in 1861, he also resigned the pastorate of Bethel Church, in June, 1852. This was a tender subject, not only with him, but also with the church. So long and so happy had been their connection in this relationship, that the church did not accept his resignation unconditionally. I happened to be present, when Messrs. Bronaugh and Garnett came to make known to him that the church desired to continue him as their pastor, and to employ an assistant, and that they still wished to pay him the salary as heretofore. To this he assented at the time from regard to the wishes and feelings of the church. But he no longer considered himself its

* Of these eminent men, brief and imperfect notices have already been given in this work.

pastor, and, I think, never accepted compensation, though so generously offered by the brethren. Thus we see the ties that had so long connected them gradually loosening, and he was forcibly reminded that they would soon be severed finally.

The Bethel Church, in this case, as in all others where he was concerned, manifested a delicacy and consideration worthy of its high character. In the pulpit of this church, he made a short public · address which proved to be his last. The date I do not remember. On entering the pulpit at the time, as he said to me, he had no thought, whatever, of saying anything, but only of joining the brethren in worship. He found himself thinking, how strange it was that some professors of religion seemed to be more willing to do any thing for their religion than *to live for it*. That they would give their time, their wealth, and in many instances die for it, yet so often failed to adorn it by a " pious life and a godly conversation," which, were it done, " men seeing their good works," would " glorify their Father in heaven ;" and, until this is done, the power and beauty of Christianity will never be fully seen and felt. Under the influence of these reflections, he rose in the pulpit and pressed the consideration of these things on the brethren. Neither he nor they supposed that he might not speak again to them, though his health was feeble, and his voice unusually weak and low.

In the year 1857, as before stated, he was at last persuaded by his children and friends to leave his home at Cedar Hill, and live in the family of your uncle, John Morrison. Their reasons for urging this upon him, were his lonely and unprotected life, and the need there was of having some one to attend to all his little wants and com-

forts which your aunt Morrison was so well suited by her
affectionate nature to superintend. Accordingly, a comfortable room being built, and as many of his conveniences
and comforts as he desired removed to it, he bade a final
adieu to the old home and all its familiar and cherished
associations, with feelings more easily imagined than
described, and removed to the place where his pilgrimage
was to end.

Here every thing was favorable to his comfort and
happiness; an affectionate daughter and her family; friends
and neighbors that delighted in showing every attention
and kindness; a community that had grown up to love and
honor him, many of them from childhood. In the later
months of the year 1859, he suffered much of dysury, and
was completely prostrated by that painful disease. During
his illness, he was cheered and comforted almost daily by
the loving ministrations of his friends and brethren. Their
conversations on these occasions assumed a religious character and many deeply interesting subjects were discussed.

CHAPTER XLII.

LAST ILLNESS AND DEATH.

In the early days of January, 1860, your grandfather's health seemed somewhat improved. On the 19th, he had his apparatus for shaving brought to him. He shaved himself with care, pared his nails, combed his hair, and put on fresh clothes. No one was in his room except his old servant Fanny, who was waiting on him. After this, as he told me, he rose to his feet, stood a moment, then fell suddenly with all his weight on the hearth, but seemed to recover a little very soon, and said: "Fanny, I have started on my long journey." There were two opinions in regard to the cause of the fall. One, that it was paralysis; the other, that it was, simply, vertigo. I have no doubt it was the latter. The fall was a hard one; turning the side which fell on the bricks black with bruises. All the family gathered around him immediately; his physician was summoned, and every thing done that kindness and affection could suggest; but inflammation and fever supervened, and it was soon apparent that his recovery was more than doubtful. We will let some extracts from letters your aunt Morrison wrote to her daughter, your cousin, Rowena Waggener, of Louisville, tell the remainder. She says:

"I am sorry to tell you that father is very ill, much more so than he has been since you left us. He had a fall, about noon last Friday, the

416

19th of January, and has not been up since. We are all very uneasy about him. He cannot move his feet at all. I am fearful it was paralysis that caused the fall, as he started across the room. We sent down for brother James, Friday, and he came up yesterday. He intends staying with your grandfather this week.   ·   ·   ·   · I will write you a few lines every day till Monday, and tell you how he is."

"*Monday morning.*—Father is no better this morning, and was very ill all last night. His mind is flighty at times. Your father came in a short time since, and told me my father had called me two or three times. I went to his room and sat by him a while, but he had fallen asleep. Your uncle James, Mr. Slaughter, Mr. E. Garnett, and your brother sat up with him last night. The neighbors are as kind and attentive to him as they can be. All seem anxious to do something for him."

"*Monday evening.*—Brother James thinks father better than he has been since he came. Dr. Porter, Mr. and Mrs. Radford came to see him to-day. All denominations love him."

"*Tuesday morning.*—Dear father is no better; was suffering a great deal all night. Edward Ross came up to see and help nurse him. Oh, that we could relieve him!"

"*January 25th.*—The doctor says he cannot live more than forty-eight hours, unless a change for the better takes place soon. He suffers a great deal, but is resigned to both suffering and death; for he is ready for the change that awaits us all. I heard him praying several times to-day that he might be permitted to die, and be at rest. His faith is unwavering, for he 'knows in whom he has put his trust.'"

"*January 26th.*—I see no change in father's condition since yesterday, except his mind seems more wandering. He smiled pleasantly while relating some of the incidents of his early life. He is perfectly helpless and requires several persons to turn him in the bed. Mr. Richard Tandy, Mr. and Mrs. Barclay, Annie Pendleton, Mr. B. Garnett, indeed all the neighbors come to inquire how he is, and offer to sit with him at night. I give you all these particulars, for I know you want to hear them."

"*January 27th.*—Father is no better to-day. His mind wanders, so that it is sad to hear him talk. The doctor says he is no longer sensible of his sufferings, and I am thankful that it is so. Mr. William Pendleton, Mr. R. Jameson, and Mr. E. Garnett, are particularly kind. Brother James is still with us, and will remain till all is over. Your

grandfather says, 'Eugene is one of the best nurses he has ever seen.'
I feel so sad! It seems to help me to tell you all these things.

"*January 28th.*—Your grandfather breathed his last this morning, a
few minutes after five o'clock, without a sigh or a groan. It is some
comfort that his last moments were so calm and easy, after all his sufferings; though he appeared to feel no pain for twenty-four hours before
his death, and was unconscious a great deal of the time. Yesterday, he
looked up at brother James, and said: 'Why, Jemmie!' and smiled,
and seemed surprised and pleased, as though he had but just come. Immediately after he fell asleep, and slept for several hours, breathing
calmly and sweetly as if he had been well. When he awoke your father
was standing by his bed. He said: 'Johnnie, if you will open the
door, I will sing you a new song.' When the door was opened, he
began:

> " ' Oh, sing to me of heaven
> When I am called to die!'

"His countenance brightened up while singing and he sung several
verses very distinctly. And these, my child, were his last audible words
on earth. I thank my Heavenly Father for the reason I have to believe
that he and my dear mother went directly to heaven when they left this
suffering world; for heaven was a theme they loved to dwell upon.
Father will be buried to-morrow at Cedar Hill, at three o'clock. Brother
James has gone down to attend to the digging of a grave by the side of
our beloved mother. How calm and peaceful and beautiful he looked,
when I beheld him for the last time! He was dressed in a suit of deep
black, without shroud or winding-sheet, as was his expressed desire. He
requested your uncle to bury him in a plain, black walnut coffin, just
like the one our mother was buried in. I wish you could have seen
him. It would have left such a pleasant recollection with you. His
features wore the same sweet, peaceful expression that rested on mother's
after death."

"*January 30th.*—Eugene and Millie have returned from Cedar Hill.
They say they never saw so many people at a burial before. A good
many joined them as they passed through Trenton and the neighborhood
below.   ·   ·   · I can't tell you how much I miss him.
He was so much company for me, and I loved to think he was safe in
his own room, even when I did not see him walking about. When
Spring comes how I shall miss him. He told me of the first visits of the

birds, and of the first blossoms of the early Spring. How often has he
brought me a little flower and said : ' See, Nannie, how pretty ! and the
weather still so cold.' Father was unquestionably a superior man in
many respects. I am his oldest child, and he was more confidential
with me, I suppose, on that account. I was with him in so many of the
sad events of his life ! I also enjoyed his happiness, when his labors
were crowned with success in the noble work to which he had devoted
himself. His life was a checkered scene, and, as I look back on it, the
prominent characteristics, as I recall them, were his dignity in the presence of men, his humility before God, and his tender sympathy for all
who were in trouble."

   " *You* have heard him preach many fine sermons, but I, who remem
ber him in his prime, considered him unsurpassed by any preacher I ever
heard. I was proud of him, and his memory will be a living pleasure
while life endures."

   Thus, my dear Marion, your aunt who loved him tenderly, described the closing scenes of your grandfather's
life, and at the same time the feelings of her own affectionate heart. They were a mutual pleasure to each other
while they lived. He loved her for her sweet temper,
gentleness, and affectionate heart; and she reverenced
him for the noble qualities he possessed. They now sleep
side by side in their quiet graves.

   At your grandfather's interment there were no religious
services, except a very touching prayer by Elder S. P.
Forgy, which seemed to impress the hearts of all present,
in which he alluded to the wide spread grief that would be
felt when the news of his death should go abroad. But on
the 23rd of July following, Elder J. M. Pendleton, to a
large audience, delivered a deeply interesting address, in
which he reviewed his life and times, and placed his character as a man, a Christian, and a minister of the gospel
before the audience, as no one who had not loved and admired him, could have done. This address appeared after-

wards in print; such was its character I doubted the propriety of writing any thing farther on the subject, but finally concluded that you and others of your grandfather's descendants would be pleased to have a more extended account of his life and of the fortunes of our family in the early times.

Elder Pendleton, though born in Virginia, was taken when an infant to Kentucky, and belongs to one of the most respectable families in that part of the country. His father and your grandfather were intimate friends, from the time of their first acquaintance. Elder Pendleton was raised under your grandfather's ministry, baptized at Bethel Church in April, 1829, began to preach in September, 1831, and was ordained at Hopkinsville, November 2, 1833, by Elders William Tandy, Robert Rutherford, William C. Warfield, and your grandfather, who, from the first, predicted a bright future for him, and rejoiced in the hope that he was destined to accomplish much in the service of the Master. From his early youth, Elder Pendleton manifested deep affection and reverence for your grandfather, and has never failed, when occasion offered, to express his admiration of his Christian character, etc. In an article I have lately seen, he says:

" The name Reuben Ross, awakened in me many tender recollections. I knew him from my childhood, and always felt a profound veneration for him. In his palmy days, he was what I will call a fine specimen of manly beauty. In person he was above the average size, of a commanding presence, and of dignified manners. No one could see him without believing him to be a remarkable man. Though not acquainted with the technical rules of logic, he was a powerful reasoner. In the realms of the pathetic, he had no superior. . . . . I have been young and now I am growing old, and must not express myself extravagantly. I have listened to great men in the South and in the North.

. . . .—Yet, I say I have heard nothing, I have seen nothing, that impressed me so deeply as the appearance of Elder Reuben Ross, when in solemn majesty, and with pathetic earnestness, he entreated sinners to be reconciled to God."

I will close this chapter by another extract from the address refered to.

"It is right *for me* to say here that Elder Ross was called in the latter part of the year 1836, to preach to this church, (Bethel) and commenced his labors in 1837. He preached for you about seventeen years. I need not tell you how he labored for your welfare, and how the Lord blessed his labors, for you know better than I. In the year 1838, you saw him on one bright morning baptize sixty-six rejoicing converts, and often in subsequent years, did he visit the baptismal waters. Venerated by all in the community, he here proclaimed the unsearchable riches of Christ. His voice always mild, and often through deep feeling, assuming a melting tenderness in its intonations, resounded again and again within these walls. In this Sanctuary he wept over you and your children, for his eyes were prodigal of tears. You will cherish his memory while you live, and transmit your impressions of his many excellencies to the generations following.

"For several years before his death, our venerable brother, owing to the infirmities of declining age, was able to preach only an occasional sermon. He lived in your midst, and you know what sufferings were his. The vigor of his manhood was gone, and disease fastened itself upon his noble form. He suffered and declined till the 28th of January, 1860, when he breathed his last, in the eighty-fourth year of his age. The day on which he passed away a great and good man died. I cannot think a purer spirit than his ever ascended to the skies. The state of his mind as he drew near the grave was characterized by tranquil trust in Christ. There was no special ecstacy, but the calmness of abiding trust in the Saviour. Thus lived and died Reuben Ross, whose name I have been accustomed from childhood to consider as the synonym of all that is good in human character.

"His eyes first saw the light in North Carolina. The greater part of his life was spent in Tennessee, and he died in Kentucky. His body was conveyed to his former home near Clarksville, Tennessee, and buried by the wife of his youth, under the spreading branches of a noble oak, and not far off a cluster of cedars, ever green, fit emblem of immortality."

19

Such was the language of a Christian brother, prompted by the mingled sentiments of love and esteem, as he reviewed the life of one who had " finished his course," and entered into his rest—one of those " who had turned many to righteousness," and of whom it is said : " They shall shine as the brightness of the firmament, and as the stars forever."

CHAPTER XLIII.

EARLY in 1861 our great civil war began, and for four unhappy years but little was heard except the " clash of resounding arms." So soon as tranquillity was, to some extent restored, the thoughts of his brethren reverted to your grandfather, and they resolved to place a monument at his grave, to perpetuate his memory and to testify their esteem and respect for him. This was accordingly done, and the memorial services on the occasion are thus noticed in the *Western Reeorder* of July 1st, 1871 :

" According to request made by the last Ministers' and Deacons' Meeting of the Bethel Association at Hopkinsville, a large number of the relatives and friends and acquaintances of the loved and lamented Father Ross met, on Tuesday morning, June 20th, 1871, at the old homestead in Montgomery County, Tennessee, in order to hold some befitting memorial service in connection with the monument lately erected to his memory, by order of the Bethel Association.

" The occasion was one of deep and impressive solemnity, full of heart-touching reminiscences, which found utterance in the silent tear, rather than the pomp of ceremony. It was a congregation of mourners, composed of the children and grandchildren of brethren and friends of life-long acquaintance, met together to pay the last earthly tribute of respect and veneration to a Father in Israel. After visiting the grave, the

423

audience repaired to the yard,—and, beneath the branches of a wide-spreading oak, the services took place in the following order:

"Elder S. A. Holland acting as Moderator, and J. W. Rust as Clerk.

"First—Hymn, 'And let this feeble body fail.'

"Second—Reading, 1 Cor. 15 : 42–58, by Elder J. L. Crutcher.

"Third—Prayer, by S. S. Mallory.

"Fourth—Hymn, 'Servant of God, well done.'

"Fifth—Memorial Address, by Elder W. W. Gardner."

The speaker delivered this address standing near the spot where, twenty-four years before, Dr. Baker addressed a similar audience on the occasion of your grandmother's funeral. Many were present now that were present then, and were, no doubt, forcibly reminded of that occasion. The day, now as then, was beautiful. The air was soft and balmy, and this, together with the deep-green foliage of the trees, the verdure of the sward beneath, the bright, unclouded sky of June above, and the subdued and noise-less multitude listening in rapt attention to the impressive words of the speaker—presented a scene long to be remembered by those present. With these tender but pleasing reminiscences fresh in our memory, we now, my dear Marion, bring to a close our Recollections of the Life and Times of your Grandfather—Elder Reuben Ross.

APPENDIX.

JAMES ROSS, the writer of the foregoing "Recollections," was born September 3, 1801. He was a bright boy, and his merry voice was sweet as music to his parents. His father knowing the value of education by the lack of it, resolved that, if possible, his son should know its worth by its possession. There were many obstacles in the way of the accomplishment of the father's purpose, but in the good providence of God it was accomplished. After enjoying the limited advantages of Primary Schools, James was, through the kindness of a friend, placed in an Institution of high grade, in which much attention was given to classical studies. He diligently improved his opportunities and acquired quite a reputation as a Latin and Greek scholar. He taught these languages for forty years, and there are, no doubt, many now living who are indebted to him for their first love of classical studies.

He was very happy in his marriage, having gained the heart and hand of Miss Barker, daughter of Charles Barker, Esq., whose residence was not far from Clarksville, Tenn. She was a woman of sprightly intellect, liberal education, attractive person, elegant manners, and sincere piety. She was the worthy wife of her worthy husband. They had seven children, four of whom are believed to be dead.* Two sons are living, one of whom is Dr. John W.

* The writer thus expresses himself, not being certain.

425

Ross, of the United States Navy, who so generously utilized his medical knowledge and experience in the Yellow Fever epidemic at Memphis a few years ago.

The only surviving daughter is Mrs. Dudley, of Logan County, Kentucky, for whose gratification the foregoing pages were written.

The death of Mrs. Ross preceded that of her husband. For some years he trod the path of life uncheered by her presence and her smiles. He never forgot his happy married life, and did not believe that the grave contained more precious dust than that of his loved one. After her death he seemed, if possible, more closely drawn to his children, and was specially gratified to see in them a reproduction of the virtues conspicuous in their mother.

The reader will think it strange that Mr. James Ross never made a public profession of religion. He was considered by those who knew him a believer in Christ—he was in principle a Baptist—but his ideal of what a Christian professor should be was so high as to deter him from making "the good profession," lest he should dishonor it. He doubtless took a mistaken view of the matter.

He died after a short illness in March, 1878, in the 77th year of his age. His robust and manly form fell under the stroke of mortality, and no one more worthy to be called an accomplished gentleman survives him. Patient in his last illness, yet suffering much, he sighed for rest. His last words were " *Requiescat in pace*," of which he gave the translation—"Let him rest in peace."

His funeral sermon was preached by A. D. Sears, D. D., and they buried him by the wife of his love.

J. M. P.

JAMES ROSS.

ERRATA.

P. 124, line twelve, for *pay* read *pass.*

P. 124, line two from bottom, for 1728 read 1808.

P. 304, line fourth, for *you and your grandfather* read, *your grand-mother and grandfather.*

P. 322, fourth line, *biographes* read *biographer.*

INDEX

Montgomery Co., 15, 53, 55,
107, 113, 114, 115, 116,
140, 155, 212, 218, 219,
270, 312, 334, 343, 411,
423
Morgan Co., 102
Nashville, 102, 103, 105,
106, 107, 118, 151, 179,
187, 208, 257, 258, 264,
265, 288
New Providence, 259
Palmyra, 248
Port Royal, 15, 107, 108,
113, 118, 153, 244, 288
Robertson Co., 15, 113, 114,
115, 116, 140, 300, 302,
319
Springfield, 115, 319
Stewart Co., 15, 114, 115,
116, 140, 168, 169, 174,
176, 177, 178, 260, 337
Sumner Co., 235, 336
Williamson Co., 151
Virginia
Abingdon, 99, 100
Albermarle Co., 336
Albemarle, 349
Lunenburg Co., 148
Roanoke, 12

Washington Co., 99

RIVERS, ETC.
Albemarle Sound, 27, 33, 70
Big Harpeth River, 147
Caney Fork River, 102, 105
Clinch River, 102
Cumberland River, 102, 107,
115, 150, 168, 178, 182, 200,
205, 207, 210, 220, 257
Dutch River, 105
Green River (Ky.), 75
Holston, 257
Kawawha, 199
Mississippi, 171, 178, 187,
208, 210, 220
Monongahela, 363
Ohio River, 118, 179, 180, 182,
257, 346
Red River, 107, 108, 118, 119,
168, 257, 258, 259
Roanoke River, 21, 25, 27, 29,
33, 59, 70, 89, 315
Saline Creek, 142
Spring Creek, 134, 155
Scioto, 198
Tar River, 94
Tennessee River, 102, 115
Thames, 201
West Fork of Red River, 155